A-Z NOR

Key to Map Pages	2-3
Large Scale City Centre	4-5
Map Pages	6-42

Index
Villag
and s

CW00499063

REFERENCE

A Road	A147
B Road	B1150
Dual Carriageway	
One-way Street Traffic flow on A Roads is also indicated by a heavy line on the driver's left.	
Road Under Construction Opening dates are correct at the time of publication.	
Proposed Road	
Restricted Access	
Pedestrianized Road	
Track / Footpath	
Residential Walkway	
Railway	Station, Level Crossing, Heritage Station
Built-up Area	MILL RD.
Local Authority Boundary	
Broads Authority Boundary	
Post Town Boundary	
Postcode Boundary (within Post Town)	
Map Continuation	16 · Large Scale City Centre 4
Airport	

Car Park (selected)	P
Church or Chapel	†
City Wall (large scale only)	
Cycleway (selected)	
Fire Station	■
Hospital	H
House Numbers (A & B Roads only)	15 8
Information Centre	i
National Grid Reference	625
Park & Ride	Harford P+R
Police Station	▲
Post Office	★
Safety Camera with Speed Limit Fixed cameras and long term road works cameras. Symbols do not indicate camera direction.	30
Toilet	▽
Educational Establishment	
Hospital or Healthcare Building	
Industrial Building	
Leisure or Recreational Facility	
Place of Interest	
Public Building	
Shopping Centre or Market	
Other Selected Buildings	

SCALE

Large Scale Pages 4-5 1:7,920

0 ⅛ ¼ Mile

0 100 200 300 Metres

8 inches (20.32cm) to 1 Mile 12.63cm to 1km

Map Pages 6-42 1:15,840

0 ¼ ½ Mile

0 250 500 750 Metres

4 inches (10.16cm) to 1 Mile 6.31cm to 1km

A-Z AZ AtoZ
registered trade marks of Geographers' A-Z Map Company Ltd

www.az.co.uk

EDITION 9 2019

Copyright © Geographers' A-Z Map Co. Ltd.

© Crown copyright and database rights 2019 OS 100017302.

Safety camera information supplied by www.PocketGPSWorld.com
Speed Camera Location Database Copyright 2019 © PocketGPSWorld.com

Every possible care has been taken to ensure that, to the best of our knowledge, the information contained in this atlas is accurate at the date of publication. However, we cannot warrant that our work is entirely error free and whilst we would be grateful to learn of any inaccuracies, we do not accept responsibility for loss or damage resulting from reliance on information contained within this publication.

KEY TO MAP PAGES

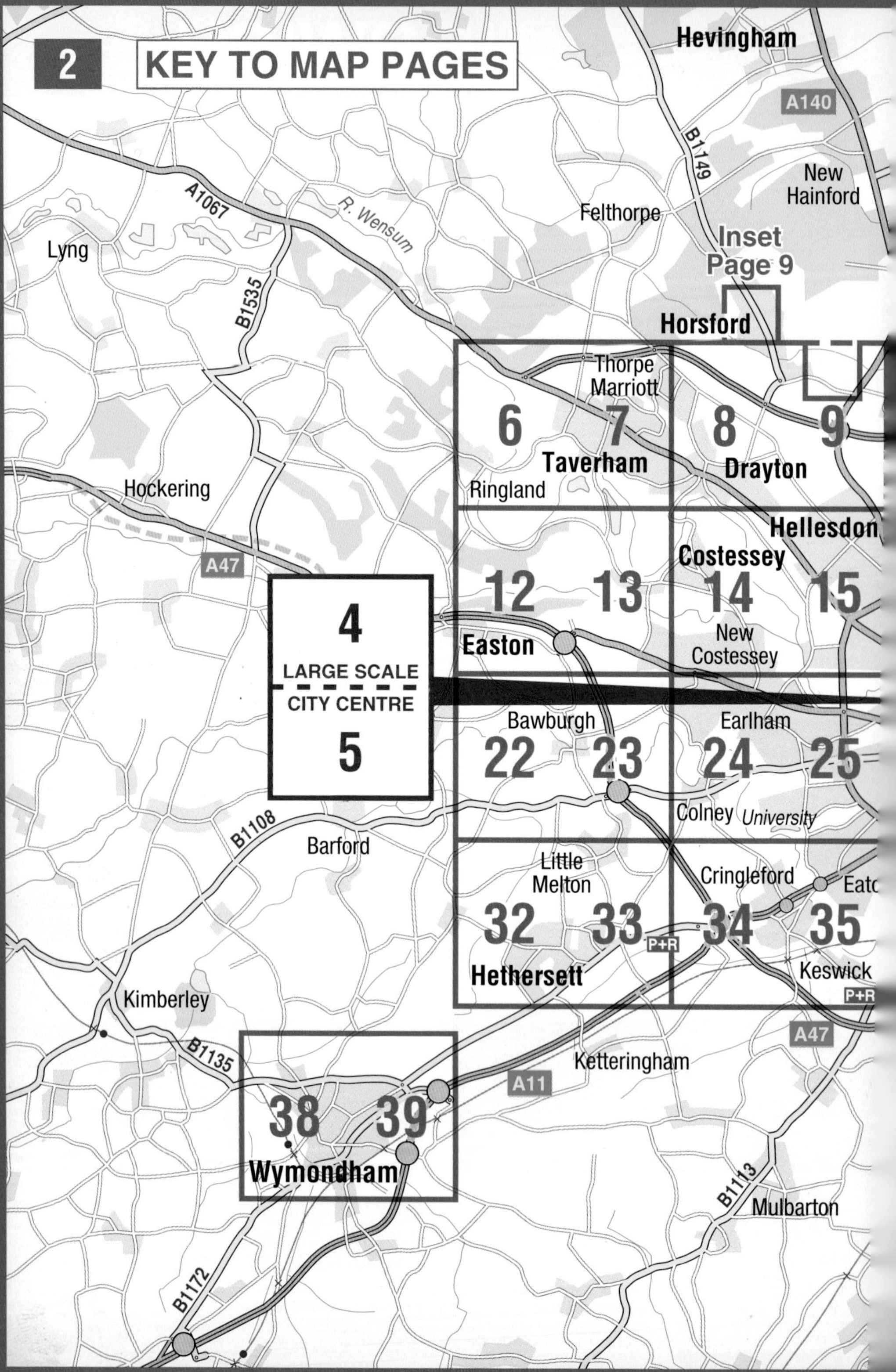

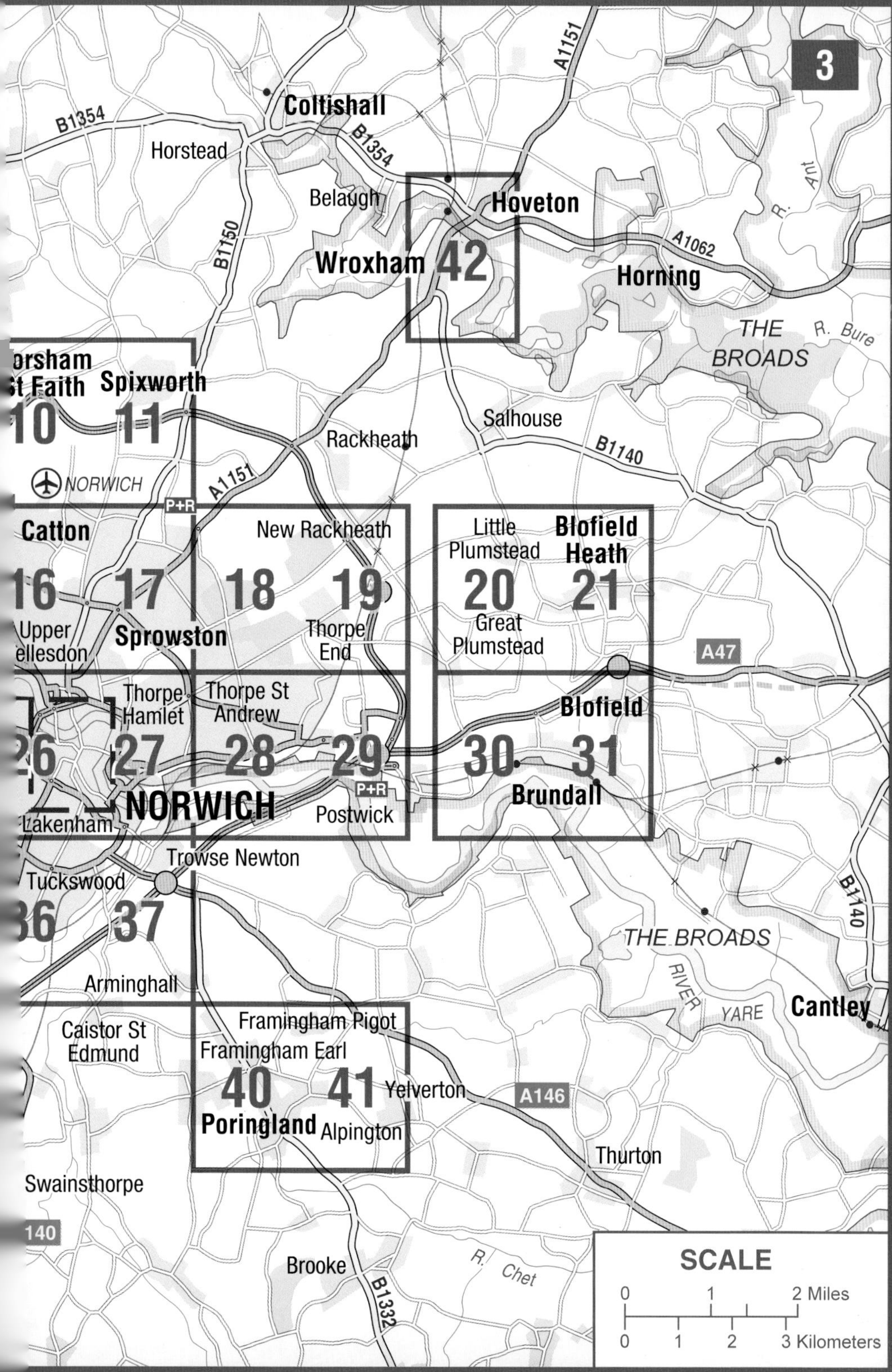
Coltishall
B1354
Horstead
B1354
Belaugh
Hoveton
Wroxham
42
Horning
A1151
A1062
R. Ant
B1150
THE BROADS
R. Bure
orsham St Faith
Spixworth
10
11
NORWICH
Salhouse
Rackheath
B1140
A1151
P+R
Catton
New Rackheath
Little Plumstead
Blofield Heath
16
17
18
19
20
21
Upper Hellesdon
Sprowston
Thorpe End
Great Plumstead
A47
Thorpe Hamlet
Thorpe St Andrew
Blofield
26
27
28
29
30
31
NORWICH
P+R
Brundall
Lakenham
Postwick
Trowse Newton
Tuckswood
36
37
B1140
THE BROADS
RIVER YARE
Arminghall
Cantley
Caistor St Edmund
Framingham Pigot
Framingham Earl
40
41
Yelverton
A146
Poringland
Alpington
Thurton
Swainsthorpe
140
Brooke
R. Chet
B1332
SCALE
0
1
2 Miles
0
1
2
3 Kilometers

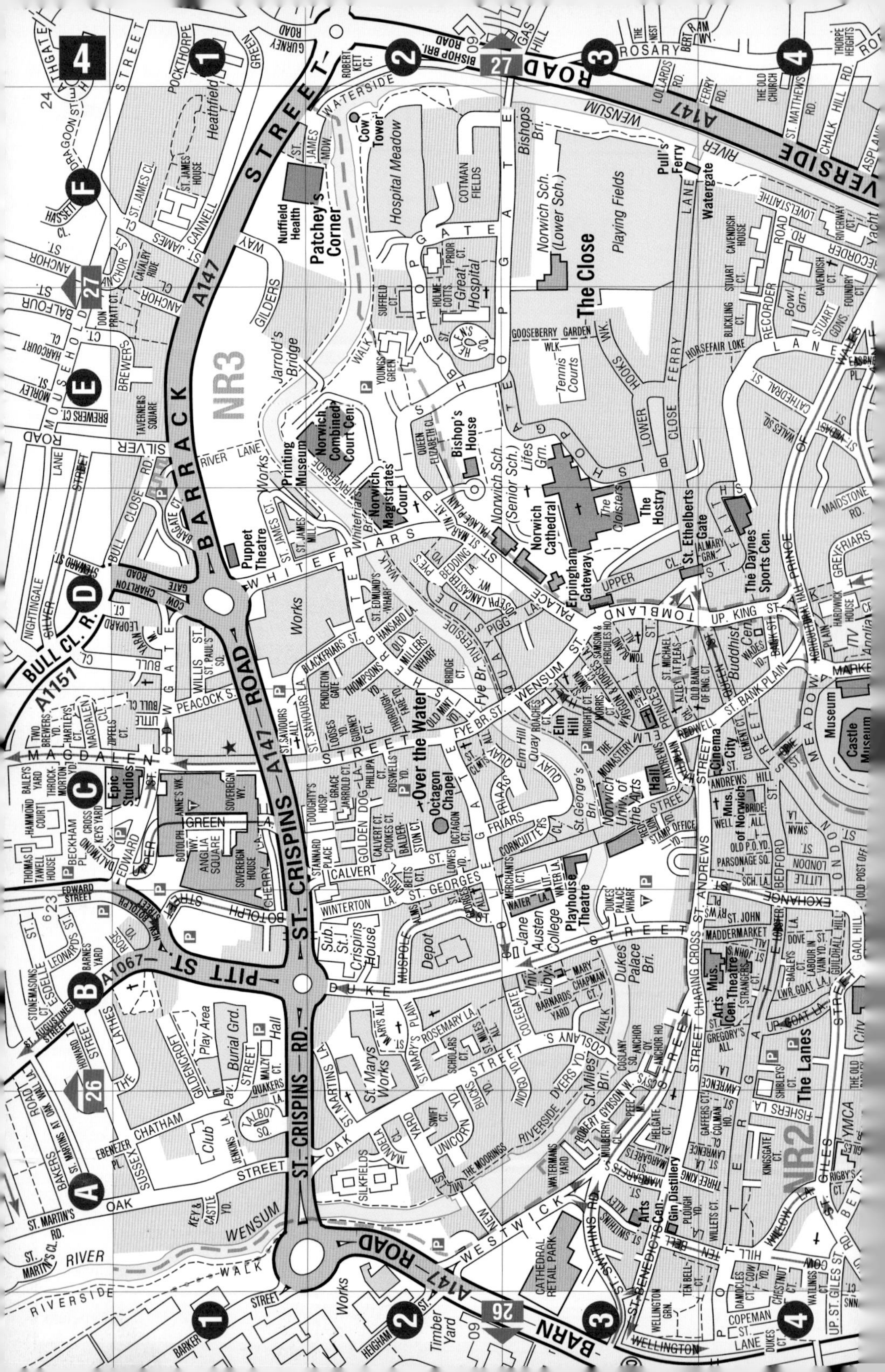
NR3
NR2
BARRACK ROAD
ST. CRISPINS ROAD
A147
A1151
A1067
PITT ST.
BARN ROAD
RIVERSIDE ROAD
RIVER WENSUM
WHITEFRIARS
MAGDALEN STREET
DUKE STREET
OAK STREET
COLEGATE
ST. GEORGES STREET
PALACE ST.
TOMBLAND
ST. ANDREWS STREET
CHARING CROSS
ST. BENEDICTS ST.
WESTWICK ST.
PRINCES ST.
ELM HILL
BISHOPGATE
The Close
Norwich Cathedral
The Cloisters
The Hostry
Bishop's House
Great Hospital
Hospital Meadow
Cow Tower
Patchey's Corner
Nuffield Health
Norwich Combined Court Cen.
Norwich Magistrates Court
Printing Museum
Puppet Theatre
Over the Water
Octagon Chapel
Anglia Square
Epic Studios
Jarrold's Bridge
Fye Br.
St. George's Br.
Dukes Palace Bri.
St. Miles' Bri.
Bishops Bri.
Pull's Ferry
Erpingham Gateway
St. Ethelberts Gate
The Daynes Sports Cen.
Norwich Univ. of the Arts
Playhouse Theatre
Jane Austen College
Mus. of Norwich
Cinema City
Maddermarket
Arts Cen.
Mus. Theatre
The Lanes
Gin Distillery
Castle Museum
Museum
Cathedral Retail Park
St. Marys Works
Sub. St. Crispins House
Depot
Works
Timber Yard
Play Area
Burial Grd.
Club
Playing Fields
Tennis Courts
Norwich Sch. (Lower Sch.)
Norwich Sch. (Senior Sch.)
Watergate
A
B
C
D
E
F
1
2
3
4
26
27

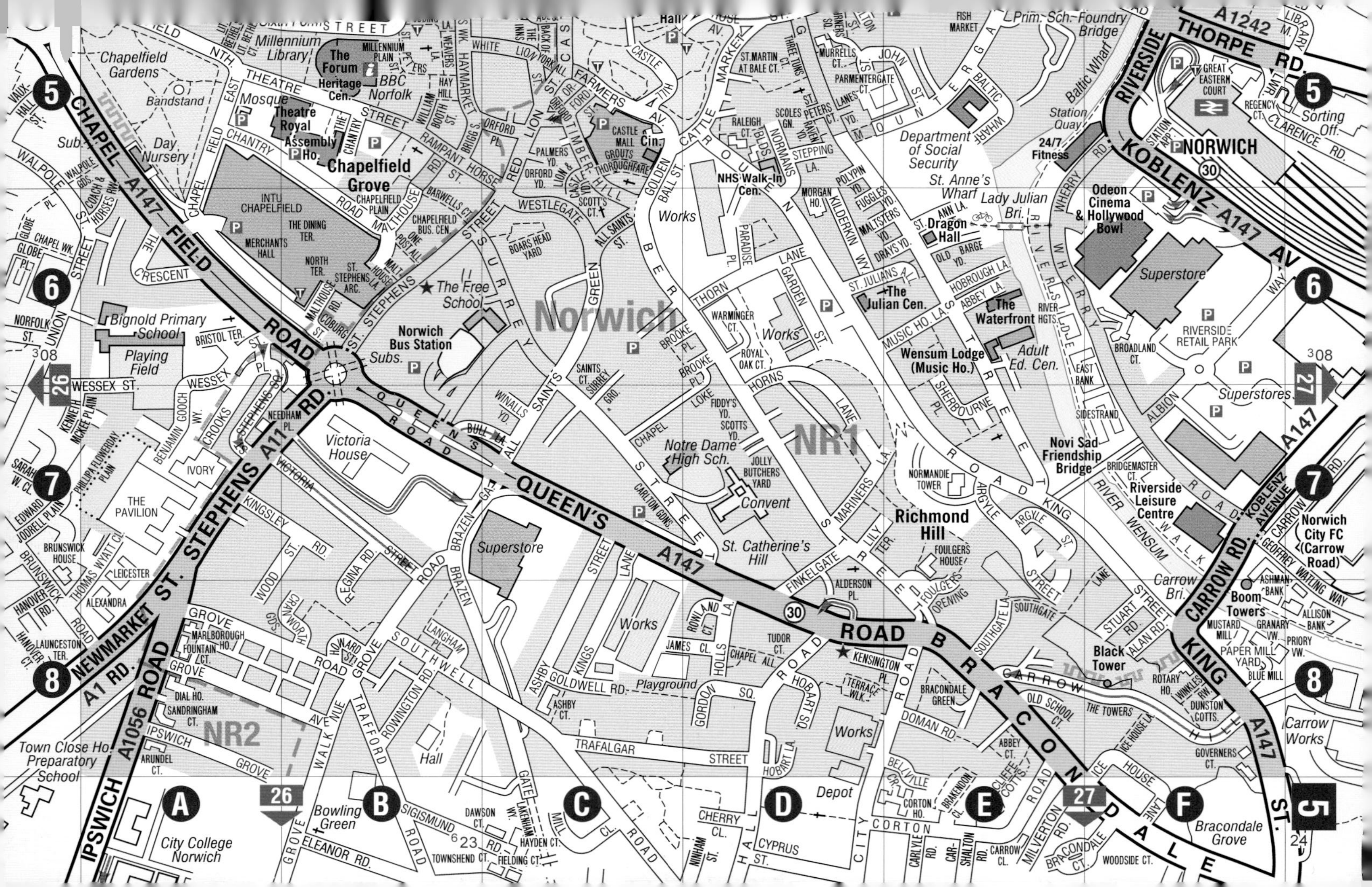
Norwich
NR1
NR2
CHAPEL FIELD ROAD
A147
ST. STEPHENS RD.
A11
QUEEN'S ROAD
BRACONDALE
KING ST.
CARROW RD.
KOBLENZ AVENUE
KOBLENZ AV.
RIVERSIDE
THORPE RD.
A1242
NEWMARKET ST.
A1 RD.
IPSWICH ROAD
A1056
NORWICH
Chapelfield Gardens
Bandstand
Day Nursery
Millennium Library
The Forum
Heritage Cen.
BBC Norfolk
Mosque
Theatre Royal
Assembly Ho.
Chapelfield Grove
INTU CHAPELFIELD
THE DINING TER.
MERCHANTS HALL
NORTH TER.
CASTLE MALL
Cin.
NHS Walk-In Cen.
Works
The Free School
Norwich Bus Station
Subs.
Bignold Primary School
Playing Field
Victoria House
THE PAVILION
Superstore
Notre Dame High Sch.
Convent
St. Catherine's Hill
Richmond Hill
NORMANDIE TOWER
FOULGERS HOUSE
The Julian Cen.
Wensum Lodge (Music Ho.)
The Waterfront
Adult Ed. Cen.
Dragon Hall
Department of Social Security
St. Anne's Wharf
Lady Julian Bri.
Odeon Cinema & Hollywood Bowl
24/7 Fitness
Station Quay
Baltic Wharf
Prim. Sch.-Foundry Bridge
RIVERSIDE RETAIL PARK
Superstores
Novi Sad Friendship Bridge
Riverside Leisure Centre
RIVER WENSUM
Carrow Bri.
Norwich City FC (Carrow Road)
Boom Towers
Black Tower
Carrow Works
Bracondale Grove
City College Norwich
Town Close Ho. Preparatory School
Bowling Green
Hall
Playground
Depot
Sorting Off.
GREAT EASTERN COURT
Town Close
5
6
7
8
A
B
C
D
E
F
26
27
308
23
24
30

6
A
B
C
D
614
15
316
A1067
FAKENHAM
Attlebridge Hills
Juniper Valley
Potato Plantation
Shooting Ground
Club Ho.
Deighton Hills
Shooting Ground
Attlebridge Hall
Crooked Oaks
BROADLAND
The Knoll
Rose Carr
The Nursery
Low Farm
NR9
Garfield Farm
A1067
15
Primrose Grove
WENSUM VALLEY
GOLF COURSE
Club House
Royal Hill
BEECH AV.
Round Wood
Beech Lodge
Brampton Bryan
RINGLAND LANE
THE STREET
Hill House Cotts.
WESTON RD.
Church Farm
LANE
Glebe Farm
Taverham Park
Snake Wood
14
BACK
Pitt Farm
PITT FM. GRN.
THE COMMON
Low Common
WENSUM
West Lodge
West Bank
HONINGHAM LA.
Manor Farm
THE STREET
FIELD
TAVERHAM
Pav.
RINGLAND
RINGLAND LANE
ROAD
Langley Preparatory School at Taverham Hall
NR8
Taverham Hall Farm
Ringland Wood
RIVER
COSTESSEY
13
Three Corner Plantation
12
Blyth's Wood
14
15
Gap
Taranaki
1
2
3
4
5
6

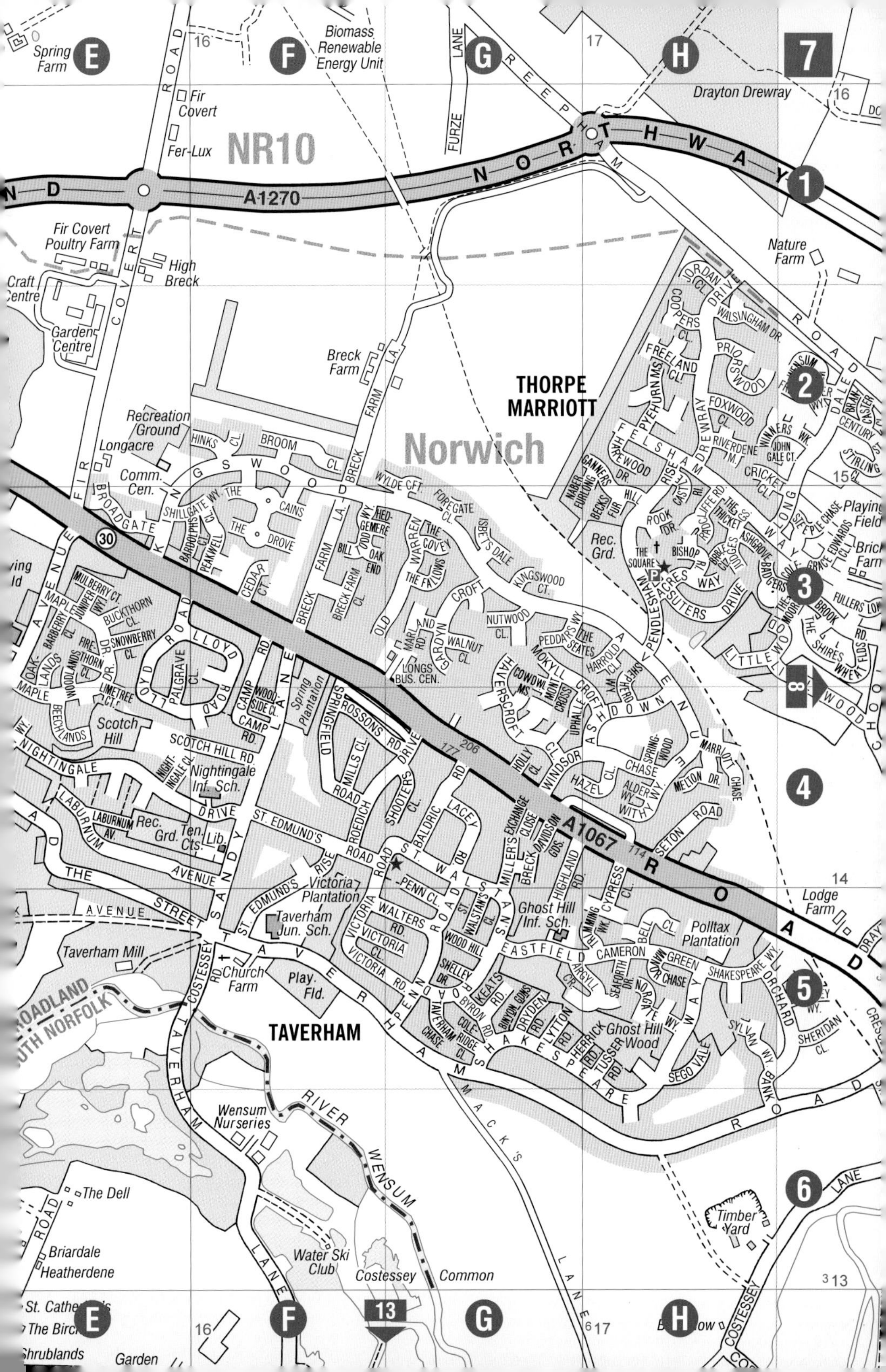
NR10
Norwich
THORPE MARRIOTT
TAVERHAM
NORTHWAY
A1270
A1067
Spring Farm
Biomass Renewable Energy Unit
Fir Covert
Fer-Lux
Drayton Drewray
Fir Covert Poultry Farm
High Breck
Craft Centre
Garden Centre
Breck Farm
Nature Farm
Recreation Ground
Longacre
Comm. Cen.
Rec. Grd.
Playing Field
Scotch Hill
Nightingale Inf. Sch.
Lib.
Ten. Cts.
Spring Plantation
Longs Bus. Cen.
Victoria Plantation
Taverham Jun. Sch.
Ghost Hill Inf. Sch.
Polltax Plantation
Lodge Farm
Taverham Mill
Church Farm
Play. Fld.
Ghost Hill Wood
Wensum Nurseries
River Wensum
Timber Yard
The Dell
Briardale
Heatherdene
Water Ski Club
Costessey Common
St. Catherine's
The Birch
Shrublands
Garden
Broadland
South Norfolk
Fir Covert Road
Sandy Lane
Breck Farm La.
Reepham Road
Furze Lane
Drayton Road
Kingswood
Broadgate
Shillgate Wy.
The Drove
Cains
Peakwell
Bardolphs Cl.
Cedar Ct.
Hinks Cl.
Broom Cl.
Wylde Cft.
Foregate Cl.
Isbets Dale
Kingswood Ct.
Hedgemere
Bill Todd Wy.
Oak End
Warren
The Covey
The Fallows
Breck Farm Cl.
Old Breck
Marl and Rd.
Gardyn Croft
Walnut Cl.
Nutwood Cl.
Peddars Wy.
The Seates
Mokyll Croft
Harrold Cl.
Shepherd Wy.
Haverscroft
Cowdwl Ms.
Montcross
Uphall
Ashdown
Windsor Cl.
Holly Cl.
Hazel Cl.
Springwood Chase
Alder Wy.
Withy Wy.
Marriott Chase
Melton Dr.
Seton Road
Pendlesham
Acres
Suters Drive
Bishop Way
The Square
Rook Dr.
Castle Rise
Radcliffe Rd.
Felsham Way
Harewood Dr.
Ganners Hill
Naber Furlong
Becks Fur.
Pyehurn Ms.
Freeland Cl.
Coopers Cl.
Jordan Cl.
Walsingham Dr.
Drewray Drive
Priorswood
Foxwood Cl.
Riverdene M.
Winners Wk.
John Gale Ct.
Cricket Cl.
Long Way
Steeple Chase
Grace Edwards Cl.
Ashgrove
Badgers Brook
Fullers Loke
The Moor
The Shires
Wheatfields
Littlewood
Stirling Cl.
Century Wy.
Mulberry Ct.
Juniper Wy.
Maple Dr.
Barberry Cl.
Buckthorn Cl.
Snowberry Cl.
Firethorn Cl.
Oaklands
Woodlands
Limetree Ct.
Beechlands
Lloyd Road
Palgrave Cl.
Camp Rd.
Woodside Cl.
Scotch Hill Rd.
Nightingale Cl.
Nightingale Drive
Laburnum Av.
Laburnum
The Avenue
The Street
Avenue
St. Edmund's Rd.
St. Edmund's Rise
Rossons Rd.
Springfield
Mills Cl.
Roedich Road
Shooters Cl.
Baldric Rd.
Lacey Rd.
Penn Cl.
Penn Road
St. Walstans Road
St. Walstan's Cl.
Walters Rd.
Victoria Cl.
Victoria Rd.
Wood Hill
Shelley Dr.
Byron Rd.
Keats Rd.
Binyon Gdns.
Dryden Rd.
Lytton Rd.
Herrick Rd.
Tusser Rd.
Taverham Chase
Coleridge Cl.
Shakespeare Way
Shakespeare Wy.
Millers Cl.
Exchange Close
Breck Davidson Gdns.
Highland Rd.
Cypress Cl.
Trimming Wk.
Bell Cl.
Eastfield
Cameron Green
Argyll Cr.
Seaforth Dr.
Chase
Norgate Wy.
Orchard
Sheridan Cl.
Sylvan Wy.
Bank
Sego Vale
Ringland Road
Taverham Road
Costessey Rd.
Costessey Lane
Mack's Lane
Costessey
Lane
A
B
C
D
E
F
G
H
1
2
3
4
5
6
8
13
14
15
16
17
30
114
177
206

8
A
B
C
D
616 18
316
Drayton Drewray
X Adventure Activities
INSET
HORSFORD
HOLT
DOG LANE
Poplars Farm
Bell Farm
Chestnut Farm
Old Manor Farm
Depot
Works
HORSBECK IND. EST.
Sewage Pumping Station
Wks.
CROWN HILL
HOWE WAY
Works
BROADLAND NORTHWAY
A1270
REEPHAM ROAD
Nature Farm
Warehouse
Norwich
The Lindens
JORDAN CL.
DRIVE
WALSINGHAM DR.
PRIORS
WENSUM
FRESHWATER WY.
DALE
BRANCASTER CL.
FOXWOOD CL.
DREWRAY
RIVERDENE M.
JOHN GALE CT.
WINNERS WK.
CENTURY
ST. MARGTS. CL.
STIRLING CL.
CRICKET CL.
FELSHAM
15
RADCLIFFE RD.
THE THICKET
ASHGROVE
LONG
STEEPLECHASE
Playing Field
GRACE EDWARDS CL.
Brick Farm
WAY
BADGERS
FULLERS LOKE
BROOK RD.
THE SHIRES
WHEAT FLDS.
THE MOORS
THORPE MARRIOTT
B1149
BREWERY LANE
The Homestead Nursery
Little Hill House
The Cottage
Bugg's Grave
LITTLEWOOD
7
Drayton Infant Sch.
SCHOOL ROAD
HIGHFIELD RD.
GLEBE CL.
CATOR RD.
NR8
Borderlands
MARRIOTT
MELTON DR.
ROAD
VAWDREY RD.
Junior School
MANOR FARM CL.
Brick Yard Farm
Scots Pine
14
FAKENHAM ROAD
Lodge Farm
Polltax Plantation
DRAYTON GRO.
BELLOMONTE CR.
FIRBANKS CL.
DRAYTON
LANE
Old Hill
Black Hill
Tall Trees
SHAKESPEARE WY.
ORCHARD
BEVERLEY WY.
SHERIDAN CL.
SYLVAN WY.
BANK
POND
THE GREEN
HALL LANE
Hall
Leisure Centre
Drayton Hall Lawn Plantation
CARTER
BONE ROAD
DRIVE
PARK RD.
DRAYTON HALL
DRAYTON HALL PARK
38
THE CRESCENT
ROAD
30
GEORGE CL.
CARTER RD.
DRAYTON HIGH RD.
GEORGE
LAYTON CL.
Canham's H
STATION RD.
DRAYTON IND. EST.
LOW
DRAYTON
A1067
HIGH ROAD
LODGE BRECK
FAIRVIEW CL.
FROST INDUSTRIAL PARK
Ten. Ct.
BIDEWELL CL.
Pav.
King George's Field
Bowl. Grn.
BRADSHAW RD.
DELANE ROAD
TAVERHAM
6
Timber Yard
BROADLAND
SOUTH NORFOLK
Low Farm
Drayton Old Lodge
LODGE
DRAYTON PK.
MAGNAY RD.
HERBERT NURSEY CL.
HURN
HOWELL RD.
COSTESSEY
13
The Bungalow
18
Bloods Dale
ROAD
19
Mill Cottages

9
E
F
G
H
INSET
HORSFORD
Norwich
NR10
Sharp's Hall Farm
Mill Lane Farm
Horsford C of E Prim. Sch.
PINELANDS INDUSTRIAL ESTATE
Pyehurn Farm
PYEHURN LANE
HOLT ROAD
B1149
Playing Field
Hall
SCHOOL
Lodge Farm
CORNER
8
St. Faith Crematorium
Lower Farm
HORSHAM ST. FAITH
ABBEY FARM COMMERCIAL PARK
St. Faith's Priory
CHURCH ST.
CROWN RD.
Cemy.
ABBEY RD.
WEST LANE
Bowling Green
10
West Farm
City of Norwich Aviation Mus.
A140
ROAD
Works
Church Farm
CHURCH STREET
Horsford Hall
Home Farm
Sparrow Cottages
NR10
HOLT ROAD
New Home Farm
CROMER ROAD
A1270
NORTHWAY
Manor Farm
Harts Hill
Manor Farm Cottages
Pav.
Cricket Ground
Harts Hill Farm
Horsford Manor
Sports Field
Bowling Green
Tennis Courts
BROADLAND
NORWICH
NR6
NORWICH AIRPORT
Terminal Building
P+R Airport
GAMBLING CL.
BUCK COURTNEY CR.
AMSTERDAM WAY
DELFT
ALKMAAR
BUSH ROAD
SADLER ROAD
COTTINGHAMS DR.
DRIVE
GOWING ROAD
GOWING CL.
Arden Grove Inf. Sch.
ARDEN GRO.
FOXCOTTE CL.
RAYMOND ROAD
BERRINGTON ROAD
DENNIS ROAD
HOLT ROAD
MEREDITH
15
1
2
3
4
5
6
14
16
17
20
21

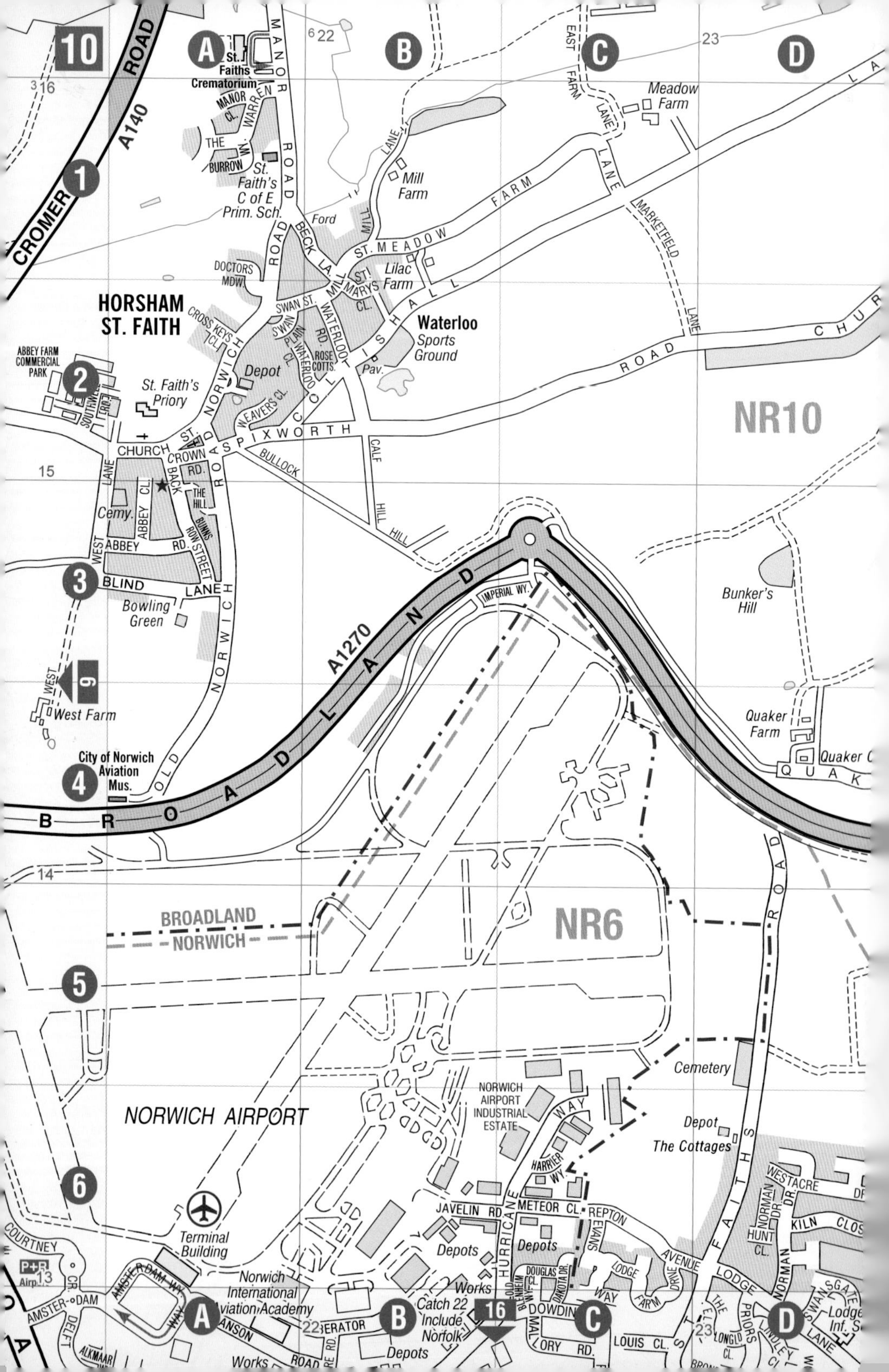
10
A
B
C
D
1
2
3
4
5
6
CROMER ROAD
A140
St. Faiths Crematorium
MANOR CL.
THE BURROW
WARREN WY.
MANOR ROAD
St. Faith's C of E Prim. Sch.
Mill Farm
MILL LANE
Ford
BECK LA.
ST. MEADOW
FARM
Lilac Farm
Meadow Farm
EAST FARM LANE
LANE
MARKETFIELD LANE
DOCTORS MDW.
HORSHAM ST. FAITH
SWAN ST.
SWAN CL.
PLAIN
WATERLOO RD.
ST. MARYS CL.
MILL
WATERLOO
COLTISHALL
ROSE COTTS.
Waterloo Sports Ground
Pav.
CHURCH ROAD
ROAD
NR10
CROSS KEYS CL.
ABBEY FARM COMMERCIAL PARK
SOUTHWELL RD.
St. Faith's Priory
Depot
NORWICH ROAD
WEAVERS CL.
PIXWORTH
BULLOCK
CALF HILL
HILL
CHURCH ST.
CROWN RD.
BACK
THE HILL
WEST LANE
ABBEY CL.
Cemy.
ABBEY RD.
BUNNS ROW STREET
BLIND LANE
Bowling Green
NORWICH
A1270
BROADLAND
IMPERIAL WY.
Bunker's Hill
WEST
9
West Farm
Quaker Farm
Quaker C
QUAK
City of Norwich Aviation Mus.
OLD
BROADLAND ROAD
14
15
316
622
23
BROADLAND
NORWICH
NR6
ROAD
Cemetery
NORWICH AIRPORT
NORWICH AIRPORT INDUSTRIAL ESTATE
WAY
HARRIER WY.
Depot
The Cottages
ST. FAITHS
WESTACRE DR.
NORMAN DR.
HUNT CL.
KILN CLOSE
NORMAN
JAVELIN RD
METEOR CL.
REPTON AVENUE
HURRICANE
OLD HURRICANE
EVANS
Depots
Terminal Building
COURTNEY CR.
P+R Airport
13
AMSTERDAM WY.
AMSTER-DAM WAY
DELFT
ALKMAAR
Norwich International Aviation Academy
Works
Catch 22 Include Norfolk
16
DOUGLAS CL.
BLENHEIM WY.
DAKOTA DR.
LODGE FARM DRIVE
LODGE
WAY
DOWDING
MALLORY RD.
LOUIS CL.
THE LONGDELL
LONGDELL CL.
PRIORS
LINDLEY
SWANSGATE
Lodge Inf. Sch.
LANE
ANSON ROAD
GENERATOR
22
Depots

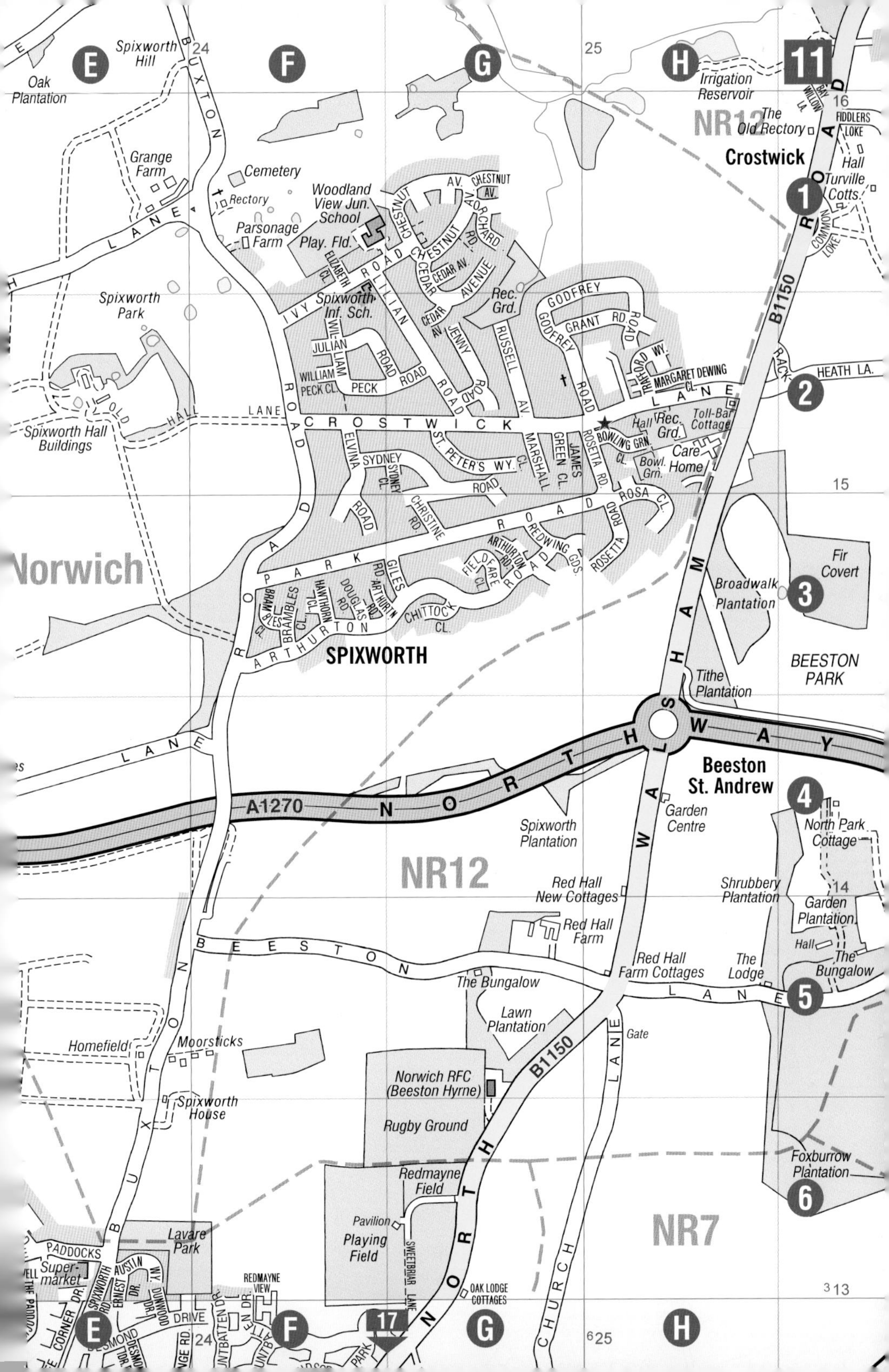
11
E
F
G
H
24
25
16
15
14
13
Spixworth Hill
Oak Plantation
BUXTON
Irrigation Reservoir
NR12
The Old Rectory
Crostwick
FIDDLERS LOKE
BAY WILLOW LA.
Hall
Turville Cotts.
COMMON LOKE
Grange Farm
Cemetery
Rectory
Parsonage Farm
Woodland View Jun. School
Play. Fld.
CHESTNUT AV.
CHESTNUT AV.
ORCHARD RD.
CHESTNUT CL.
CEDAR CL.
CEDAR AV.
AVENUE
Rec. Grd.
LANE
ELIZABETH CL.
IVY ROAD
Spixworth Inf. Sch.
LILLIAN CL.
LILLIAN ROAD
CEDAR AV.
JENNY ROAD
RUSSELL AV.
GODFREY
GODFREY ROAD
GRANT RD.
ROAD
TRAFFORD WY.
MARGARET DEWING CL.
Spixworth Park
WILLIAM
JULIAN
ROAD
WILLIAM PECK CL.
PECK ROAD
ROAD
B1150
RACK
HEATH LA.
CROSTWICK LANE
OLD HALL LANE
Spixworth Hall Buildings
ELVINA ROAD
SYDNEY
SYDNEY CL.
ST. PETER'S WY.
MARSHALL CL.
GREEN CL.
JAMES
ROSETTA RD.
BOWLING GRN. CL.
Hall
Rec. Grd.
Toll-Bar Cottage
Care Home
Bowl. Grn.
ROAD
ROSA CL.
CHRISTINE RD.
ROAD
PARK ROAD
ROSETTA ROAD
Norwich
ARTHURTON RD.
REDWING GDS.
ROSETTA
FIELDFARE CL.
ROAD
GILLES RD.
ARTHURTON RD.
DOUGLAS RD.
HAWTHORN CL.
BRAMBLES CL.
BRAMBLES CL.
CHITTOCK CL.
ARTHURTON ROAD
SPIXWORTH
HAMSTEAD ROAD
Broadwalk Plantation
Fir Covert
BEESTON PARK
Tithe Plantation
NORTH WALSHAM ROAD
NORTHWAY
LANE
Beeston St. Andrew
A1270
Garden Centre
Spixworth Plantation
North Park Cottage
NR12
Red Hall New Cottages
Shrubbery Plantation
Red Hall Farm
Garden Plantation
Hall
BEESTON LANE
Red Hall Farm Cottages
The Lodge
The Bungalow
The Bungalow
Lawn Plantation
Gate
Homefield
Moorsticks
B1150
Norwich RFC (Beeston Hyrne)
Rugby Ground
Spixworth House
BUXTON ROAD
CHURCH LANE
Redmayne Field
Foxburrow Plantation
Pavilion
Playing Field
SWEETBRIAR LANE
NR7
Lavare Park
PADDOCKS
Super-market
SPIXWORTH RD.
ERNEST
AUSTIN DR.
DUNWOOD DR.
WY.
REDMAYNE VIEW
OAK LODGE COTTAGES
THE PADDOCKS
CORNER DR.
DRIVE
DESMOND
17
PARK

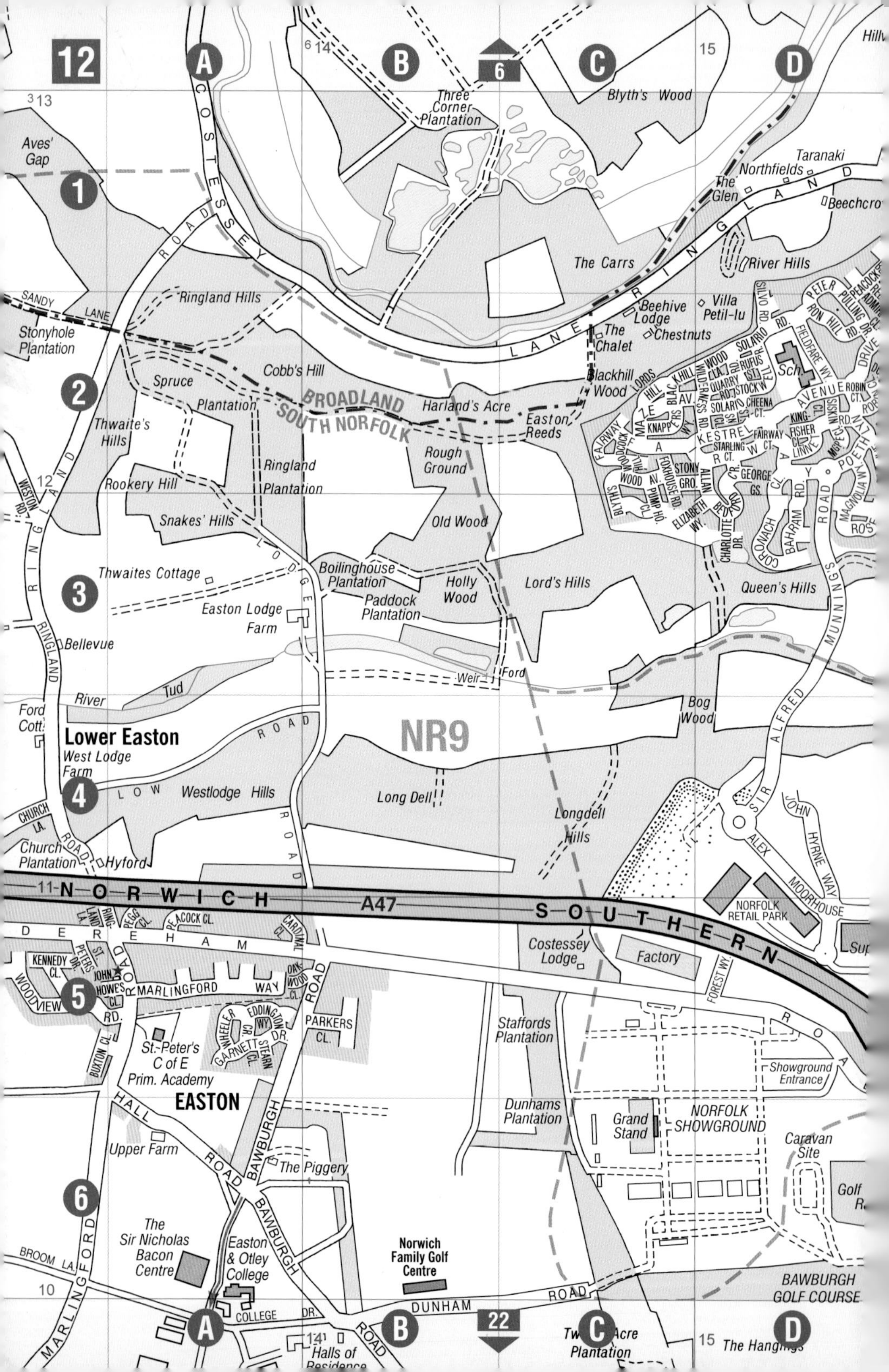
A
B
C
D
1
2
3
4
5
6
6
22
Aves' Gap
Three Corner Plantation
Blyth's Wood
Hillv
Taranaki
Northfields
The Glen
Beechcro
The Carrs
River Hills
COSTESSEY
ROAD
SANDY LANE
Stonyhole Plantation
Ringland Hills
Beehive Lodge
Villa Petil-lu
Chestnuts
The Chalet
RINGLAND LANE
Cobb's Hill
Spruce Plantation
BROADLAND
SOUTH NORFOLK
Harland's Acre
Blackhill Wood
Easton Reeds
Thwaite's Hills
Rough Ground
Ringland Plantation
Rookery Hill
Snakes' Hills
Old Wood
WESTON RD.
RINGLAND ROAD
Thwaites Cottage
Boilinghouse Plantation
Holly Wood
Lord's Hills
Queen's Hills
Paddock Plantation
Easton Lodge Farm
LODGE
Bellevue
Weir
Ford
River Tud
Ford Cott.
Bog Wood
NR9
Lower Easton
West Lodge Farm
LOW ROAD
Westlodge Hills
Long Dell
Longdell Hills
CHURCH LA.
Church Plantation
Hyford
SIR ALFRED MUNNINGS ROAD
ALEX MOORHOUSE WAY
JOHN HYRNE WAY
NORFOLK RETAIL PARK
Sup
NORWICH SOUTHERN
A47
11
DEREHAM ROAD
KENNEDY CL.
PETERS ST.
JOHN HOWES CL.
WOODVIEW RD.
MARLINGFORD WAY
PEACOCK CL.
CARDINAL CL.
OAK WOOD CL.
PARKERS CL.
WHEELER CR.
EDDINGTON WY.
GARNETT CL.
STEARN DR.
BUXTON CL.
St. Peter's C of E Prim. Academy
EASTON
Costessey Lodge
Factory
FOREST WY.
Staffords Plantation
Showground Entrance
Dunhams Plantation
Grand Stand
NORFOLK SHOWGROUND
Caravan Site
Golf R
HALL ROAD
BAWBURGH ROAD
Upper Farm
The Piggery
The Sir Nicholas Bacon Centre
Easton & Otley College
Norwich Family Golf Centre
BROOM LA.
MARLINGFORD ROAD
COLLEGE DR.
DUNHAM ROAD
BAWBURGH GOLF COURSE
Halls of Residence
The Hangings
Two Acre Plantation
FAIRWAY
WOODCOCK HILL
MAZE AV.
KNAPPERS WY.
BLACKHILL WOOD
LORDS HILL
WILDERNESS RD.
SOLARIO RD.
QUARRY RD.
RUFUS ST.
STOCK WELL
CHEENA CT.
KESTREL AVENUE
STARLING CT.
FAIRWAY CT.
FISHER CL.
KING CL.
NIXSIS RD.
ROBIN CT.
LINNET CL.
BLYTH'S WOOD AV.
FOXHOUSE RD.
STONY GRO.
ALLAN CR.
GEORGE GS.
PUMP HO. CL.
ELIZABETH WY.
BEDFORD
CHARLOTTE DR.
CORONACH CL.
BAHRAM RD.
POETH
MAGNOLIA WY.
ROSE
PETER PULLING RD.
RON HILL RD.
FIELDFARE WY.
PEACOCK
DRIVE
Sch.

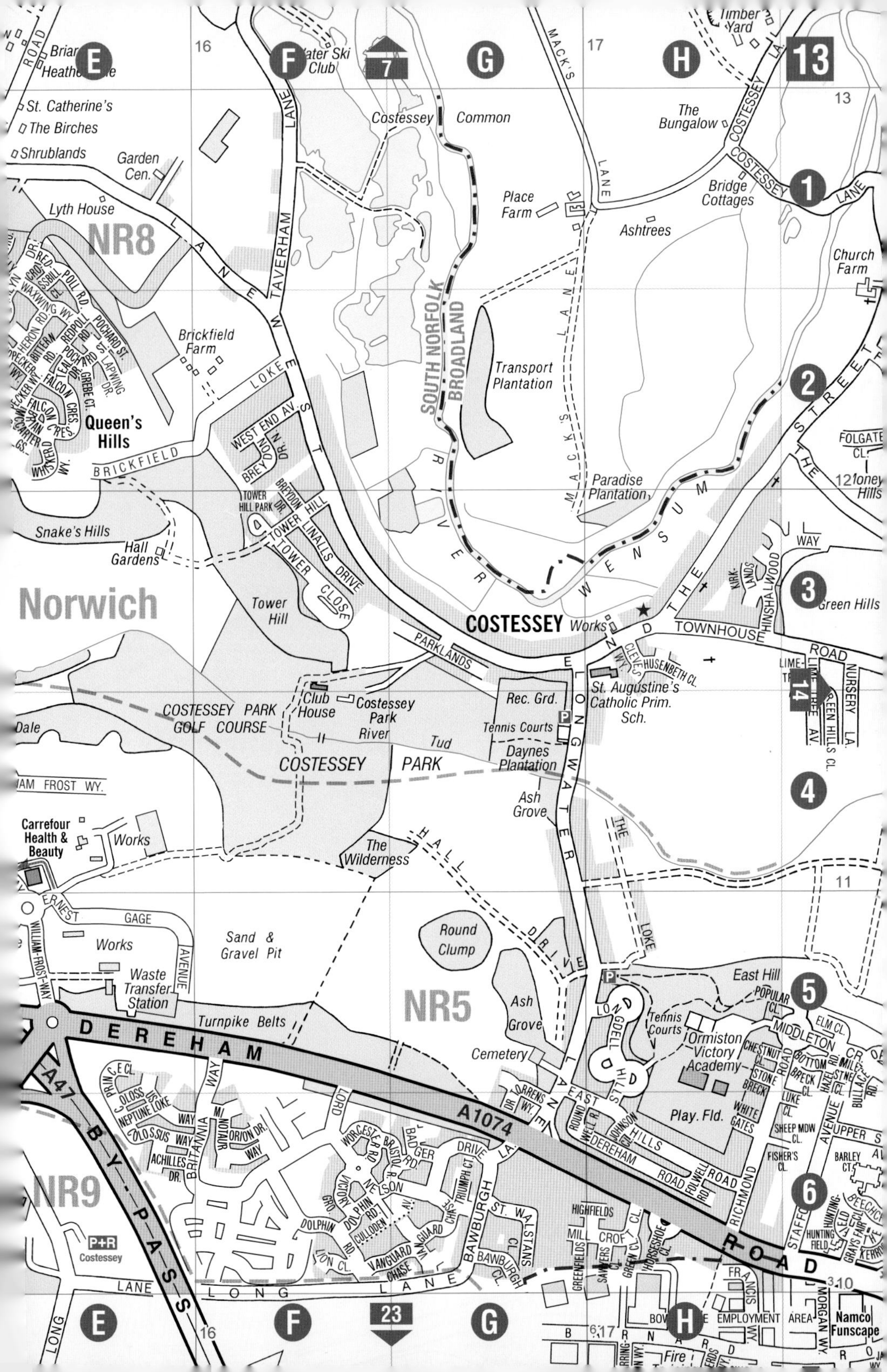
E
F
G
H
16
17
13
7
23
14
1
2
3
4
5
6
11
12
Water Ski Club
Costessey Common
Timber Yard
The Bungalow
Bridge Cottages
Ashtrees
Place Farm
Church Farm
St. Catherine's
The Birches
Shrublands
Garden Cen.
Lyth House
NR8
Brickfield Farm
Queen's Hills
BRICKFIELD
Snake's Hills
Hall Gardens
Norwich
TAVERHAM LANE
WEST END AV.
BREYDON DR. N.
TOWER HILL PARK
TOWER HILL
LINALLS DRIVE
TOWER CLOSE
Tower Hill
LOKE
MACK'S LANE
COSTESSEY LANE
SOUTH NORFOLK
BROADLAND
Transport Plantation
Paradise Plantation
RIVER WENSUM
THE STREET
FOLGATE CL.
Honey Hills
WAY
KIRKLANDS
HINSHALWOOD
Green Hills
COSTESSEY
Works
TOWNHOUSE ROAD
PARKLANDS
CLEVES WY.
HUSENBETH CL.
St. Augustine's Catholic Prim. Sch.
LIME TREE AV.
GREEN HILLS CL.
NURSERY LA.
Club House
Costessey Park
River Tud
Rec. Grd.
Tennis Courts
COSTESSEY PARK GOLF COURSE
COSTESSEY PARK
Daynes Plantation
Ash Grove
LONGWATER LANE
Dale
WILLIAM FROST WY.
Carrefour Health & Beauty
Works
ERNEST GAGE AVENUE
Works
Waste Transfer Station
Sand & Gravel Pit
The Wilderness
HALL DRIVE
Round Clump
THE LOKE
East Hill
POPULAR CL.
Tennis Courts
Ormiston Victory Academy
MIDDLETON CR.
ELM CL.
CHESTNUT CL.
STONE BRECK
WHITE GATES
Play. Fld.
RICHMOND ROAD
NR5
Ash Grove
Cemetery
Turnpike Belts
DEREHAM ROAD
A1074
A47
BY-PASS
NR9
P+R Costessey
PRINCE CL.
COLOSSUS LOKE
NEPTUNE
COLOSSUS WAY
ACHILLES DR.
BRITANNIA WAY
MINOTAUR
ORION DR.
LORD
WORCESTER RD.
BRISTOL RD.
BADGER RD.
DRIVE
NELSON
VICTORY GRO.
DOLPHIN RD.
DOLPHIN
CULLODEN
VANGUARD
VANGUARD CHASE
LION CL.
TRIUMPH CT.
BAWBURGH LA.
BAWBURGH CL.
ST. WALSTANS CL.
DR. TORRENS WY.
EAST HILLS
ROUND WELL RD.
JOHNSON
FOLWELL RD.
HIGHFIELDS
MILL CROFT
GREENFIELDS
SAWYERS CL.
GREEN CL.
HORSESHOE CL.
FRANCIS
EMPLOYMENT AREA
MORGAN WY.
Namco Funscape
LONG LANE
LONG
LANE
BRECK CL.
LUKE CL.
SHEEP MDW CL.
FISHER'S CL.
AVENUE
UPPER
BARLEY CT.
HUNTING FIELD
GRAYS FAIR
BULLACE
Fire

14
A
B
C
D
1
2
3
4
5
6
8
13
24
NR8
NR5
Norwich
NEW COSTESSEY
Timber Yard
The Bungalow
Bridge Cottages
COSTESSEY LA.
Mill Cottages
The Rookery
Old Costessey House
Church Farm
Old Lodge
Bloods Dale
DRAYTON ROAD
A1067
MAGNAY RD.
HOWELL RD.
HURN RD.
ST. EDMUND'S CL.
FOLGATE
FOLGATE CL.
VICARAGE CL.
Money's Hills
SIDNEY RD.
THE CROFT
WINDMILL LA.
HALWOOD WY.
KIRKWOODS
HINSHALWOOD WY.
Green Hills
HIGHLANDS
THE GLADE
CARR'S HILL CL.
Windmill Farm
Carr's Hill
TOWNHOUSE ROAD
LIME TREE AV.
GREEN HILLS CL.
NURSERY LA.
MYRTLE AV.
HILL TOP DR.
STIMPSON LOKE
KOST RD.
PICCOLI CL.
Floral Acres Nursery
Point Cottages
Wensum Mount Farm
RIVER
BROADLAND
SOUTH NORFOLK
Rogers Farm
River Tud
Red Bridge
RED BRIDGE LANE
GUNTON LANE
Play. Fld.
OTTAWAY CL.
MEADOW VALE
MEADOW RD.
CHAPEL RD.
MEADOW CL.
HALL RD.
HILLVUE CL.
ELDER CL.
VICTORIA WY.
HILDA BROOKES WY.
FOXES CT.
HAWTHORN RD.
SWINDELLS CL.
HILL CREST
ASHTREE
KABIN ROAD
RUSKIN RD.
MITHDALE R.
MARGARET RD.
GLENDA CT.
GLENDA CRES.
GLENDA CL.
GLENDA ROAD
OLIVE RD.
OLIVE CL.
East Hill
POPLAR CL.
ELM CL.
MIDDLETON CRESCENT
Ormiston Victory Academy
CHESTNUT CL.
STONE BRECK
WHITE GATES
BOTTOM BRECK CL.
HAZEL CL.
MILESTONE CL.
OAK CL.
Playground
FARMLAND RD.
VALLEY VW.
GROVEDALE CL.
WEST CL.
WEST RD.
WOODLANDS RD.
Bunkers Hill
HIGHLOW RD.
GREENWOOD VW.
GURNEY AVENUE
GEORGE LOWE CL.
RICHMOND ROAD
SHEEP MDW CL.
FISHER'S CL.
FOLWELL RD.
UPPER STAFFORD AV.
DARLEY CT.
ROWAN CT.
BEECHCROFT
HUNTINGFIELD
GRAYS FAIR
THE KERRODS
THREE MILE LANE
UPPER BRECKLAND RD
BRECKLAND ROAD
Lib.
Youth Centre
Costessey Jun. Sch.
Play. Fld.
JERNINGHAM ROAD
THE LINNETS
DE GREY CL.
CROWN RD.
BEAUMONT
Costessey Inf. Sch.
HENDON CL.
GROVE ROAD
SUNNY CL.
SUNNY GRO.
SUNNY CT.
SANTOLINA CL.
THE DRIVE
EVERSON CL.
NORTHVIEW RD.
LINDEN RD.
VALLEY ROAD
OVAL AV.
WOODHILL RISE
Play. Fld.
Valley Acad.
DEREHAM ROAD
A1074
FRANCIS WY.
EMPLOYMENT AREA
MORGAN WY.
JARROLD WY. IND. EST.
Ten. Cts.
Bowthorpe Park
Bowl
The FDC
AUTUMN DR.
MARSHALL CL.
GURNEY CL.
NORWICH ROAD

HELLESDON
LOWER HELLESDON
MILE CROSS
NR6
Hellesdon Hospital
Hellesdon High Sch.
Kinsale Infant & Junior Schools
Firside Jun. Sch. Play. Fld.
Recreation Ground
Comm. Cen.
Lib.
Tennis Courts
Arden Grove Inf. Sch.
Superstore
Hotel
David Lloyd
Boundary Cross
Hellesdon Park Industrial Estate
Sweet Briar Retail Park
Sweet Briar Ind. Est.
Rabbits' Hill
Burial Ground
Works
Factory
Warehouse
Chemical Works
Hill House
Sloughbottom Park
BMX Track
Cycle Speedway
Playing Field
Recycling Centre
Depots
Water Works
Norman Rec. Cen.
Mile Cross Prim. Sch.
Sports Ground
Bowl. Grn.
Play. Fld.
Hellesdon Bri.
Airport
Drayton Wood
NORWICH
A1067
A140
A1024
HIGH ROAD
REEPHAM ROAD
BOUNDARY ROAD
DRAYTON ROAD
SWEET BRIAR ROAD
HOLT RD.
CROMER ROAD
MILE CROSS ROAD
HELLESDON HALL ROAD
HELLESDON LANE
HOSPITAL LANE
GOWING ROAD
WOODLAND ROAD
DRAYTON WOOD ROAD
WESTWOOD DRIVE
NEYLOND CRESCENT
LINKS AVENUE
PINEWOOD CLOSE
MEADOW WAY
HAWTHORNE AVENUE
BOWERS AVENUE
GALLEY HILL
SLOUGHBOTTOM PARK
AYLMER TOWER
MARKHAM TOWER
SEAMAN TOWER
E F G H
1 2 3 4 5 6
9
16
25
20 21 12 13 11 10

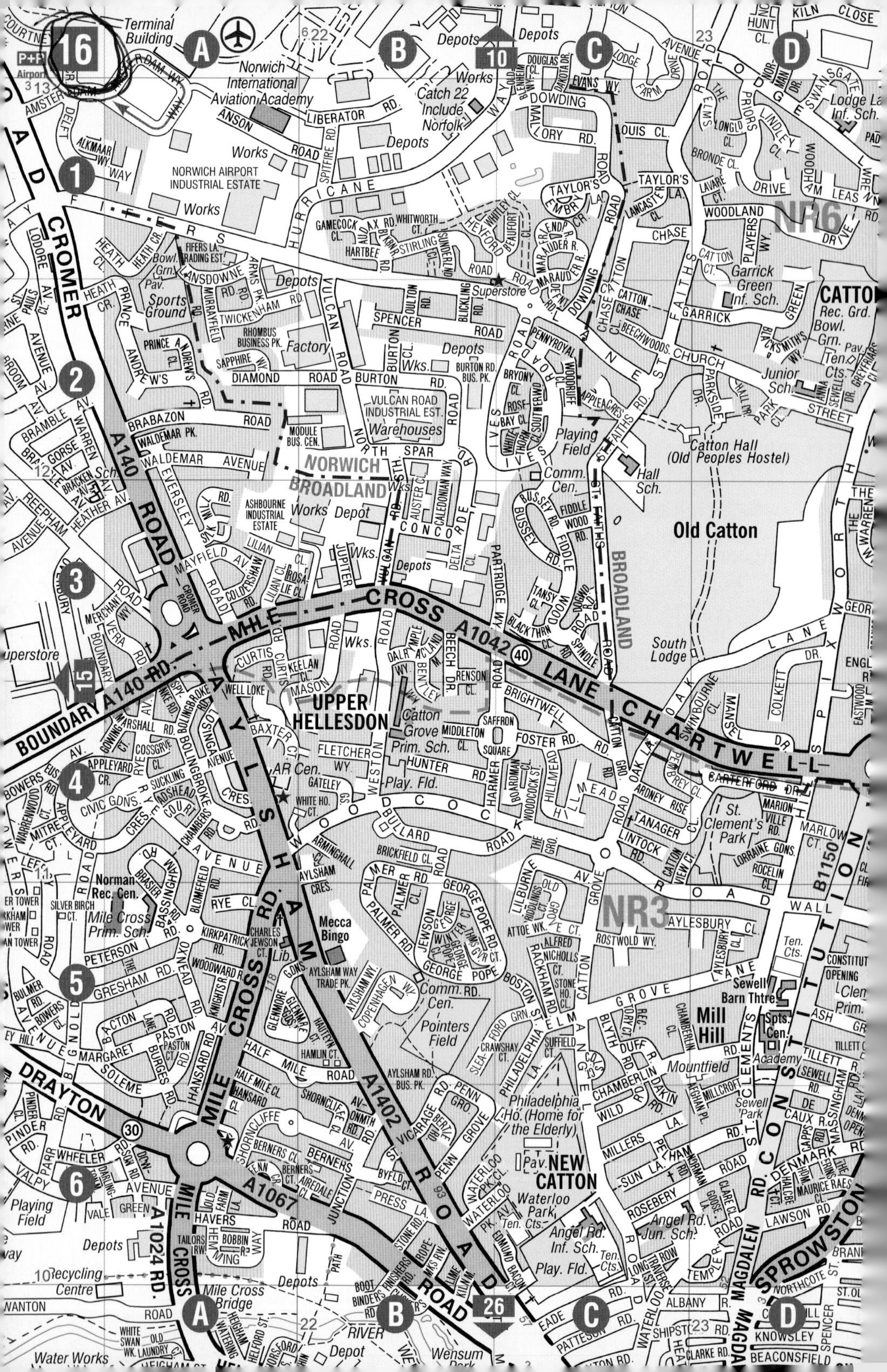
Terminal Building
Norwich International Aviation Academy
NORWICH AIRPORT INDUSTRIAL ESTATE
Depots
Works
10
Catch 22 Include Norfolk
A
B
C
D
1
2
3
4
5
6
NR6
CATTON
Garrick Green Inf. Sch.
Junior Sch.
Catton Hall (Old Peoples Hostel)
Hall Sch.
Old Catton
South Lodge
VULCAN ROAD INDUSTRIAL EST.
Warehouses
NORWICH
BROADLAND
ASHBOURNE INDUSTRIAL ESTATE
RHOMBUS BUSINESS PK.
Factory
Sports Ground
Superstore
15
UPPER HELLESDON
Catton Grove Prim. Sch.
Play. Fld.
AR Cen.
St. Clement's Park
NR3
Norman Rec. Cen.
Mile Cross Prim. Sch.
Mecca Bingo
AYLSHAM WAY TRADE PK.
Lib.
Comm. Cen.
Pointers Field
Philadelphia Ho. (Home for the Elderly)
NEW CATTON
Waterloo Park
Angel Rd. Jun. Sch.
Angel Rd. Inf. Sch.
Mill Hill
Sewell Barn Thtre.
Mountfield
Sewell Park
Academy
Playing Field
Recycling Centre
Mile Cross Bridge
Water Works
Depot
26
CROMER ROAD A140
BOUNDARY A140 RD.
MILE CROSS A1042 LANE
CHARTWELL
AYLSHAM RD. A1402
DRAYTON A1067
MILE CROSS A1024 RD.
CONSTITUTION B1150
SPROWSTON
ST. FAITHS ROAD
WOODCOCK ROAD
HURRICANE WAY
FIFERS LANE

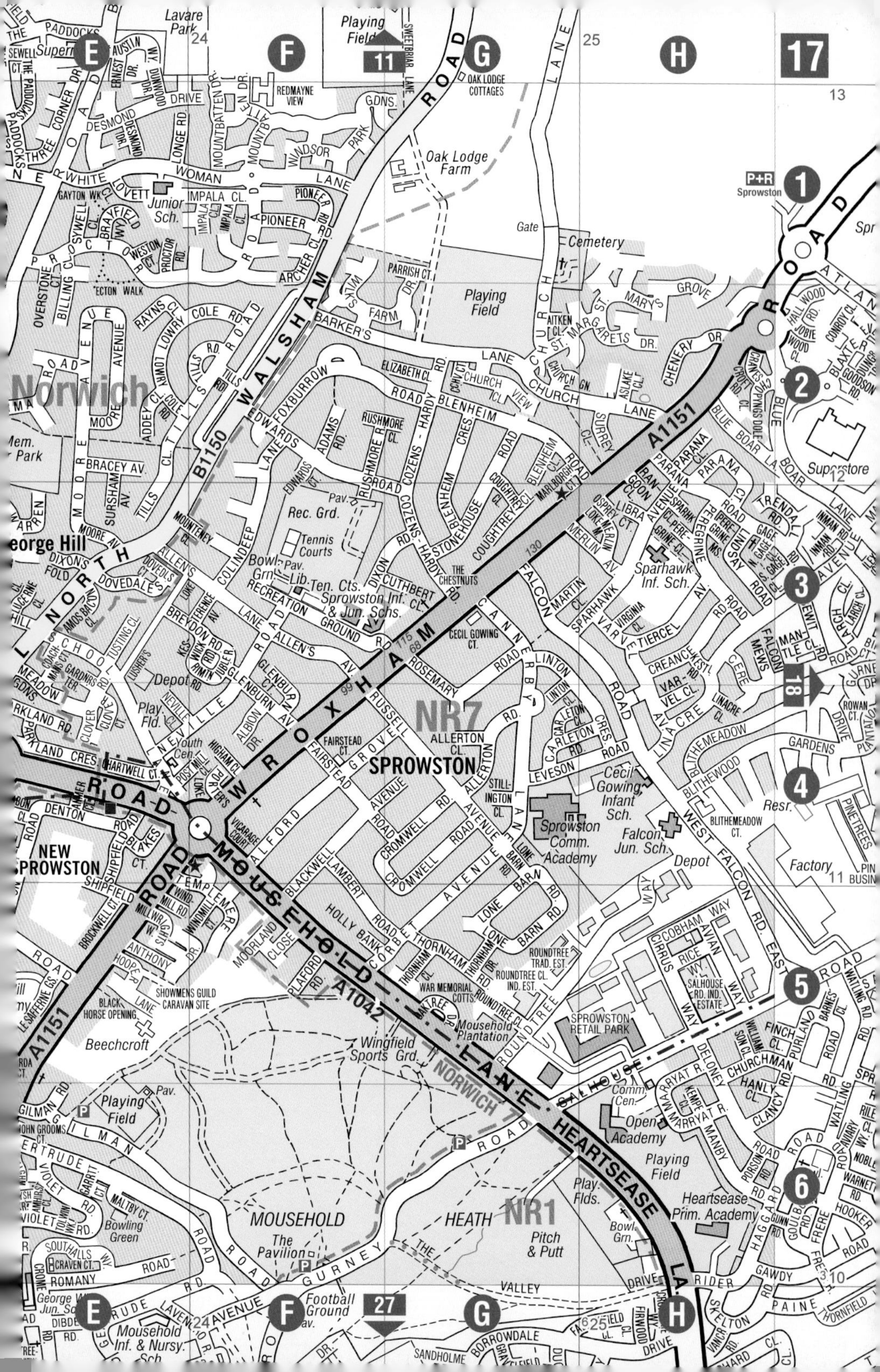

Norwich
SPROWSTON
NEW SPROWSTON
NR7
NR1
MOUSEHOLD
HEATH
George Hill
Lavare Park
Playing Field
Oak Lodge Farm
OAK LODGE COTTAGES
Cemetery
Junior Sch.
Rec. Grd.
Tennis Courts
Sprowston Inf. & Jun. Schs.
Sparhawk Inf. Sch.
Superstore
Cecil Gowing Infant Sch.
Sprowston Comm. Academy
Falcon Jun. Sch.
Depot
Factory
SPROWSTON RETAIL PARK
Open Academy
Heartsease Prim. Academy
Wingfield Sports Grd.
Mousehold Plantation
Beechcroft
The Pavilion
Pitch & Putt
Football Ground
Mousehold Inf. & Nursy. Sch.
SHOWMENS GUILD CARAVAN SITE
ROUNDTREE TRAD. EST.
SALHOUSE RD. IND. ESTATE
WAR MEMORIAL COTTS.
WALSHAM ROAD
NORTH WALSHAM ROAD
WROXHAM ROAD
MOUSEHOLD LANE
HEARTSEASE LA.
WHITE WOMAN LANE
BLUE BOAR LANE
WEST FALCON RD.
FALCON ROAD
CHURCH LANE
BARKER'S LANE
BLENHEIM ROAD
FOXBURROW ROAD
RECREATION GROUND RD.
GURNEY ROAD
VALLEY DRIVE
SALHOUSE ROAD
A1151
A1042
B1150
P+R Sprowston
E
F
G
H
1
2
3
4
5
6
11
18
27
24
25
13
12
11
10

A
B
C
D
1
2
3
4
5
6
313
26
27
12
11
10
Sprowston Plantation
Park Cotts.
Cock Shoot
Rackheath Park
Newman's Strip
SPROWSTON MANOR GOLF COURSE
Club House
Golf Driving Range
P+R Sprowston
A1151
WROXHAM ROAD
Sprowston Manor (Hotel)
The Owlery
ATLANTIC AVENUE
NR7
Arnup's Belt
Paine's Yard Wood
GROVE
HALL WOOD RD.
JOBIE WOOD CL.
CONROY CL.
BLAXTER WY.
DUNGEE RD.
GOODSON RD.
CLOSE
MOORHEN CL.
LURKINS CRES.
HERON CL.
COOT DR.
WAY
GREBE DR.
POND WY.
BLUE BOAR LANE
Superstore
MUTE CR.
SWAN LA.
White House Farm Cotts.
White House Farm
PARANA CL.
PARANA
TRENDALL RD.
PEREGRINE RD.
GAGE RD.
GAGE CL.
INMAN RD.
MALLARD
Boar Plantation
SHELDUCK WY.
GREYLAG CL.
BEAN GOOSE RW.
EGYPTIAN GOOSE RD.
BITTERN
WOODCOCK DR.
CARTER RD.
OVERSTRAND WY.
LAUNDRY LA.
Sports Grnd.
Pav.
OVERSTRAND
ELLIS CL.
RANDALL
MALLET CL.
HANSON CL.
SOUTHALL RD.
Round Hill Plantation
Bulmer Coppice
AVENUE
BEWIT
MANTLE CL.
FALCON MEWS
LARCH CL.
YEW CT.
BEAM CL.
BIRCH CT.
GURNEY DR.
MERE
LINACRE CL.
17
Garden Cen.
ROWAN CT.
PLANTATION DR.
PINE CT.
DRIVE
BOLTON
BOBOLINK RW.
BOURGES CT.
The Breck
Grange Farm Bungalow
Grange Farm
BLITHEMEADOW
GARDENS
BLITHEWOOD
COTTAGE PLANTATION
Harrison's Plantation
Sprowston Grange Cottage
Reservoir
BLITHEMEADOW CT.
WEST FALCON RD.
PINETREES
Depot
Factory
PINETREES BUSINESS PARK
SALHOUSE
HAMMOND WY.
HARRISONS DR.
GREENWOOD WAY
WOODCROFT CL.
GREENBOROUGH
BRECK RD.
Heath Farm
CASTON IND. EST.
BROADLAND
NORWICH ROAD
WOODSIDE ROAD
SALE ROAD
LISHMAN RD.
AVIAN WY.
RICE WY.
SALHOUSE RD. IND. ESTATE
EAST
ASHBOURNE TWR.
BURLEIGH TWR.
COMPASS TWR.
Rec. Grd.
RACECOURSE PLANTATION
Slaughter House
WATLING RD.
FINCH CL.
PURLAND ROAD
BARNES CL.
MUNNINGS RD.
WILLIAMSON CL.
DELONEY
CHURCHMAN RD.
HANLY CL.
CLANCY RD.
MARRYAT R.
KEMPE CL.
WOODFORDE RD.
SPRINGFIELD RD.
BARCLAY ROAD
FUGILL GRN.
RACECOURSE
ARMSTRONG RD.
PASTON WY.
POUND LANE
Brown's Plantation
RILEY CL.
TINGHAM
CHIPPERFIELD RD.
LAUREL CT.
GOODWOOD
REDFERN
MANBY
ROAD
NOBLE CL.
COLLS WK.
GRAHAM SQ.
PIPER RD.
PINE RD.
FIRTREE RD.
LAUREL
Belmore Plantation
Bowl. Grn.
WARNETT RD.
HOOKER RD.
WITARD RD.
DE HAVILLAND PL.
THURLING PLAIN
TRACEY RD.
DRIVE
SOUTH HILL ROAD
Woodland Studio
Heartsease Prim. Academy
HAGGARD RD.
GOULBURN RD.
GUNN RD.
FRERE RD.
GAWDY
RIDER
PAINE
THORNFIELD WY.
HOLMES CL.
PLUMSTEAD ROAD
SKELTON RD.
BEECHWOOD
BELMORE RD.
CASTON RD.
BOOTY ROAD
FIRMAN CT.
HANSELL RD.
LONGFIELDS
PRIOR RD.
WOODLANDS CR.
Youth & Comm.
FURZE ROAD
THE COTTAGE DR.
STH. HILL
28
Thorpe St. Andrew
ROAD
Playing Field

BROADLAND
A1270
NORTHWAY
Norwich
NR13
NEW RACKHEATH
THORPE END
Dussindale Park
Mahoney Grn
Works
Green Lane
May Farm
Long's Cres.
Newman Rd.
Cherry Tree Farm
Yew Tree Farm
Gazebo Farm
Heath Wood
Rhododendron Covert
Pig's Park
March Covert
Brillig
Slipper's Bottom
Rackheath Prim. Sch.
Salhouse Road
West Green Lane
Green Lane East
Wilkinson
Tagg Wy.
Fuller Cl.
Wilde Rd.
Webb Dr.
Willoughby Wy.
Luscombe
Cornwall Cl.
Devon Cl.
Way
Canfor Rd.
Craske Dr.
Eva Rd.
Palmer Rd.
Sam Smith
Field Wy.
Green Wy.
Lighthouse Rd.
Norwich Rd.
Mousehold Farm
Vera Rd.
Burton Dr.
Lonsdale Rd.
Vera Cl.
Bernard Cl.
Broad Lane
Factory
Road
Norwich Rd.
Mousehold House
Reeve's Corner
Brooklyn House
Newman's Farm
The Belt
Hallgate
Alton-Gate
North Gate
Padgate
Seppings Wy.
Broadmead Grn.
Broadmead Gn.
Broadland Dr.
Broad Vw.
Barker Wy.
Beechbank Dr.
Heather Wood
Heather Cl.
Drive
Plumstead Road
The Boulevard
The Lawn Cr.
Drive
Woodland
Sth. Wlk.
Percy Howes Cl.
St. Davids Dr.
Heath Rd.
East Green Lane
Triangle Wood
Broad La.
Hare Lane
Lane
Road
Orchard Cottage
Oaks Farm
Oak Farm Cottage
Toad Lane
Broome Cottage
Hall Farm
Middle Road
The Lodge
Red House
Great Plumstead Hall
Laurel Farm Cotts.
Low Road
North Road
Brook Fm.
Green La. Sth.
Meadow View
South Lodge Farm
Nursery
Pikeman Place
Pym Cl.
Pride Wy.
Cornet Cl.
Hyde Ct.
Waller Cl.
Dowsing Ct.
Lynn Cl.
Joyce Wy.
Marvel Gn.
Leven Cl.
Skippon Way
Fleetwood Dr.
Desborough Way
Maidens Cl.
Fairfax Dr.
Insborough Rise
E
F
G
H
1
2
3
4
5
6
13
12
11
10
28
29

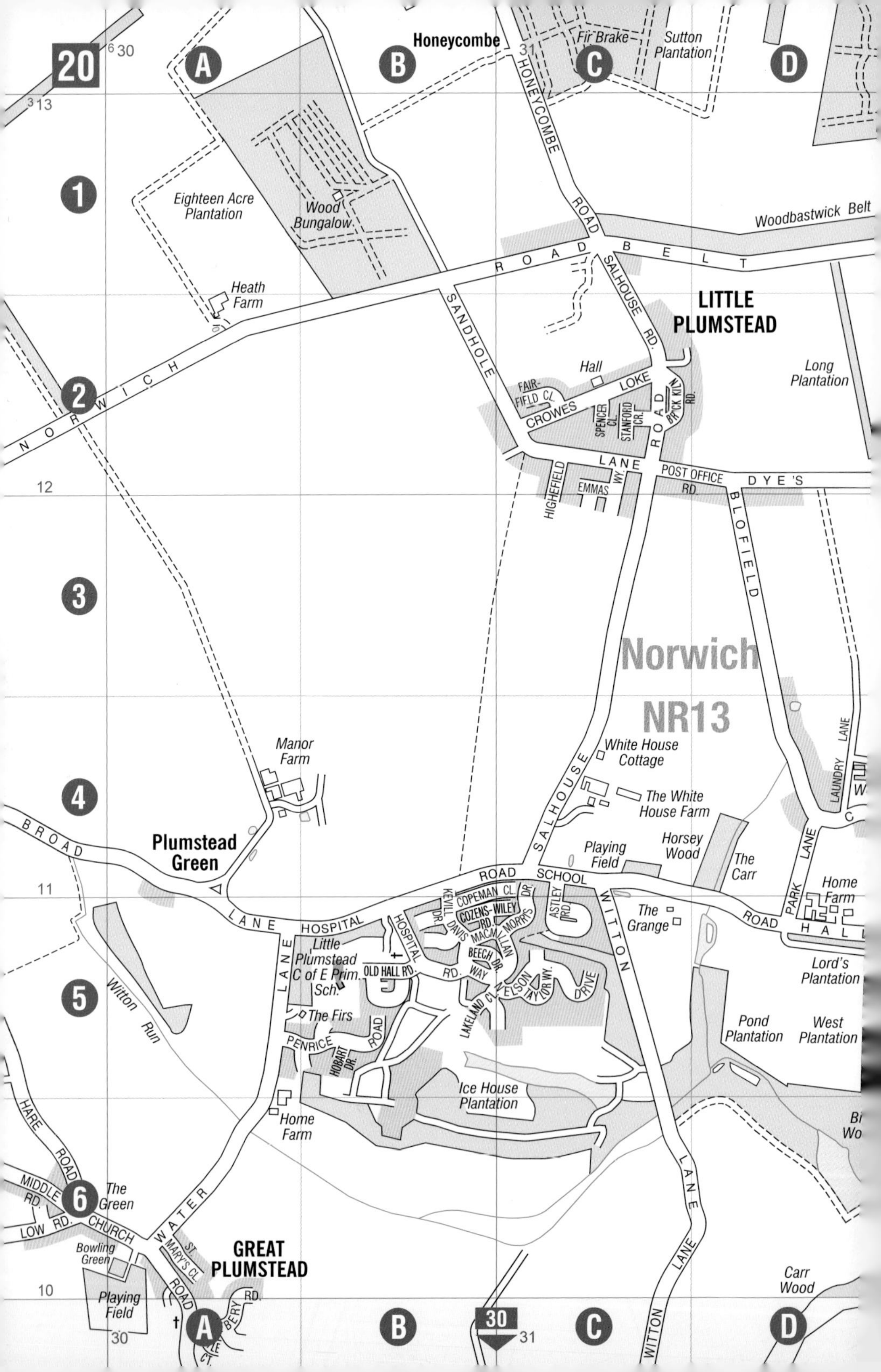

Honeycombe
Fir Brake
Sutton Plantation
HONEYCOMBE ROAD
Eighteen Acre Plantation
Wood Bungalow
Woodbastwick Belt
ROAD BELT
Heath Farm
SANDHOLE
SALHOUSE RD.
LITTLE PLUMSTEAD
Hall
Long Plantation
NORWICH ROAD
FAIR-FIELD CL.
LOKE
CROWES
SPENCER CL.
STANFORD CR.
ROAD
BRICK KILN RD.
FAIR
LANE
POST OFFICE RD.
DYE'S
HIGHFIELD
EMMAS WY.
BLOFIELD
Norwich
NR13
Manor Farm
White House Cottage
SALHOUSE
The White House Farm
LAUNDRY LANE
BROAD
Plumstead Green
Playing Field
Horsey Wood
The Carr
PARK LANE
Home Farm
ROAD SCHOOL
LANE HOSPITAL
HOSPITAL RD.
COPEMAN CL.
KEVILL DR.
COZENS-WILEY RD.
DAVIS
MACMILLAN
MORRIS DR.
ASTLEY RD.
WITTON
The Grange
ROAD HALL
Little Plumstead C of E Prim. Sch.
OLD HALL RD.
BEECH DR.
WAY
NELSON
TAYLOR WY.
DRIVE
LAKELAND CL.
Lord's Plantation
Witton Run
The Firs
PENRICE ROAD
HOBART DR.
Pond Plantation
West Plantation
Ice House Plantation
Home Farm
HARE ROAD
MIDDLE RD.
The Green
LOW RD.
CHURCH
WATER
ST. MARY'S CL.
ROAD
GREAT PLUMSTEAD
Bowling Green
Playing Field
BERY RD.
CT.
WITTON LANE
Carr Wood
30
31
13
12
11
10
A
B
C
D
1
2
3
4
5
6

30

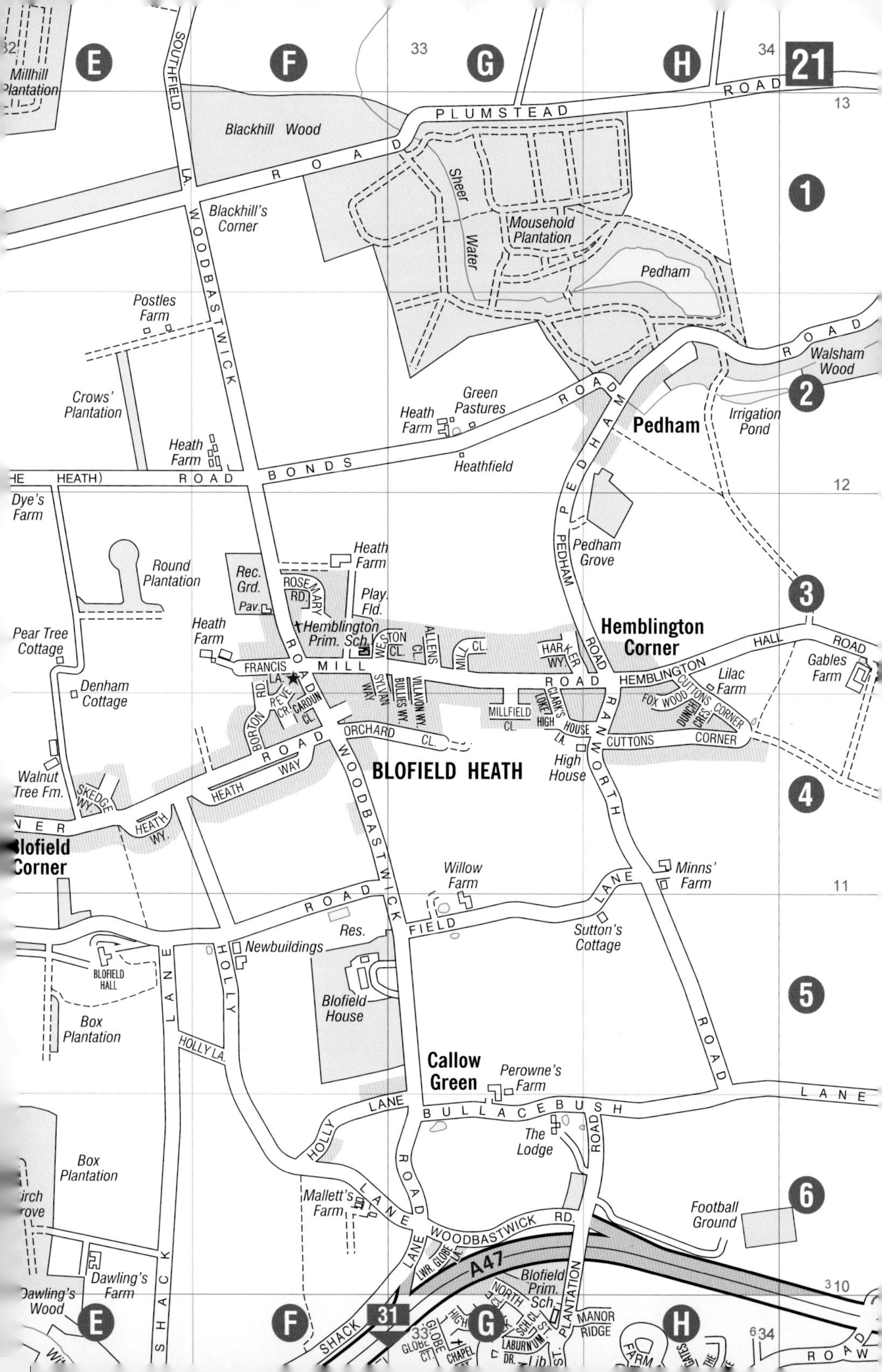
E
F
G
H
33
34
13
12
11
10
1
2
3
4
5
6
Millhill Plantation
SOUTHFIELD LA.
Blackhill Wood
PLUMSTEAD ROAD
Blackhill's Corner
Sheer Water
Mousehold Plantation
Pedham
WOODBASTWICK
Postles Farm
Crows' Plantation
Heath Farm
Green Pastures
Heathfield
BONDS ROAD
(THE HEATH) ROAD
Walsham Wood
Irrigation Pond
Pedham
PEDHAM ROAD
Pedham Grove
Dye's Farm
Round Plantation
Rec. Grd.
Pav.
ROSEMARY RD.
Play. Fld.
Hemblington Prim. Sch.
Pear Tree Cottage
Denham Cottage
FRANCIS LA.
MILL ROAD
WESTON CL.
ALLENS CL.
MILL CL.
HARKER WY.
Hemblington Corner
HEMBLINGTON HALL ROAD
Gables Farm
Lilac Farm
FOX WOOD
CUTTONS CORNER
DUNCH CRES.
BORTON RD.
REVE CR.
CARDUN CL.
SYLVAN WAY
BULLIES WY.
VILLAVON WY.
ORCHARD CL.
MILLFIELD CL.
LOKE
CLARK'S
HIGH HOUSE LA.
CUTTONS CORNER
High House
RANWORTH ROAD
BLOFIELD HEATH
Walnut Tree Fm.
SKEDGE WY.
HEATH WAY
HEATH WY.
Blofield Corner
Willow Farm
Minns' Farm
FIELD LANE
Sutton's Cottage
Res.
Newbuildings
BLOFIELD HALL
Box Plantation
HOLLY LA.
Blofield House
SHACK LANE
Callow Green
Perowne's Farm
BULLACEBUSH LANE
The Lodge
Box Plantation
Mallett's Farm
WOODBASTWICK RD.
LWR. GLOBE LA.
A47
31
Blofield Prim. Sch.
PLANTATION ROAD
Football Ground
Birch Grove
Dawling's Farm
Dawling's Wood
MANOR RIDGE
NORTH ST.
SCH. CL.
LABURNUM
DR.
HIGH ST.
GLOBE CT.
CHAPEL
Lib.
FARM
GATES
THE
ROAD

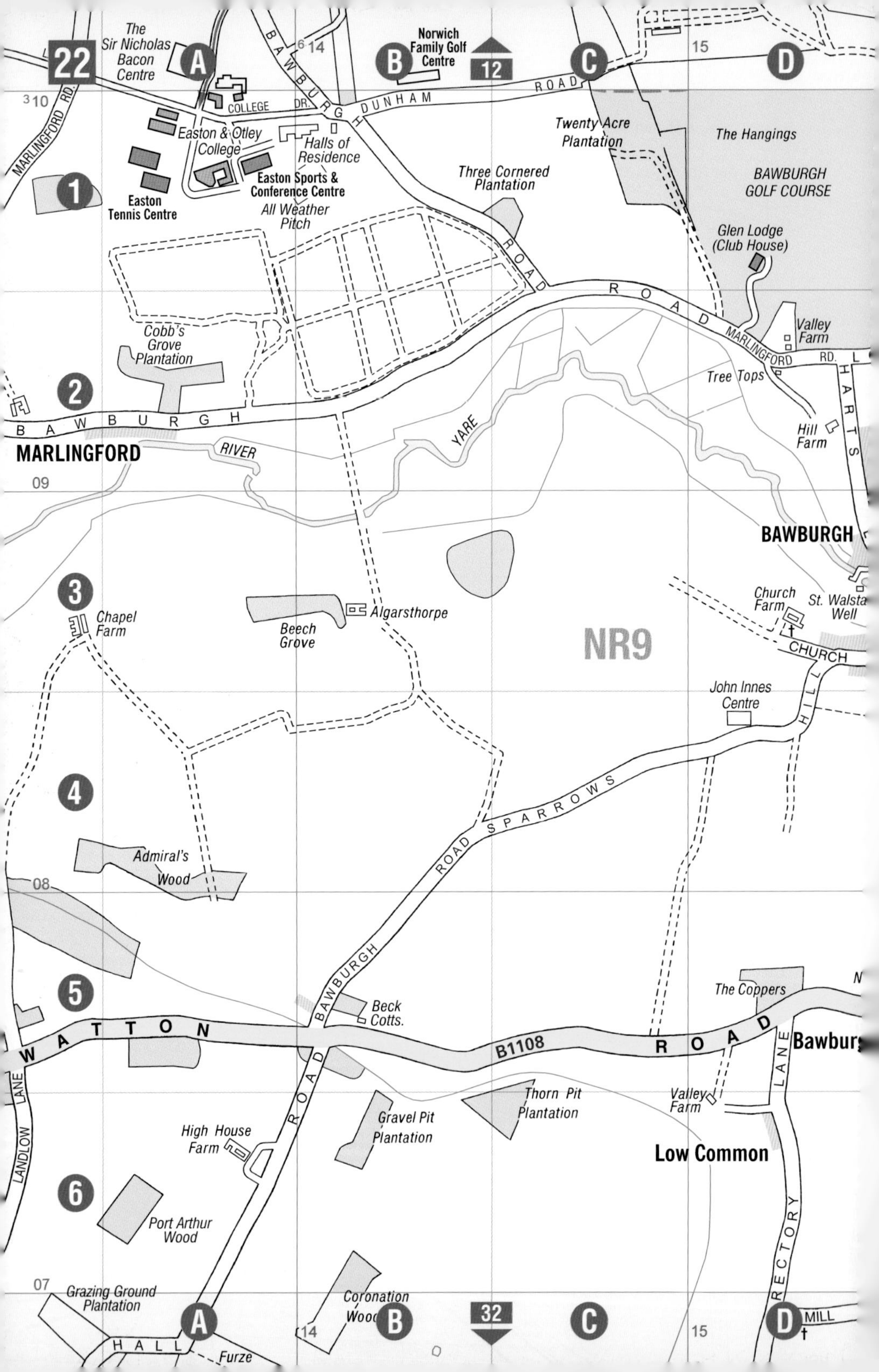
12
The Sir Nicholas Bacon Centre
Norwich Family Golf Centre
Easton & Otley College
Halls of Residence
Easton Sports & Conference Centre
Easton Tennis Centre
All Weather Pitch
COLLEGE DR.
MARLINGFORD RD.
BAWBURGH DUNHAM ROAD
Twenty Acre Plantation
The Hangings
BAWBURGH GOLF COURSE
Three Cornered Plantation
Glen Lodge (Club House)
Valley Farm
ROAD
MARLINGFORD RD.
Tree Tops
Hill Farm
HARTS
Cobb's Grove Plantation
BAWBURGH
MARLINGFORD
RIVER YARE
BAWBURGH
Chapel Farm
Algarsthorpe
Beech Grove
Church Farm
St. Walsta Well
NR9
CHURCH HILL
John Innes Centre
SPARROWS ROAD
Admiral's Wood
BAWBURGH
Beck Cotts.
The Coppers
WATTON B1108 ROAD
Bawburg
LANE
Valley Farm
Thorn Pit Plantation
Gravel Pit Plantation
High House Farm
Low Common
LANDLOW LANE
BAWBURGH ROAD
Port Arthur Wood
RECTORY LANE
Grazing Ground Plantation
Coronation Wood
MILL
HALL
Furze
32

23
13
33
24
E
F
G
H
1
2
3
4
5
6
16
17
10
09
08
07
P+R Costessey
Norwich
NR5
NR4
NORWICH SOUTHERN BY-PASS
A47
B1108
WATTON ROAD
NEW ROAD
LONG LANE
HOCKERING LANE
STOCKS HILL
GREEN LANE
SCHOOL LANE
LITTLE MELTON LANE
MILL ROAD
HETHERSETT LANE
DEREHAM ROAD
BARNARD ROAD
CHAPEL BREAK ROAD
HARPSFIELD
THREE SCORE ROAD
NORWICH BREAK
SOUTH NORFOLK
Beech Plantation
Long Lane Farm
The Rookery
Holmleigh
Hall Farm
Clinkhill Plantation
Lodge Farm
The Bawburgh Sch.
Sand & Gravel Pit
Summer House Plantation
COLNEY WOOD
Colney Hall
RIVER YARE
Colney Wood Burial Pk.
The Bungalow
Lower Hall Farm
Vicarage
Villa San Lorenzo
Villa Farm
Vine Cottage
Nursery
Ryebeck Plantation
Ryebeck
Limekiln Wood
Plantation
Milestone
Moonrakers
Village Hall
Manor Farm
Hospital Farm
LITTLE MELTON
Little Melton Prim. Sch.
Fire Training Cen.
BOWTHORPE EMPLOYMENT AREA
Namco Funscape
Junior School
Sch.
Hall
OAK HO.

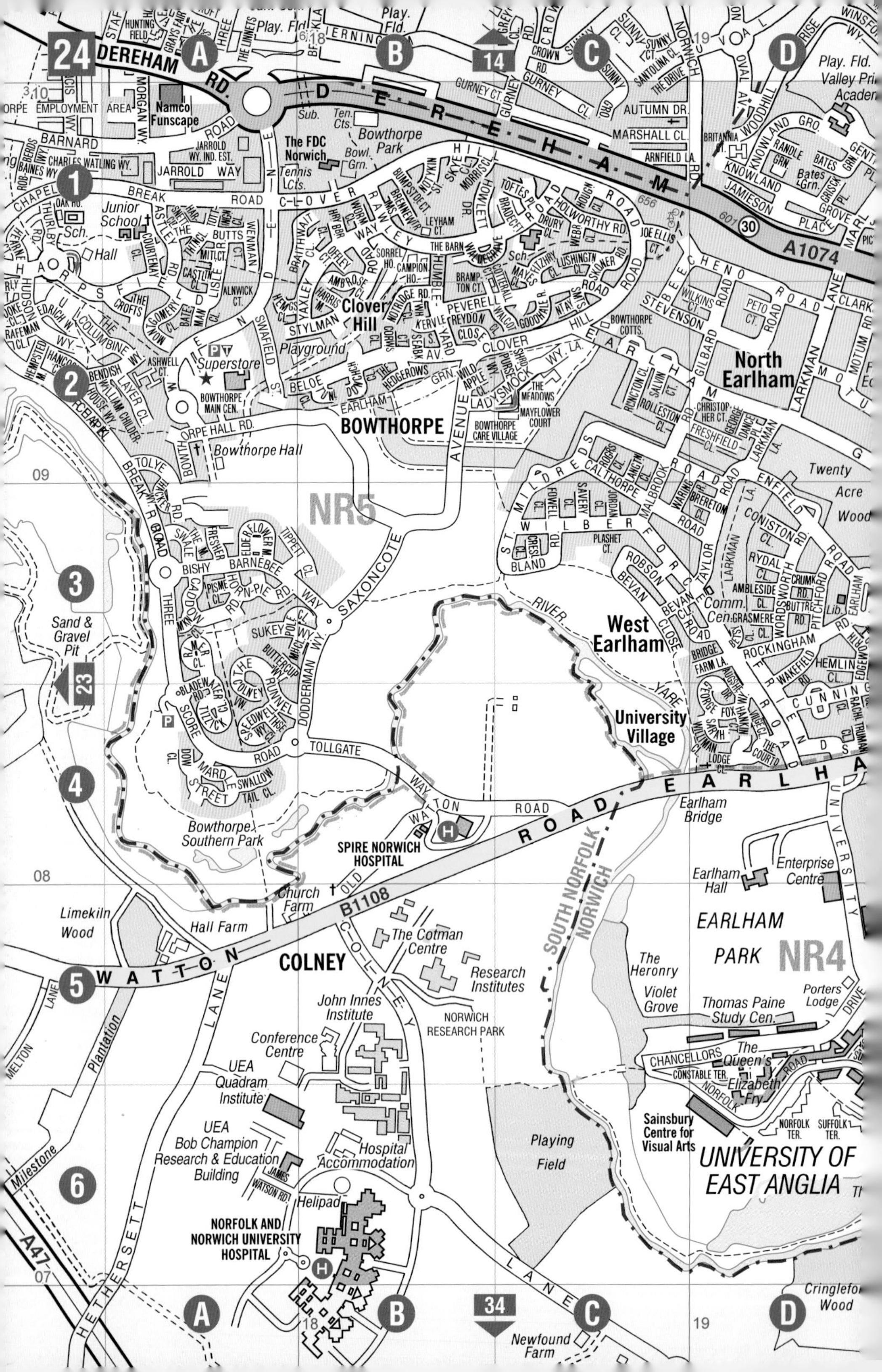

DEREHAM RD.
DEREHAM
A1074
Namco Funscape
EMPLOYMENT AREA
BARNARD
CHARLES WATLING WY.
JARROLD WY. IND. EST.
JARROLD WAY
The FDC Norwich
Bowthorpe Park
Bowl. Grn.
Tennis Cts.
Ten. Cts.
Sub.
CLOVER ROAD
BREAK ROAD
RAWLEY ROAD
Junior School
Sch.
Hall
Clover Hill
Playground
Superstore
BOWTHORPE MAIN CEN.
BOWTHORPE HALL RD.
Bowthorpe Hall
BOWTHORPE
BOWTHORPE CARE VILLAGE
MAYFLOWER COURT
THE MEADOWS
SAXONCOTE
DODDERMAN WY.
TOLLGATE WAY
NR5
North Earlham
West Earlham
Twenty Acre Wood
Comm. Cen.
Lib.
University Village
Sand & Gravel Pit
Bowthorpe Southern Park
WATTON ROAD
SPIRE NORWICH HOSPITAL
Church Farm
Hall Farm
Limekiln Wood
B1108
EARLHAM ROAD
Earlham Bridge
COLNEY
The Cotman Centre
Research Institutes
John Innes Institute
NORWICH RESEARCH PARK
Conference Centre
UEA Quadram Institute
UEA Bob Champion Research & Education Building
Hospital Accommodation
Helipad
NORFOLK AND NORWICH UNIVERSITY HOSPITAL
COLNEY LANE
HETHERSETT LANE
Plantation
Milestone
A47
SOUTH NORFOLK
NORWICH
Playing Field
Earlham Hall
Enterprise Centre
EARLHAM PARK
NR4
The Heronry
Violet Grove
Thomas Paine Study Cen.
Porters Lodge
CHANCELLORS DRIVE
The Queen's
Elizabeth Fry
Sainsbury Centre for Visual Arts
UNIVERSITY OF EAST ANGLIA
Cringleford Wood
Newfound Farm
Play. Fld.
Valley Primary Academy
Bates Grn.
14
23
34

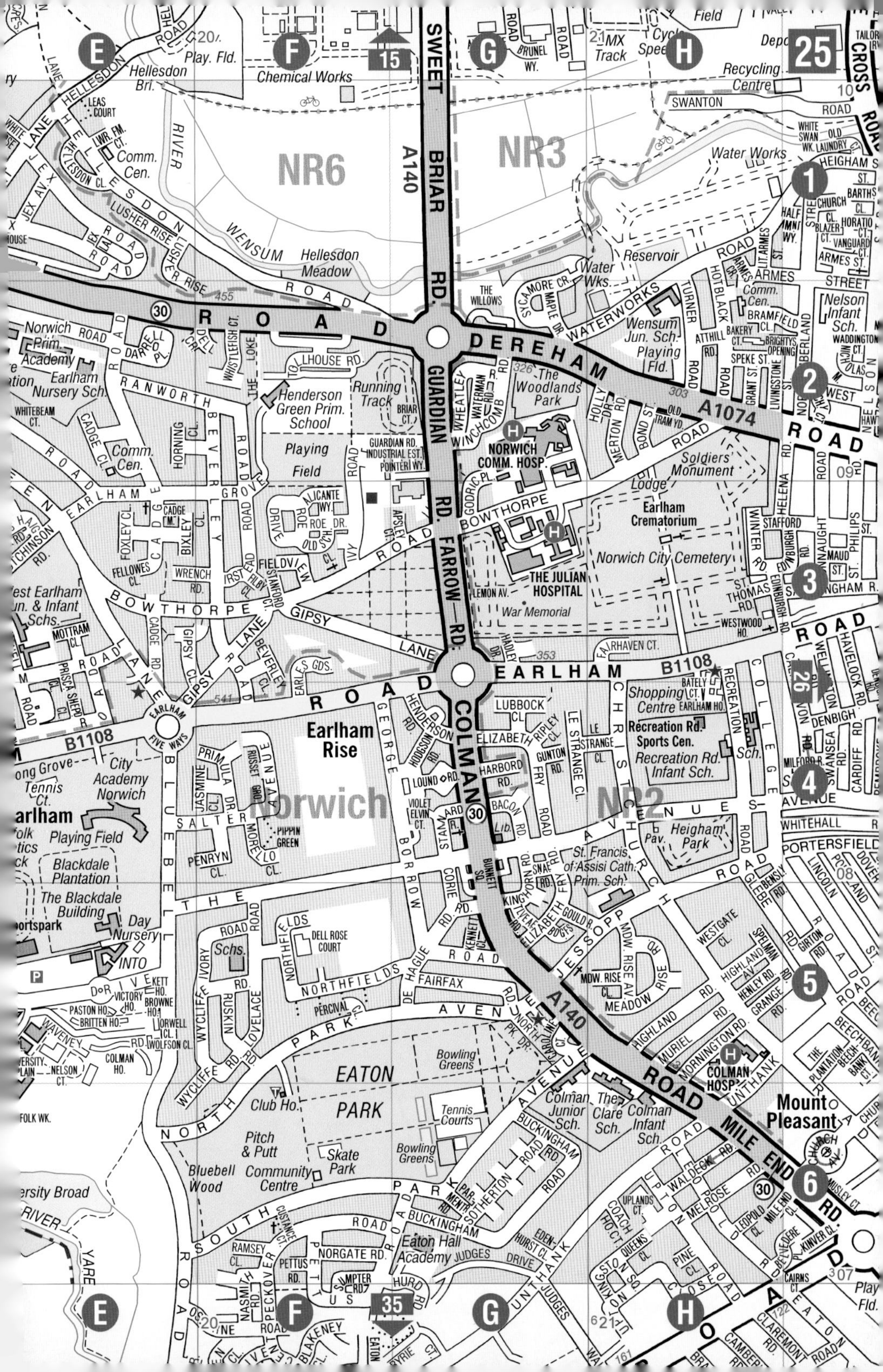
E
F
G
H
15
Chemical Works
Play. Fld.
Hellesdon Bri.
MX Track
Cycle Speedway
Recycling Centre
SWANTON ROAD
NR6
NR3
RIVER WENSUM
Hellesdon Meadow
Water Works
Reservoir
SWEET BRIAR RD.
A140
HELLESDON LANE
HELLESDON ROAD
LUSHER RISE
Comm. Cen.
1
2
3
4
5
6
26
35
DEREHAM ROAD
A1074
Norwich Prim. Academy
Earlham Nursery Sch.
RANWORTH
Henderson Green Prim. School
Running Track
Playing Field
GUARDIAN RD.
The Woodlands Park
NORWICH COMM. HOSP.
Wensum Jun. Sch. Playing Fld.
WATERWORKS
Nelson Infant Sch.
Soldiers' Monument
Lodge
Earlham Crematorium
Norwich City Cemetery
THE JULIAN HOSPITAL
War Memorial
BOWTHORPE ROAD
GIPSY LANE
FARROW RD.
EARLHAM ROAD
B1108
West Earlham Jun. & Infant Schs.
EARLHAM FIVE WAYS
Earlham Rise
Norwich
NR2
COLMAN ROAD
City Academy Norwich
Playing Field
Blackdale Plantation
The Blackdale Building
Day Nursery
INTO
Shopping Centre
Recreation Rd. Sports Cen.
Recreation Rd. Infant Sch.
Heigham Park
St. Francis of Assisi Cath. Prim. Sch.
THE AVENUES
BLUEBELL ROAD
NORTHFIELDS
DELL ROSE COURT
EATON PARK
Bowling Greens
Tennis Courts
Club Ho.
Pitch & Putt
Skate Park
Community Centre
Bluebell Wood
NORTH PARK AVENUE
SOUTH PARK AVENUE
Colman Junior Sch.
The Clare Sch.
Colman Infant Sch.
COLMAN HOSP.
UNTHANK ROAD
MILE END RD.
Mount Pleasant
Eaton Hall Academy
JUDGES DRIVE
BUCKINGHAM ROAD
RIVER YARE
Play Fld.

A
B
C
D
1
2
3
4
5
6
16
25
36
4
5
HAVERS ROAD
A1024
MILE CROSS ROAD
Mile Cross Bridge
Depots
Recycling Centre
Water Works
WATERWORKS RD.
HEIGHAM ST.
HEIGHAM ST.
OLD PALACE RD.
DRAYTON RD.
A1067
AYLSHAM RD. A140
RIVER WENSUM
Wensum Park
Depot
Angel Rd. Jun. Sch.
Angel Rd. Inf. Sch.
ANGEL RD.
LONG ROW
TEMPLE RD.
MAGDALEN RD.
SPROWSTON RD.
ALBANY RD.
SHIPSTONE RD.
CHURCHILL RD.
KNOWSLEY RD.
BEACONSFIELD RD.
MARLBOROUGH RD.
Silver Triangle
MAGPIE RD.
BULL CL. RD.
MAGDALEN ST.
WATERLOO RD.
PATTESON RD.
BUXTON RD.
EADE RD.
ST. MARTIN'S RD.
Warehouse
Tower (Rems. of)
Works
RIVERSIDE WALK
OAK ST.
SUSSEX ST.
CHATHAM ST.
PITT ST.
COWGATE
ST. CRISPINS ROAD
BARN RD.
A147
DEREHAM RD.
A1074
Nelson Infant Sch.
NELSON ST.
ARMES ST.
Comm. Cen.
HEIGHAM ST.
PADDOCK ST.
BARKER ST.
RUSSELL ST.
CLIFTON ST.
DEVONSHIRE ST.
HASLIPS CL.
ELY ST.
MIDLAND ST.
Belvedere Cen.
DISTILLERY SQ.
Heigham Grove
Care Home
WEST POTTERGATE
GRAPES HILL
SANDRINGHAM R.
STAFFORD ST.
CONNAUGHT RD.
PHILIPS RD.
ALEXANDRA RD.
GLADSTONE ST.
BELVOIR ST.
Cemetery
EARLHAM
B1108
EARLHAM RD.
NR2
PARK LA.
Cath.
Day Nursy.
The Vauxhall Cen.
CLARENDON RD.
NEVILLE ST.
GROSVENOR RD.
Bowl. Grn.
UNTHANK RD.
CHAPEL FIELD ROAD
Chapelfield Gardens
Chapelfield Grove
ST. BENEDICTS ST.
CHARING CROSS
ST. ANDREWS ST.
POTTERGATE
The Lanes
ST. GILES ST.
City Hall
Mus.
The Forum
BBC
THEATRE ST.
Thtre.
INTU CHAPELFIELD
ST. STEPHENS ST.
Norwich Bus Sta.
Coll.
Univ. Lib.
COLEGATE
ST. GEORGES ST.
DUKE ST.
WHITEFRIARS
FISHERGATE
QUAYSIDE
PALACE ST.
The Hostry
Spts. Cen.
Shire Hall
Mus.
CASTLE MEADOW
CASTLE MALL
ROUEN RD.
BER ST.
QUEEN'S RD.
A147
Superstore
Notre Dame High Sch.
Convent
ST. STEPHENS RD.
Victoria Ho.
Bignold Sch.
Fellowes Plain
GROVE RD.
GROVE AVENUE
TRAFFORD RD.
SOUTHWELL RD.
ASHBY ST.
TRAFALGAR ST.
CHERRY CL.
HOBART RD.
CYPRUS ST.
HARFORD ST.
Sch.
HOSPITAL LA.
Rec. Grd.
LINDLEY ST.
HALL RD.
Comm. Cen.
Rec. Grd.
KEYES
City Coll. Norwich
NR1
ELEANOR RD.
LADY MARY RD.
BRIAN AVENUE
PATRICIA RD.
ST. ALBAN'S RD.
LADY BETTY RD.
CECIL RD.
Cen. Halls
Cromwell
ROAD
The Hewett
IPSWICH ROAD
A1056
Town Close Ho. Prep. School
TOWN CLOSE RD.
A11 ROAD
NEWMARKET RD.
Norwich High Sch. for Girls
THE CEDARS
BEECH DR.
Golden Triangle
CAMBRIDGE ST.
TRINITY ST.
ESSEX ST.
YORK ST.
NEWMARKET ST.
UNTHANK RD.
AVENUE ROAD
WHITEHALL RD.
PORTERSFIELD RD.
Heigham Park
COLLEGE RD.
LINCOLN ST.
PORTLAND ST.
DOVER ST.
Mount Pleasant
CHRISTCHURCH RD.
COLMAN HOSP.
MILE END RD.
DANIELS RD.
Play.
Club Tennis Cts.
HORNOR CL.
ROSEACRE
NEWMARKET RD.
Sch.
Play. Fld.
Playgrd.

27
E
F
G
H
1
2
3
4
5
6
17
4
5
28
37
MOUSEHOLD
HEATH
Pitch & Putt
Prim. Academy
Bowling Green
VIOLET RD.
SILVER ROAD
CROME ROAD
ROMANY
George White Jun. Sch.
GERTRUDE
LAVENGRO
AVENUE
Mousehold Inf. & Nursy. Sch.
MOUSEHOLD
CAMPBELL CT.
NR3
Football Ground
Pav.
VALLEY
DRIVE
RIDER
HEARTSEASE LA.
A1042
SKELTON
PAINE
HORNFIELD
BORROWDALE
SANDHOLME CL.
MOSSFIELD CL.
GRAVELFIELD
DUGARD AV.
RIDGEWAY
GERALD CL.
STEEPGREEN CL.
RISEWAY CL.
TIMOTHY CL.
FALLOWFIELD CL.
FIRWOOD
CROFTHOLME
ORCHARD CL.
PLUMSTEAD RD. E.
AERODROME RD.
BODMIN CT.
Bowl. Grn.
The County Arts Bowl Club
ST. WILLIAMS WY.
MARGETSON AV.
HARVEY CL.
PILLING RD.
GORDON AVENUE
HENBY WY.
HOWARD
BOULTON RD.
LIME TREE AV.
WHITE FARM LA.
ROCKLAND DR.
SCHOOL LA.
Sports
Playing Field
The Oaks
Bowl. Grn.
Thorpe Tower
BEECH DR.
MONS AV.
BRITANNIA
Sports Field
Pav.
HMP & YOI NORWICH
KNOX AV.
KNOX CL.
HM Remand Cen.
HILARY AV.
ALDRYCHE RD.
VALLEY SIDE RD.
LLOYD RD.
ABERDARE CT.
ROAD
SUPPLE CLOSE
MORSE RD.
Lib.
SIENNA M.
VINCENT ROAD
BARRACK RD.
PLUMSTEAD B1140
KETT'S HILL
LION WOOD RD.
CUBITT RD.
WOMERSLEY RD.
WELLESLEY AV. NTH.
NEWBEGIN RD.
MORSE AV.
PILLING PARK ROAD
Comm. Cen.
EASTLODGE
THE PINELODGES
Woodrow Pilling Park
Ten. Cts.
HOLMWOOD RISE
Thorpe Lodge (Broadland DC Offs.)
HARVEY LANE
STANLEY AV.
OAK LODGE
EDEN CL.
VIENNA APARTS.
YARMOUTH RD.
STANNARD CT.
THORPE HALL CL.
FERRYMANS CT.
Lionwood Junior Sch.
MOUSEHOLD HO.
WOODROW PL.
Lion Wood
Reservoirs (covered)
Telegraph Plantation
TELEGRAPH LANE
CINTRA RD.
WELLESLEY AV. STH.
QUEBEC RD.
PRIMROSE RD.
Lionwood Infant & Nusry. Sch.
STAN PETERSEN CL.
Rosary Cemetery
HIGH GRN.
RANSON RD.
HEATHSIDE RD.
MATLOCK RD.
THE HEIGHTS
COTMAN RD.
FERNHILL
EASTGATE HOUSE
ROSEVILLE CL.
FROGS HALL LANE
THE DENES
CREMORNE LA.
SALISBURY RD.
A1242
NR7
BROADLAND
NEW
08
Whitlingham Adventure
WHITLINGHAM COUNTRY PARK
Whitlingham Park Quay
Visitor Cen.
LANE
NORWICH
STH. NORFOLK
ALDER COTTS.
Depot
Elm Cotts.
Willow Cotts.
THE BROADS
Coronation Belt
NR14
YARE
WHITLINGHAM LANE
Norfolk Snowsports Club
Cemetery
TROWSE NEWTON
WHITLINGHAM HALL
RIVER
Depot
NORWICH
BARRACK
A147
GILDERS WY.
Nuffield Health
Patchey's Cnr.
Cow Twr.
Play. Fld.
COTMAN FIELDS
BISHOP BRI. ROAD
ST.
WATERSIDE
30
GAS HILL
Thorpe Hamlet
THE NEST
NORWICH
The Close
Pull's Ferry
Water-gate
RIVERSIDE RD.
WENSUM
THORPE
24/7 Fitness
Sort. Off.
CLARENCE RD.
STRACEY RD.
MARLBOROUGH CT.
SQUIRE'S HAVEN
CARROW RD.
KOBLENZ AV.
Odeon Cin. & Hollywood 'Bowl
RIVERSIDE RETAIL PK.
Super-store
Depot
CANARY WAY
BROADSMAN CL.
Wensum Lodge
Novi Sad Friendship Bri.
Norwich City FC (Carrow Rd.)
KERRISON RD.
KERRISON RD. IND. EST.
Works
Wensum Depot
HARDY RD.
COZENS
RAILWAY COTTS.
CANARYFIELDS
WATLING WY.
Boom Twrs.
PAPER MILL YARD
ROAD
WENSUM
RIVER
Richmond Hill
KING ST.
BRACONDALE
A147
Bracondale Grove
Carrow Abbey
St. Mary's Priory (rems.)
Stable Cott.
County Hall
LAKENHAM
Register Office
A1054
MARTINEAU LA.
Tennis Cts.
Bowling Grn.
Long John's
Trowse
EUROPE
MILLGATE
CONESFORD DR.
CARSHALTON RD.
HARRIET CT.
Depot
Bowl. Grn.

A
B
C
D
1
2
3
4
5
6
18
27
26
Prim. Academy
GUNN RD.
GOULBURN RD.
FRERE RD.
HOOKER ROAD
BARCLAY GRN.
BARCLAY CL.
THORPE PLAIN
WITARD RD.
WITARD CL.
EAST DRIVE
BEECHWOOD
CASTON RD.
BOOTY ROAD
RIDER
WDY
KELTON
PAINE
THORNFIELD WY.
HOLMES CL.
NORWICH ROAD
BROADLAND
VANCE RD.
ORCHARD CL.
LANE
PLUMSTEAD ROAD
BODMIN CT.
AERODROME RD.
AERODROME CR.
GORSE ROAD
BROOM AV.
FURZE ROAD
FURZE AV.
FURZE RD.
Playing Fld.
WILLIAMS LOKE
CHURCHFIELD GRN.
Lib.
St. Williams Prim. Sch.
Bowl. Grn.
The County Arts Bowl Club
ST. WILLIAMS WAY
A1042
RING
BRENDA JAMES CL.
HUNDER
BELMORE
BELMORE CL.
BELMORE RD.
THE COTTAGE DR.
ACACIA RD.
SPINNEY
SPINNEY CL.
THORPE AV.
OAK AV.
JANET SMITH CL.
HILL
SOUTH HILL ROAD
STH. HILL CL.
FIRMAN CT.
FROST CL.
HANSELL ROAD
THOMPSON RD.
ANNE CL.
ST. CATHERINES RD.
LONGFIELDS
PRIOR RD.
POUND
Youth and Comm. Cen.
Thorpe St. Andrew Sch.
Playing Field
AVENUE
CHARLES
THORPE CL.
CYRIL RD.
PRINCE EDWARD CL.
DAVIDSON CL.
DAVIDSON RD.
LAUNDRY
LAUNDRY CL.
BIRKBECK
THOMAS VERE RD.
Playgrd.
Pav.
Bowl. Grn.
Ten. Cts.
EASTERN CL.
EASTERN AV.
EASTERN CRES.
EASTERN
Recreation Ground
Cycle Track
Garglehill Plantation
GARGLE HILL
PHELPS RD.
MARGARET CR.
ELIZABETH AV.
BOULDERSIDE CL.
Comm. Cen.
NR7
MARGETSON AV.
HARVEY CL.
PILLING RD.
THOR LOKE
THOR CL.
THOR RD.
GORDON AVENUE
HENBY WAY
HENBY WY.
BLAKESTONE GREEN DR.
HOWARD CL.
HILLCREST
BOULTON RD.
LIME TREE AV.
WHITE FARM LA.
ROCKLAND DR.
SCHOOL LA.
LODGE PL.
HILLY PLANTATION
ROAD
THORPE ST. ANDREW
WESTON WOOD RD.
WESTON WOOD CL.
Sports Ground
Tennis Courts
Weston Wood
High House
HIGHFIELD CL.
PRIMROSE CR.
ST. ANDREWS CL.
ST. ANDREWS AV.
BIRCHWOOD
Hillside Avenue Prim. Sch.
HILLSIDE AVENUE
HILLSIDE CL.
MEADOW LA.
SCHOOL AV.
Playing Field
Bowl. Grn.
Newlands
Thorpe Tower
Thorpe Lodge (Broadland DC Offs)
WESTERN AV.
STANMORE RD.
CLOSE
BISHOPS
TOWER HILL
STANNARD CT.
EARNSHAW CT.
DALES LOKE
BUCK YD.
CHAPEL LA.
SOUTH AVENUE
RIVER GREEN CT.
RICHMOND CT.
OLD RECTORY CL.
BARBER PL.
YARMOUTH ROAD
A1242
ROXLEY
DALES PL.
COMMON
THORPE MS.
CATHERINE GS.
Cemy.
LANE
BUNGALOW LANE
THORPE HALL CL.
FERRYMANS CT.
YARE CT.
WATER LA.
GIRLINGS LA.
WHITLINGHAM LA.
Whitlingham Junction
Norwich
THE BROADS
NEW CUT
The Carr
Whitlingham Broad
WHITLINGHAM COUNTRY PARK
Rough Marsh Plantation
RIVER YARE
Tower Cotts.
WHITLINGHAM LANE
Visitor Cen.
Riversdale Cotts.
White House
Old Chalkpit Plantation
Old Wood
NORWICH SOUTHERN BYPASS
A47
Holmemead
Hill Cottages
Whitlingham Hall
Beech Plantation
The Swaley
Duckpond Plantation
NR14
Red Barn Plantation
Red Barn
Red Barn Cottages
WHITLINGHAM HALL

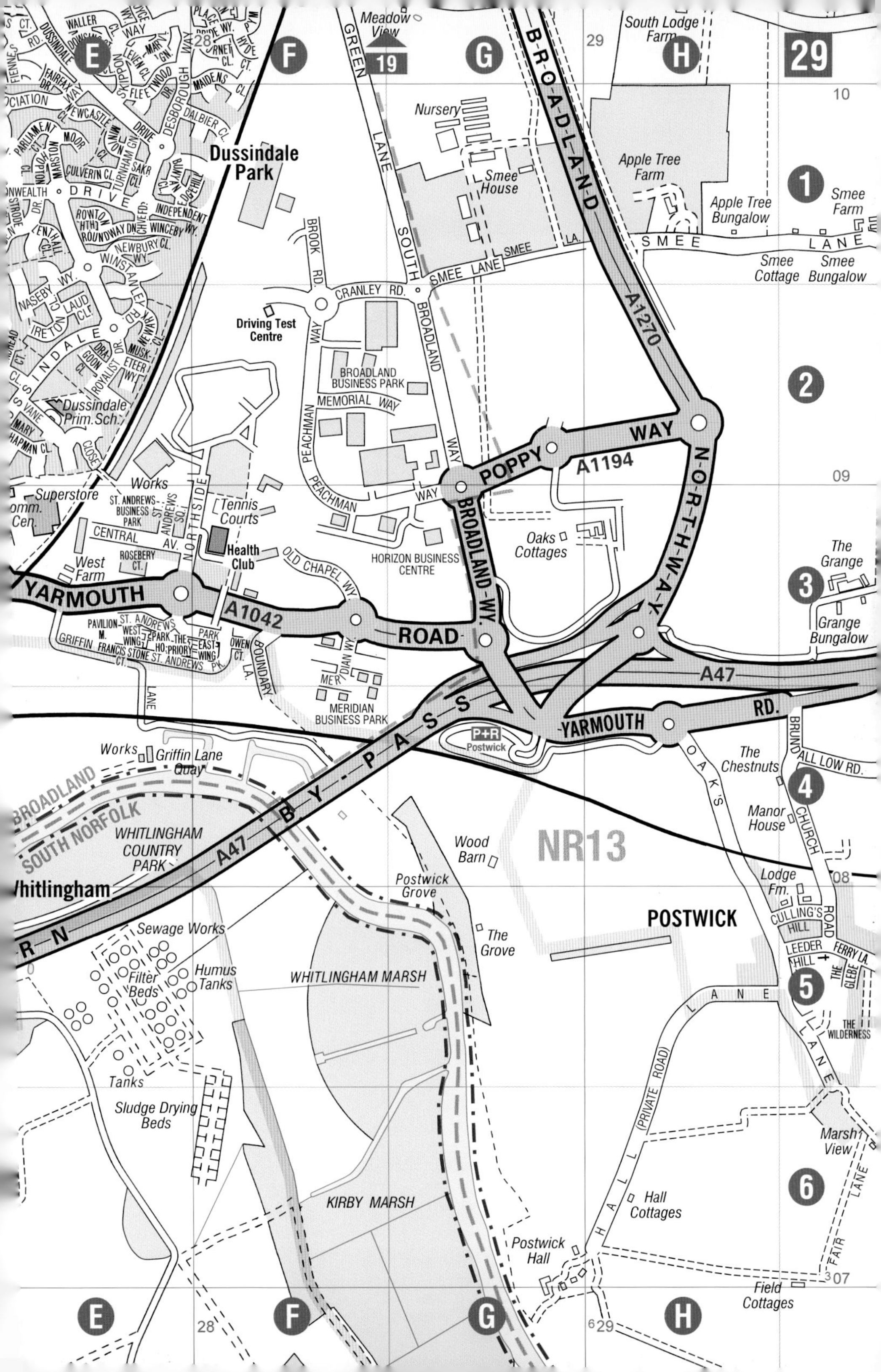

E
F
G
H
Meadow View
19
South Lodge Farm
28
29
10
Dussindale Park
Nursery
Smee House
Apple Tree Farm
Apple Tree Bungalow
Smee Farm
1
SMEE LANE
Smee Cottage
Smee Bungalow
SMEE LANE
SMEE LA.
BROADLAND
A1270
SOUTH GREEN LANE
BROOK RD.
CRANLEY RD.
Driving Test Centre
BROADLAND BUSINESS PARK
MEMORIAL WAY
PEACHMAN WAY
BROADLAND WAY
2
POPPY WAY
A1194
NORTHWAY
09
Oaks Cottages
HORIZON BUSINESS CENTRE
OLD CHAPEL WY.
Tennis Courts
Health Club
NORTHSIDE
Works
Superstore
Comm. Cen.
ST. ANDREWS BUSINESS PARK
ST. ANDREWS SQ.
CENTRAL AV.
ROSEBERY CT.
West Farm
YARMOUTH ROAD
A1042
The Grange
3
Grange Bungalow
PAVILION M.
ST. ANDREWS WEST WING
PARK HO.
THE PRIORY
PARK EAST WING
OWEN CT.
BOUNDARY LA.
GRIFFIN LANE
FRANCIS STONE CT.
ST. ANDREWS PK.
MERIDIAN WY.
MERIDIAN BUSINESS PARK
BROADLAND WY.
A47
YARMOUTH RD.
P+R Postwick
BRUNDALL LOW RD.
The Chestnuts
4
OAK'S LANE
Works
Griffin Lane Quay
BROADLAND
SOUTH NORFOLK
WHITLINGHAM COUNTRY PARK
Whitlingham
A47
SOUTHERN BY-PASS
Wood Barn
NR13
Manor House
CHURCH
Lodge Fm.
08
Postwick Grove
The Grove
POSTWICK
CULLING'S HILL
ROAD
LEEDER HILL
FERRY LA.
THE GLEBE
5
THE WILDERNESS
Sewage Works
Filter Beds
Humus Tanks
WHITLINGHAM MARSH
Tanks
Sludge Drying Beds
HALL LANE (PRIVATE ROAD)
Marsh View
6
FAIR LANE
KIRBY MARSH
Hall Cottages
Postwick Hall
07
Field Cottages

GREAT PLUMSTEAD
A
B
C
D
20
31
Bowling Green
30
Playing Field
ST. MARY'S
CHURCH
ROSEBERY RD.
HALE CT.
310
Carr Wood
1
Smee Farm
SMEE
LANE
ROAD
The Grove
CHURCH
WITTON
The Green
Cherry Tree Farm
LANE
WITTON
HALL
Witton
Witton Hall
Witton Lodge
Witton House
ROAD
2
R-O-A-D
GRAY CL.
MAURECOURT DR.
VARVEL CL.
MAURECOURT
COOPER RW.
DR.
CUCUMBER
09
ROAD
A47
MILL
BEVERLEY
PARKER
CL.
FOSTER CL.
ROAD
LEVINE CL.
SPRINGDALE
3
Norwich
CRES.
SPRINGDALE RD.
Y-A-R-M-O-U-T-H
Mast
Mast
Postwick Transmitting Station (BBC)
HOLMESDALE ROAD
LANE
LANE
Brundall Barn
LANE
POSTWICK
ROAD
WEST AV.
WEST END
DR.
Brundall Gardens
ROMAN DR.
LAKE VIEW DR.
REDCLIFFE
LAUREL
LOW
WEST
BRUNDALL
4
LANE
Brundall Gardens
Brundall Broad
STATION HALT
Boat Yard
Brundall Marsh
YARE
08
Newman's Hole
BROADLAND
SOUTH NORFOLK
Moore's Water
FERRY
LANE
5
FERRY
LANE
Bunney's Broad
SURLINGHAM-BROAD
FERRY
Marsh View
ROAD
Ferry Corner
RIVER
6
THE
ROAD
COMMON RD.
The Common
COMMON
LEACH'S
Surlingham Church Marsh Nature Reserve
NR14
07
Rifle Range
FERRY
30
31
THE STREET

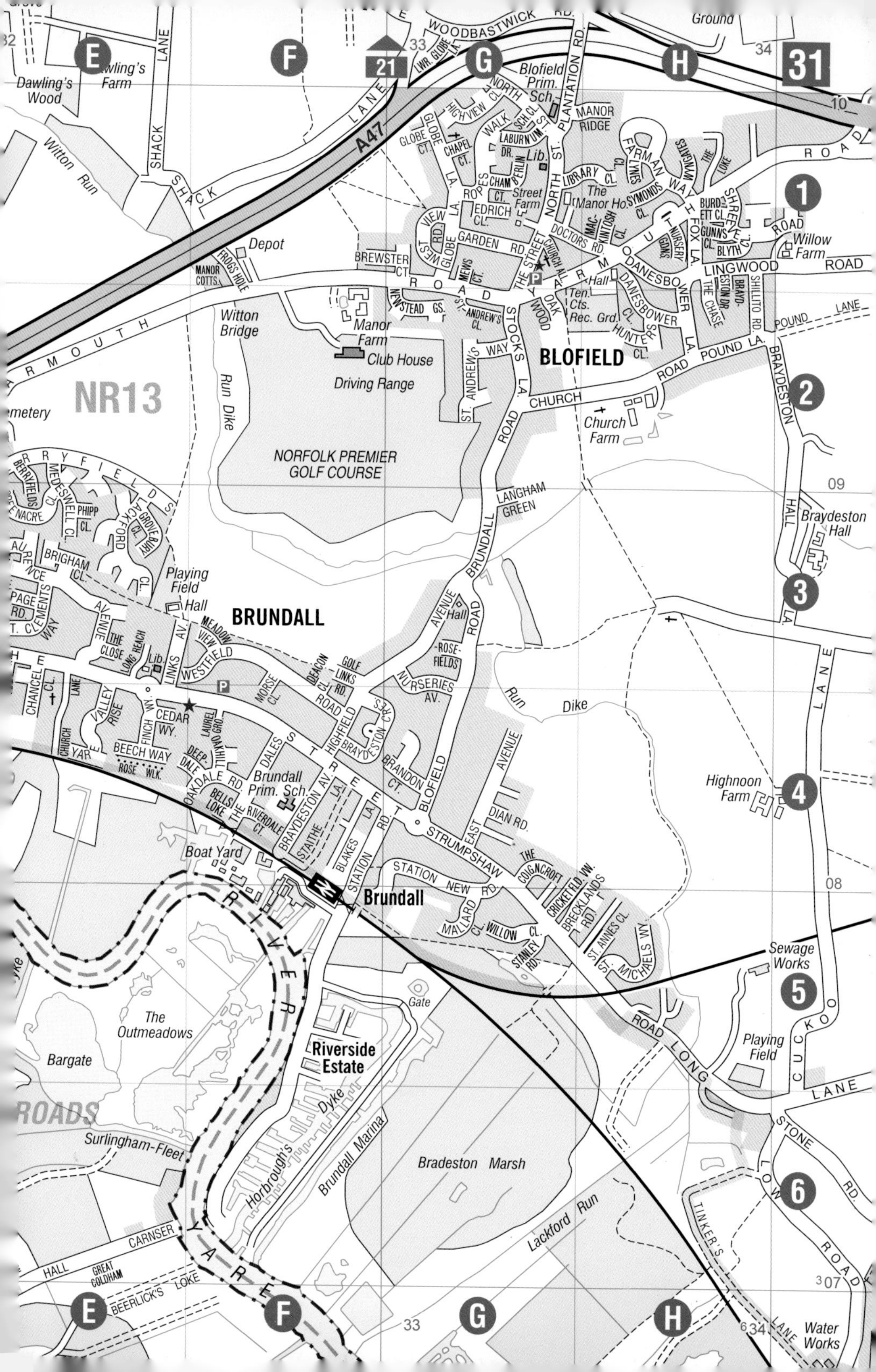
E
F
G
H
21
33
34
WOODBASTWICK RD.
Ground
Dawling's Wood
Dawling's Farm
SHACK LANE
Witton Run
A47
LANE
Blofield Prim. Sch.
PLANTATION RD.
MANOR RIDGE
NORTH ST.
LWR. GLOBE LA.
GLOBE CT.
HIGHVIEW CL.
CHAPEL CT.
WALK
SCH. CL.
LABURNUM
DR.
BERLIN
Lib.
FARMAN
WAY
LYNES
WINGATES
THE LOKE
ROAD
10
1
2
3
4
5
6
ROPES
CHAM CT.
Street Farm
EDRICH CL.
WEST VIEW RD.
GLOBE LA.
GARDEN RD.
LIBRARY CL.
The Manor Ho.
SYMONDS CL.
MAC-KINTOSH CL.
NURSERY GDNS.
FOX LA.
BURDETT CL.
GUNNS CL.
BLYTH CL.
SHREEVE CL.
ROAD
Willow Farm
LINGWOOD ROAD
DOCTORS RD.
Depot
MANOR COTTS.
FROGS HOLE
BREWSTER CT.
MEWS CT.
THE STREET
CHURCH AL.
YARMOUTH ROAD
Hall
DANESBOWER
DANESBOWER LA.
THE CHASE
ESTON DR.
BRAYD.
SHILLITO RD.
POUND LANE
NEWSTEAD GS.
ST. ANDREW'S CL.
OAK WOOD
Ten. Cts.
Rec. Grd.
HUNTERS CL.
Witton Bridge
Manor Farm
Club House
Driving Range
ST. ANDREW'S WAY
STOCKS LA.
BLOFIELD
POUND LA.
BRAYDESTON
CHURCH ROAD
Church Farm
NR13
Cemetery
Run Dike
NORFOLK PREMIER GOLF COURSE
BRUNDALL ROAD
LANGHAM GREEN
09
HALL
Braydeston Hall
BERRYFIELDS
MEDESWELL CL.
PHIPP CL.
LACKFORD CL.
GROVE BURY
FENACRE
LAURENCE
BRIGHAM CL.
Playing Field
Hall
PAGE RD.
ST. CLEMENTS WAY
AVENUE
THE CLOSE
LONG REACH
LINKS AV.
MEADOW VIEW
WESTFIELD
BRUNDALL
AVENUE
Hall
ROSEFIELDS
NURSERIES AV.
ROAD
LANE
Lib.
CHANCEL CL.
LANE
VALLEY RISE
FINCH WY.
CEDAR WY.
LAUREL GRO.
MORSE CL.
DEACON CL.
GOLF LINKS RD.
ROAD
HIGHFIELD
BRAYDESTON CR.
Run Dike
CHURCH
YAR
BEECH WAY
ROSE WLK.
DEEPDALE
OAKHILL
DALES
BRANDON CT.
BLOFIELD
AVENUE
Highnoon Farm
OAKDALE RD.
BELLS LOKE
THE RIVERDALE CT.
Brundall Prim. Sch.
BRAYDESTON AV.
STAITHE LA.
LA.
DIAN RD.
EAST
STRUMPSHAW
Boat Yard
BLAKES
STATION RD.
STATION NEW RD.
THE COIGN
CROFT
CRICKETFIELD VW.
BRECKLANDS RD.
08
Brundall
MALLARD CL.
WILLOW CL.
STANLEY RD.
ST. ANNES CL.
ST. MICHAELS WY.
Sewage Works
RIVER
Gate
ROAD LONG
Playing Field
CUCKOO LANE
The Outmeadows
Riverside Estate
Bargate
ROADS
Surlingham-Fleet
Dyke
Horbrough's
Brundall Marina
Bradeston Marsh
STONE RD.
LOW ROAD
TINKER'S LANE
Lackford Run
YARE
CARNSER
HALL
GREAT COLDHAM
BEERLICK'S LOKE
07
Water Works

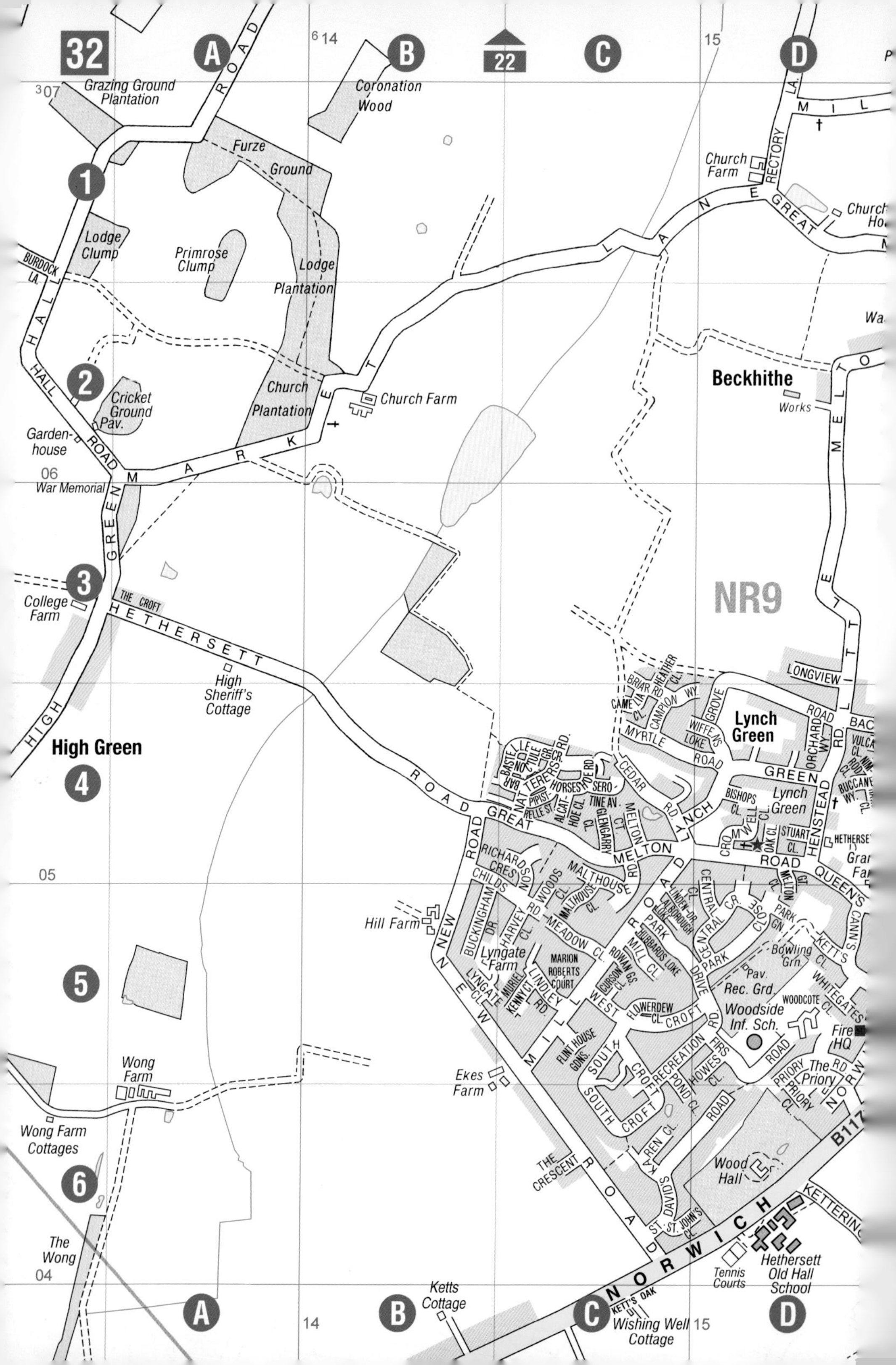
32
A
B
C
D
22
614
15
307
06
05
04
14
1
2
3
4
5
6
Grazing Ground Plantation
Coronation Wood
Furze Ground
Lodge Clump
Primrose Clump
Lodge Plantation
Church Plantation
Church Farm
Cricket Ground
Pav.
Garden-house
War Memorial
BURDOCK LA.
HALL ROAD
ROAD
MARKET LANE
RECTORY LA.
MILL
GREAT MELTON ROAD
Church Farm
Church Ho.
Beckhithe
Works
NR9
College Farm
THE CROFT
HETHERSETT ROAD
HIGH GREEN
High Sheriff's Cottage
High Green
LONGVIEW
Lynch Green
LYNCH GREEN
LYNCH ROAD
CEDAR RD.
MYRTLE
CAMPION WY.
BRIAR RD.
HEATHER CL.
WIFFENS LOKE
GROVE
ORCHARD WY.
HENSTEAD RD.
BUCCANEER WY.
VULCAN CL.
Lynch Green
BISHOPS CL.
CROMWELL CL.
OAK CL.
STUART CL.
HETHERSETT
QUEEN'S
RICHARDSONS CRES.
CHILDS
BUCKINGHAM DR.
HARVEY CL.
WOODS RD.
MALTHOUSE CL.
MALTHOUSE RD.
MELTON CT.
GLENGARRY CL.
TINE AV.
ALCATHOE CL.
HORSESHOE RD.
MEADOW CL.
Lyngate Farm
MARION ROBERTS COURT
LINDLEY RD.
MURIEL
KENNY CL.
LYNGATE CL.
ROWAN GS.
CURSON
MILL CL.
HUBBARDS LOKE
ALBOROUGH LOKE
LINDEN DR.
CENTRAL CR.
CENTRAL PARK
PARK DRIVE
PARK GN.
Bowling Grn.
Pav.
Rec. Grd.
Woodside Inf. Sch.
WOODCOTE CL.
KETT'S CL.
WHITEGATES
CANN'S
Fire HQ
FLOWERDEW CL.
WEST CROFT
FLINT HOUSE GDNS.
SOUTH CROFT
RECREATION RD.
POND CL.
HOWES CL.
FIRS ROAD
PRIORY CL.
The Priory
Wood Hall
KAREN CL.
ST. DAVID'S
ST. JOHN'S CL.
THE CRESCENT
NEW ROAD
NEW MILL ROAD
Hill Farm
Ekes Farm
Wong Farm
Wong Farm Cottages
The Wong
Ketts Cottage
KETT'S OAK
Wishing Well Cottage
NORWICH
B1172
KETTERING
Tennis Courts
Hethersett Old Hall School

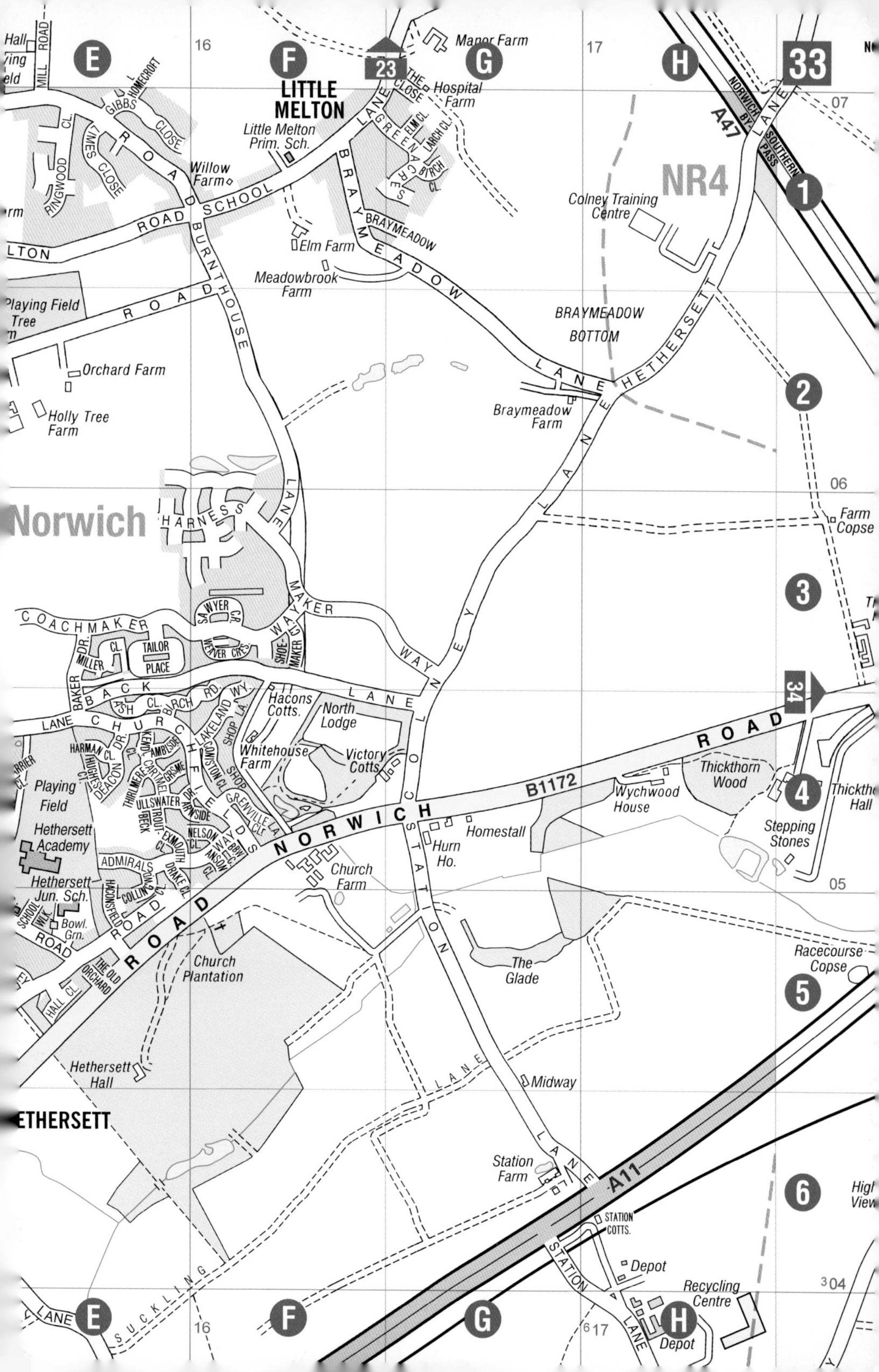
33
23
34
E
F
G
H
16
17
07
06
05
3 04
1
2
3
4
5
6
LITTLE MELTON
Little Melton Prim. Sch.
Manor Farm
Hospital Farm
Willow Farm
Elm Farm
Meadowbrook Farm
Orchard Farm
Holly Tree Farm
Playing Field
Hall
MILL ROAD
HOMECROFT
GIBBS CLOSE
LIMES CLOSE
RINGWOOD CL.
SCHOOL ROAD
BURNTHOUSE LANE
THE CLOSE
GREENACRES
ELM CL.
LARCH CL.
BIRCH CL.
BRAYMEADOW
BRAYMEADOW LANE
NR4
NORWICH SOUTHERN BY-PASS
A47
HETHERSETT LANE
Colney Training Centre
BRAYMEADOW BOTTOM
Braymeadow Farm
Norwich
HARNESS
COACHMAKER WAY
SAWYER CR.
TAILOR PLACE
WEAVER CRES.
SHOEMAKER CL.
MILLER CL.
BAKER DR.
BACK LANE
ASH CL.
BIRCH RD.
LAKELAND WY.
SHOP LA.
CHURCHFIELDS
HARMAN CL.
HUGHES CT.
DEACON DR.
KENDAL CL.
AMBLESIDE
CARTMEL
GRASMERE
CONISTON CL.
THIRLMERE
ULLSWATER
TROUTBECK
ARNSIDE
EXMOUTH
NELSON CL.
ANSON CL.
DRAKE CL.
GRENVILLE CL.
ADMIRALS WAY
COLLINS CL.
HACONSFIELD
Hacons Cotts.
Whitehouse Farm
North Lodge
Victory Cotts.
COLNEY LANE
NORWICH ROAD
B1172
Homestall
Hurn Ho.
Wychwood House
Thickthorn Wood
Thickthorn Hall
Stepping Stones
Farm Copse
Playing Field
Hethersett Academy
Hethersett Jun. Sch.
SCHOOL WLK.
Bowl. Grn.
Church Farm
Church Plantation
The Glade
Racecourse Copse
THE OLD ORCHARD
HALL CL.
Hethersett Hall
HETHERSETT
STATION LANE
LANE
Midway
Station Farm
A11
STATION COTTS.
Depot
Recycling Centre
SUCKLING LANE
High View

A
B
C
D
24
33
1
2
3
4
5
6
307
06
05
04
18
19
NORFOLK AND NORWICH UNIVERSITY HOSPITAL
Newfound Farm
Cringleford Wood
COLNEY
LANE
HETHERSETT
NORWICH
A47
Norwich
HOUSE WAY
ROUND HOUSE WAY
STRATFORD CRES.
YARE VALLEY DR.
GURNEY DR.
SOFTLEY
OAKLANDS DR.
ST. LAWRENCE DR.
NEWFOUND DR.
HARMER LANE
CRINGLEFORD CHASE
ASHCROFT CL.
BEECHCROFT CT.
ALMOND DR.
MAPLE-TREE CL.
SYCAMORE CT.
CHESTNUT PL.
CEDARWOOD CL.
JUNIPER CL.
HARTS LANE
DRAGONFLY
ROWAN WY.
LAVENDER DR.
DAFFODIL DR.
ROSE
HOLLY WK.
VERBENA DR.
THE PINES
DUNLIN
WOODPECKER
NIGHTINGALE DR.
BRAMBLING LA.
PEREGRINE M.
ORIOLE DR.
KINGFISHER CL.
DRAGON-FLY
JASMINE
FERN DR.
TULIP GS.
CATKIN CL.
LOBELIA
POPPY CL.
WILLOWCROFT
VIOLA CL.
FREESIA WAY
Prim. Sch.
Rec. Grd.
Farm Copse
Thickthorn Farm
NEWMARKET ROAD
NEWMARKET
A11
B1172
ROAD
NORWICH
P+R
Thickthorn
Wards Wood
Thickthorn Wood
Thickthorn Hall
Stepping Stones
NR9
(Proposed)
SOUTHERN
CANTLEY LANE
WELCH CT.
MARILYN
LANGLEY CL.
BRETTINGHAM
TAYLOR
PATTESON CL.
KEDLESTON DR.
ARMITAGE CL.
WOODGATE
SIDELL CL.
BANFF CT.
QUEBEC CL.
MEADOW FARM
Meadow Farm
Meadow Farm Cottages
Cantley Wood
Racecourse Copse
Bridge Cottages
All Saints' Church (site of)
Cantley Farm
High View
Little Wood
Home Farm
Lilac Plantation
Small Wood
High Noon Cottages
The White House
Recycling Centre

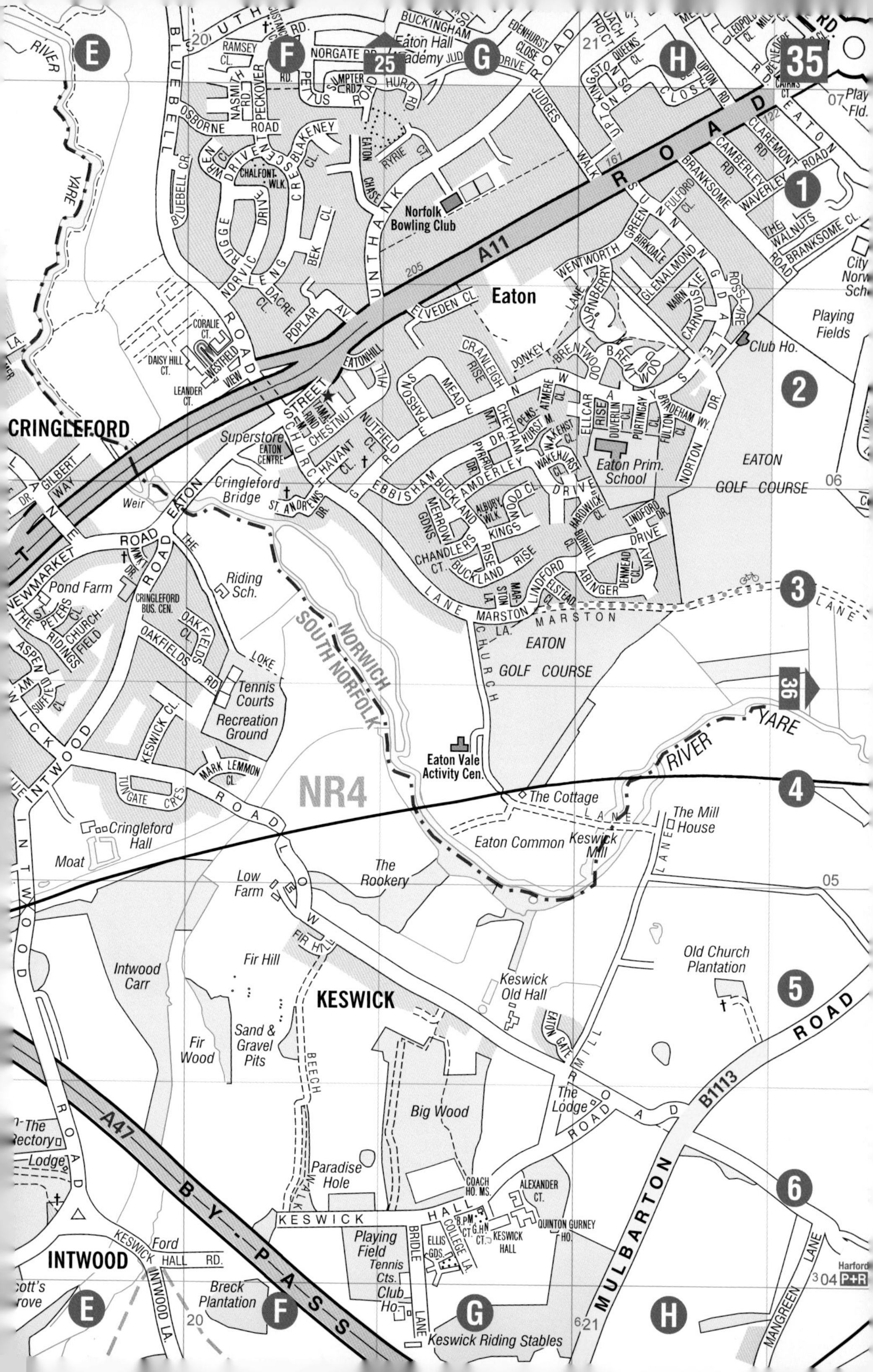
E
F
G
H
25
Eaton Hall Academy
35
1
2
3
4
5
6
Eaton
CRINGLEFORD
KESWICK
INTWOOD
NR4
A11
ROAD
Norfolk Bowling Club
City of Norwich School
Playing Fields
Club Ho.
EATON GOLF COURSE
Eaton Prim. School
Superstore
EATON CENTRE
Cringleford Bridge
Weir
Pond Farm
CRINGLEFORD BUS. CEN.
Riding Sch.
Tennis Courts
Recreation Ground
NORWICH SOUTH NORFOLK
Eaton Vale Activity Cen.
The Cottage
The Mill House
Eaton Common
Keswick Mill
RIVER YARE
36
Cringleford Hall
Moat
Low Farm
The Rookery
Fir Hill
Intwood Carr
Old Church Plantation
Keswick Old Hall
Sand & Gravel Pits
Fir Wood
Big Wood
The Lodge
B1113
MULBARTON ROAD
Paradise Hole
A47 BY-PASS
The Rectory
Lodge
Ford
KESWICK HALL RD.
INTWOOD ROAD
INTWOOD LA.
Breck Plantation
Playing Field
Tennis Cts.
Club Ho.
Keswick Riding Stables
KESWICK HALL
QUINTON GURNEY HO.
ALEXANDER CT.
COACH HO. MS.
BRIDLE LANE
MANGREEN LANE
Harford P+R
MARSTON LANE
CHURCH LANE
UNTHANK ROAD
NEWMARKET ROAD
BLUEBELL ROAD
LOW ROAD
MILL ROAD
BEECH WALK
FIR HILL
EATON GATE
GOLF COURSE

NEWMARKET RD.
A11
DANIELS RD.
A140
LAKENHAM RD.
BARRETT RD.
A146
A1056
Play. Fld.
Cromwell House
Harford Manor Sch.
Ten. Cts.
The Hewett Academy
Lakenham Playing Fields
The Wherry Sch.
Goals Norwich
City of Norwich School
Playing Fields
Club Ho.
Tennis Cts.
Youth & Comm. Cen.
Edith Cavell Academy & Nursery
Norwich Business Park
Tuckswood Academy
Tuckswood
Comm. Cen.
The Locksley Sch.
Harford Park
Bowl. Gn.
Lib.
Factory
Depots
White Lodge Business Estate
Danby Open Space
Adult Training Centre
Old Lakenham
Lea Bridges Park
Eaton Golf Course
Marston Lane
River Yare
Hotel
Norwich Livestock Market
Superstore
Wks.
Train. Cen.
Yarefield Park
University Technical College Norfolk
The Mill House
Harford Bridge
Old Church Plantation
B1113
Mulbarton Road
Ipswich Road
(Harford Hill)
Norwich
South Norfolk
Chapel Hill
Hill Cottages
Harford Farm
Markshall Farm Rd.
Markshall Farm Road
Markshall
Markshall Farm
Markshall Cottages
Mangreen Lane
Harford P+R
A47
Norwich
Caistor St. Edmu
NR4
NR1
26
35
30

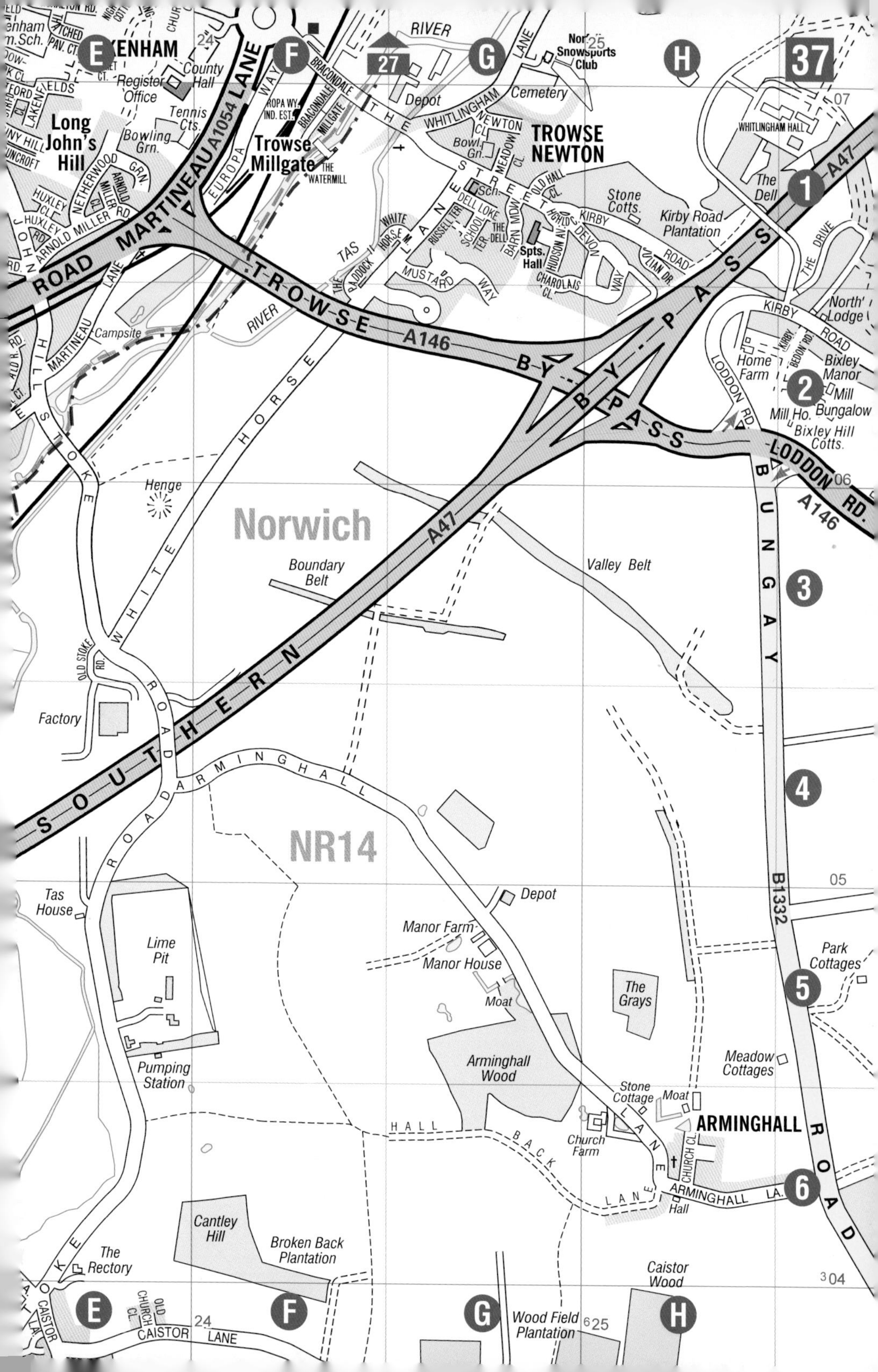

Long John's Hill
Trowse Millgate
TROWSE NEWTON
Norwich
NR14
ARMINGHALL
Register Office
County Hall
Tennis Cts.
Bowling Grn.
Depot
Cemetery
Norfolk Snowsports Club
WHITLINGHAM HALL
The Dell
Stone Cotts.
Kirby Road Plantation
North Lodge
Home Farm
Bixley Manor
Mill Bungalow
Mill Ho.
Bixley Hill Cotts.
Sch.
Spts. Hall
THE WATERMILL
ROPA WY. IND. EST.
Campsite
Henge
Boundary Belt
Valley Belt
Factory
Tas House
Lime Pit
Pumping Station
Manor Farm
Manor House
Moat
The Grays
Arminghall Wood
Park Cottages
Meadow Cottages
Stone Cottage
Church Farm
Hall
Cantley Hill
Broken Back Plantation
The Rectory
Caistor Wood
Wood Field Plantation
MARTINEAU LANE
A1054
ROAD
TROWSE BY-PASS
A146
A47
SOUTHERN BY-PASS
WHITE HORSE ROAD
STOKE ROAD
ARMINGHALL LANE
BUNGAY ROAD
B1332
LODDON RD.
KIRBY ROAD
HALL BACK LANE
ARMINGHALL LA.
CAISTOR LANE
OLD CHURCH CL.
CHURCH CL.
OLD STOKE RD.
WHITLINGHAM LANE
BRACONDALE
MILLGATE
EUROPA WAY
THE STREET
THE PADDOCK
WHITE HORSE LA.
MUSTARD WAY
RUSSELL TER.
SCHOOL TER.
DELL LOKE
THE DELL
BARN MDW.
HUDSON AV.
CHAROLAIS CL.
DEVON WAY
OLD HALL CL.
NEWTON CL.
MEADOW CL.
Bowl. Grn.
THE DRIVE
RIVER
TAS
E F G H
1 2 3 4 5 6
24 25 07 06 05 04

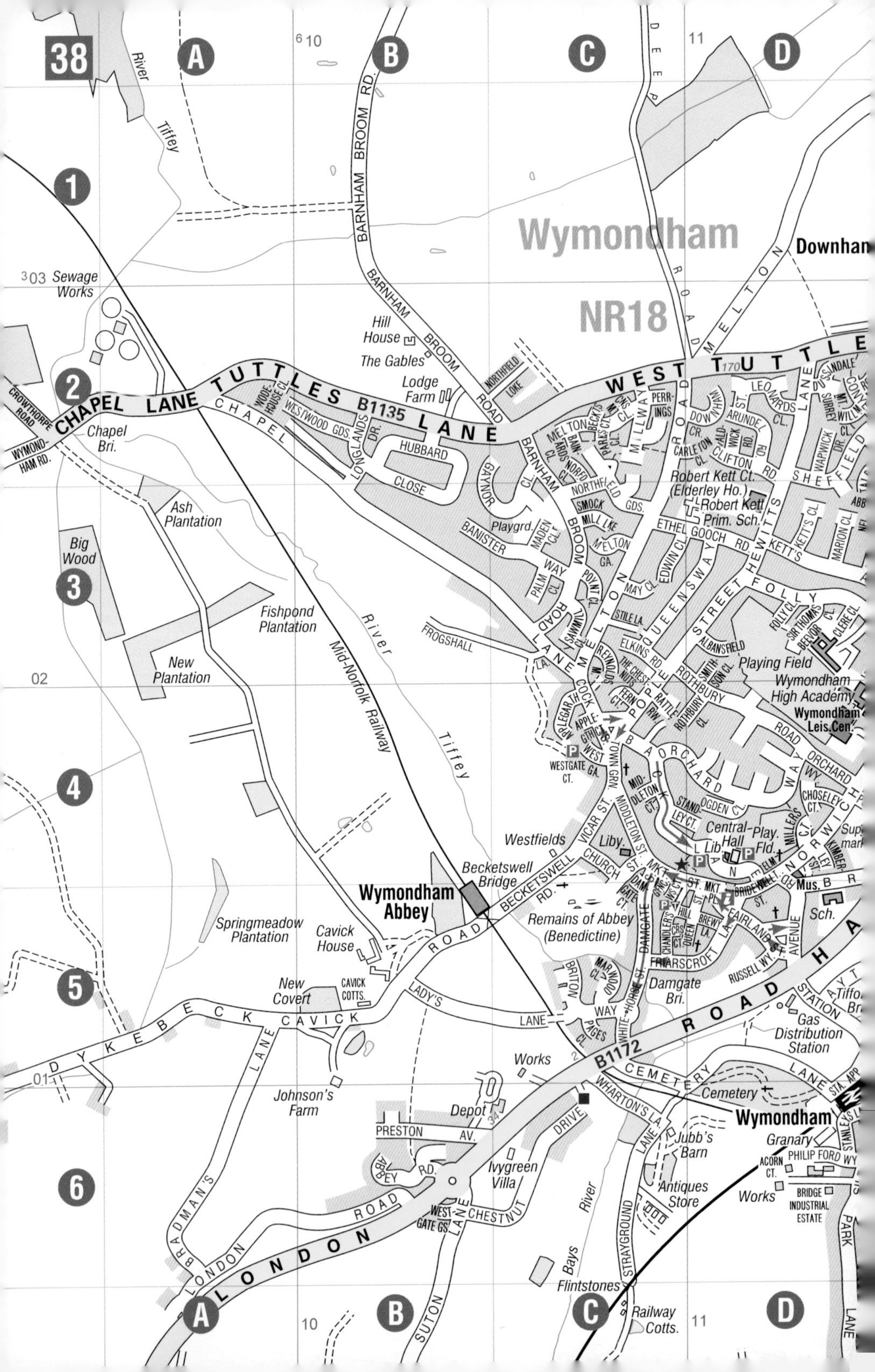
A
B
C
D
610
11
1
2
3
4
5
6
303
02
01
River Tiffey
Sewage Works
BARNHAM BROOM RD.
BARNHAM BROOM ROAD
DEEP ROAD
MELTON
Wymondham
Downham
NR18
Hill House
The Gables
Lodge Farm
NORTHFIELD LOKE
CROWTHORPE ROAD
WYMONDHAM RD.
CHAPEL LANE
TUTTLES B1135 LANE
WEST TUTTLES
170
Chapel Bri.
CHAPEL
WODEHOUSE CL.
WESTWOOD GDS.
LONGLANDS DR.
HUBBARD CLOSE
GAYNOR CL.
BARNHAM BROOM ROAD
MELTON CL.
BECKETS CT.
PERRINGS
MILLWAY
DOWNHAM CR.
CARLETON CL.
ALDWICK RD.
ARUNDEL
LEONARDS CL.
CLIFTON RD.
LANE
DUSSINDALE
SURREY
WARWICK DR.
SHEFFIELD
Robert Kett Ct. (Elderley Ho.)
Robert Kett Prim. Sch.
NORTHFIELD GDS.
SMOCK MILL LOKE
MELTON GA.
ETHEL GOOCH RD.
KETT'S CL.
MARION CL.
HEWITTS
Ash Plantation
Big Wood
Playgrd.
BANISTER WAY
MADEN CL.
PALM CL.
POYNT CL.
MAY CL.
EDWIN CL.
QUEENSWAY
STREET
FOLLY
FOLLY CL.
SIR THOMAS BEEVOR CL.
CLERE CL.
Fishpond Plantation
New Plantation
River
Mid-Norfolk Railway
FROGSHALL LA.
LANE
SAWMILL CL.
STILE LA.
ELKINS RD.
ALBANSFIELD
SMITHSON CL.
Playing Field
Wymondham High Academy
Wymondham Leis.Cen.
COCK
APPLEGARTH CT.
APPLEGARTH
REYNOLDS CT.
THE CHESTNUTS
FERN CT.
RATTLE RW.
ROTHBURY RD.
ROTHBURY CL.
ROAD
POPE
Tiffey
WESTGATE CT.
WEST GA.
TOWN GRN.
MIDDLETON CT.
ORCHARD
ORCHARD WY.
WAY
CHOSELEY CT.
STANDLEY CT.
OGDEN CL.
Central Hall
Play. Fld.
MILLERS
Westfields
VICAR ST.
Liby.
MIDDLETON ST.
Lib.
NORWICH
Super mark
Becketswell Bridge
Wymondham Abbey
BECKETSWELL RD.
CHURCH ST.
MKT.
ST. MKT. PL.
BRIDEWELL ST.
ELM
KIMBERLEY
Mus.
Sch.
Remains of Abbey (Benedictine)
DAMGATE
DAMGATE CT.
CHANDLER'S CT.
HILL
BREWERY LA.
QUEEN ST.
FAIRLAND ST.
AVENUE
FRIARSCROFT LA.
RUSSELL WY.
Springmeadow Plantation
Cavick House
ROAD
New Covert
CAVICK COTTS.
BRITON
MARWOOD CL.
WHITE HORSE ST.
Damgate Bri.
DYKEBECK
CAVICK
LADY'S LANE
LANE
WAY
PAGES CL.
B1172 ROAD
STATION
Gas Distribution Station
Works
CEMETERY LANE
Cemetery
STA. APP.
Johnson's Farm
Depot
PRESTON AV.
WHARTON'S LA.
DRIVE
LANE
Jubb's Barn
Wymondham
Granary
STANLEY
PHILIP FORD WY.
ACORN CT.
ABBEY RD.
Ivygreen Villa
Works
Antiques Store
BRIDGE INDUSTRIAL ESTATE
PARK
BRADMAN'S
LONDON ROAD
LONDON
WESTGATE GS.
CHESTNUT
LANE
River
STRAYGROUND
Bays
Flintstones
Railway Cotts.
SUTON
10
11

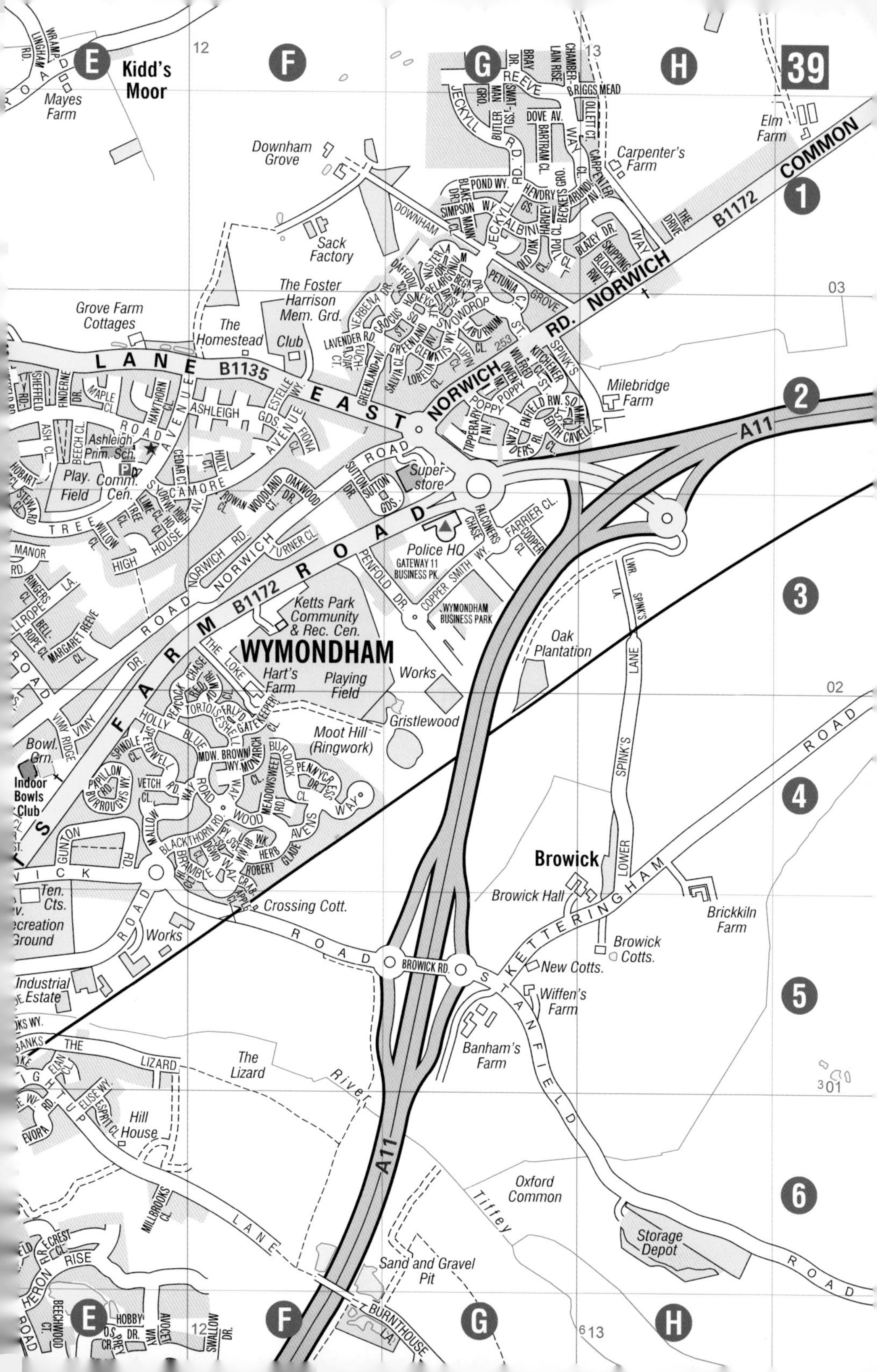
E
F
G
H
1
2
3
4
5
6
12
13
03
02
01
Kidd's Moor
Mayes Farm
Downham Grove
Sack Factory
The Foster Harrison Mem. Grd.
Grove Farm Cottages
The Homestead
Club
Elm Farm
Carpenter's Farm
COMMON
B1172
NORWICH
RD.
THE DRIVE
DOWNHAM
JECKYLL
REEVE
BRIGGS MEAD
DOVE AV.
BARTRAM CL.
POND WY.
SIMPSON WY.
HENDRY
ALBINI
OLD OAK
BLAZEY DR.
SKIPPING BLOCK RW.
PETUNIA CL.
GROVE
LABURNUM
LAVENDER RD.
GREENLAND AV.
CROCUS
DAFFODIL
VERBENA DR.
SNOWDROP
LUPIN CL.
LOBELIA
CLEMATIS WY.
SALVIA CL.
HONEYSUCKLE
253
LANE
B1135
EAST
ESTELLE WY.
ASHLEIGH
FIONA CL.
AVENUE
Milebridge Farm
A11
SPINK'S LA.
KITCHENER
WILFRED OWEN
POPPY
TIPPERARY AV.
FLANDERS RI.
ENFIELD RW.
EDITH CAVELL
SHEFFIELD RD.
FINDERNE DR.
MAPLE CL.
HAWTHORN CL.
ASH CL.
BEECH CL.
Ashleigh Prim. Sch.
Play. Field
Comm. Cen.
HOBART
STEWARD CL.
CEDAR CT.
HOLLY CT.
SYCAMORE
ROAD
TREE
WILLOW CL.
LIME TREE CL.
HIGH HOUSE
ROWAN CL.
WOODLAND CT.
OAKWOOD DR.
SUTTON DR.
SUTTON GDS.
Superstore
Police HQ
GATEWAY 11 BUSINESS PK.
FALCONERS CHASE
FARRIER CL.
COOPER CL.
SMITH WY.
COPPER
PENFOLD DR.
WYMONDHAM BUSINESS PARK
NORWICH RD.
TURNER CL.
MANOR RD.
RINGERS CL.
BELL-ROPE CL.
MARGARET REEVE CL.
FARM
B1172
Ketts Park Community & Rec. Cen.
WYMONDHAM
Hart's Farm
Playing Field
Works
Gristlewood
Oak Plantation
LWR. SPINK'S LA.
THE LOKE
PEACOCK CHASE
TORTOISESHELL
GATEKEEPER
HOLLY BLUE
SPEEDWELL
SPINDLE CL.
VIMY RIDGE
VIMY DR.
Bowl. Grn.
Indoor Bowls Club
PAPILLON RD.
BURROUGHS WY.
VETCH CL.
MDW. BROWN WY.
MONARCH CL.
BURDOCK
MEADOWSWEET RD.
PENNYCRESS DR.
Moot Hill (Ringwork)
WAY
MALLOW
WOOD
BLACKTHORN RD.
BRAMBLE
HERB ROBERT
AVENS GLADE
GUNTON RD.
WICK
Ten. Cts.
Recreation Ground
Crossing Cott.
ROAD
Works
BROWICK RD.
Browick
Browick Hall
LOWER SPINK'S LANE
KETTERINGHAM
Brickkiln Farm
Browick Cotts.
New Cotts.
Wiffen's Farm
Banham's Farm
STANFIELD
Industrial Estate
BANKS
THE LOKE
LIZARD
The Lizard
River Tiffey
ELAN CL.
ELISE WY.
ESPRIT CL.
EVORA
Hill House
Oxford Common
Storage Depot
MILLBROOKS CL.
LANE
FIRCREST CL.
RISE
HERON
BEECHWOOD CT.
HOBBY DR.
OSPREY CR.
AVOCET WAY
SWALLOW DR.
Sand and Gravel Pit
BURNTHOUSE LA.

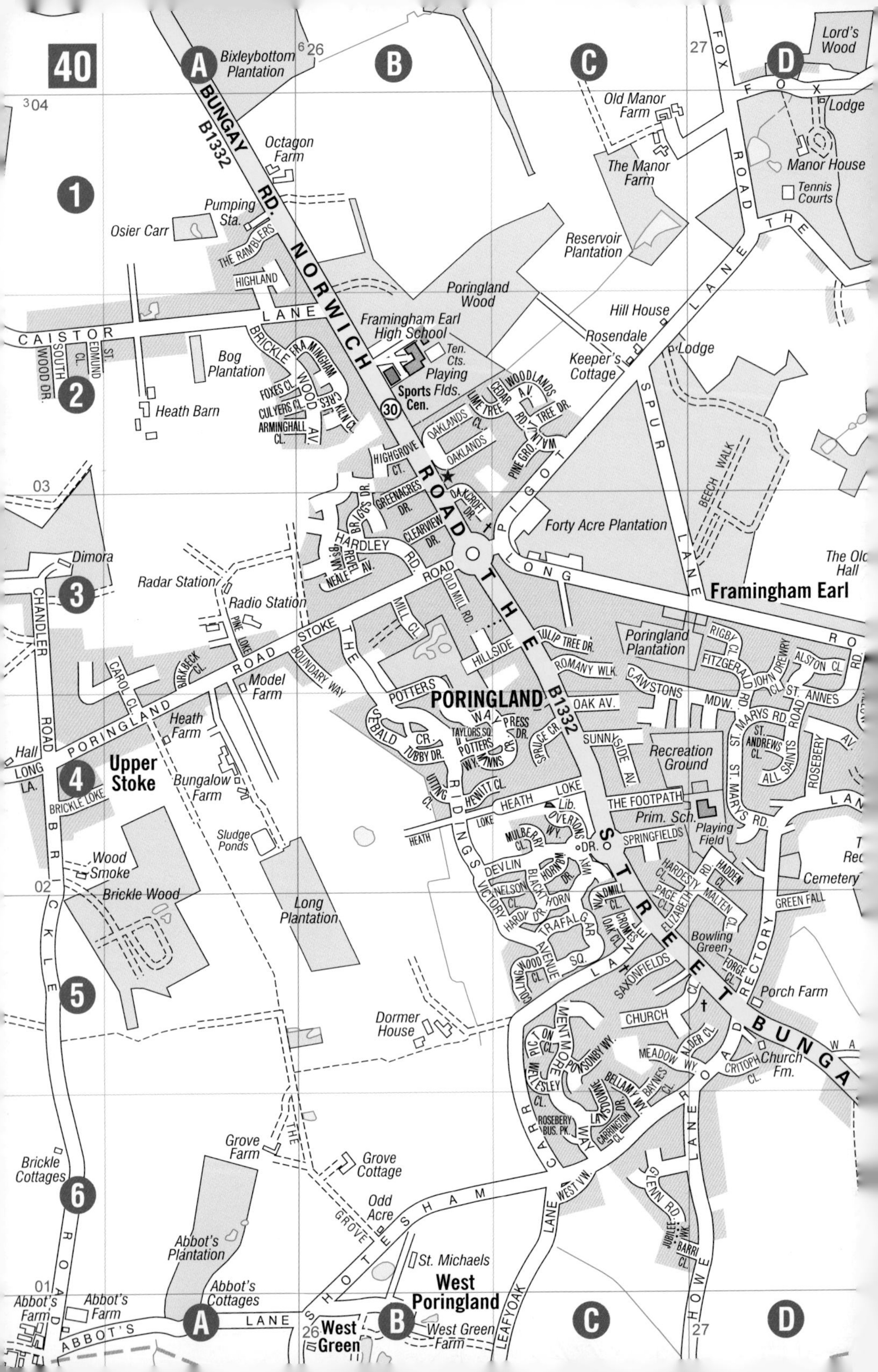
A
B
C
D
1
2
3
4
5
6
626
27
304
03
02
01
Bixleybottom Plantation
Lord's Wood
Old Manor Farm
FOX LANE
Lodge
FOX ROAD
Manor House
Tennis Courts
The Manor Farm
BUNGAY RD.
B1332
NORWICH ROAD
Octagon Farm
Pumping Sta.
Osier Carr
THE RAMBLERS
HIGHLAND
Reservoir Plantation
Poringland Wood
CAISTOR LANE
SOUTH WOOD DR.
EDMUND CL.
ST.
Framingham Earl High School
Ten. Cts.
Playing Flds.
Sports Cen.
30
Hill House
Rosendale
Keeper's Cottage
Lodge
BRICKLE
FRAMINGHAM WOOD
CRES.
KILN CL.
FOXES CL.
CULYERS CL.
ARMINGHALL CL.
AV.
Bog Plantation
Heath Barn
WOODLANDS AV.
CEDAR RD.
LIME TREE CL.
TREE DR.
WALNUT
PINE GRO.
OAKLANDS
HIGHGROVE CT.
GREENACRES DR.
BRIGGS DR.
OAKCROFT DR.
PIGOT LANE
SPUR LANE
BEECH WALK
Forty Acre Plantation
CLEARVIEW DR.
HARDLEY RD.
REVELL AV.
BS WAY
NEALE
Dimora
Radar Station
Radio Station
CHANDLER ROAD
LONG ROAD
The Old Hall
Framingham Earl
STOKE ROAD
OLD MILL RD.
MILL CL.
PINE LOKE
BIRKBECK CL.
CAROL CL.
BOUNDARY WAY
THE RIDINGS
HILLSIDE
TULIP TREE DR.
Poringland Plantation
RIGBY CL.
FITZGERALD RD.
JOHN DREWRY CL.
ALSTON CL.
ROMANY WLK.
CAWSTONS MDW.
ST. ANNES ROAD
Model Farm
POTTERS WAY
PORINGLAND
PRESS DR.
OAK AV.
ST. MARYS RD.
PORINGLAND ROAD
Heath Farm
CEBALD CR.
TAYLORS SQ.
POTTERS WY.
MINNS CR.
SPRUCE CR.
SUNNYSIDE AV.
Recreation Ground
ST. ANDREWS CL.
ALL SAINTS
ROSEBERY AV.
Hall
LONG LA.
Upper Stoke
Bungalow Farm
TUBBY DR.
UTTING CL.
HEWITT CL.
HEATH LOKE
THE FOOTPATH
Lib.
Prim. Sch.
Playing Field
BRICKLE LOKE
Sludge Ponds
HEATH LOKE
MULBERRY CL.
OVERTONS WY.
DR.
SPRINGFIELDS
ST. MARYS RD.
Wood Smoke
DEVLIN
HORNBEAM DR.
WAY
HARDESTY CL.
HADDEN CL.
Cemetery
Brickle Wood
NELSON CL.
VICTORY
BLACKTHORN
WINDMILL CL.
PAGE CL.
ELIZABETH
MALTEN CL.
GREEN FALL
Long Plantation
HARDY DR.
TRAFALGAR
CROMES OAK CL.
THE STREET
Bowling Green
BRICKLE ROAD
COLLINGWOOD CL.
AVENUE
SQ.
LANE
SAXONFIELDS
FORGE CL.
RECTORY
Porch Farm
Dormer House
MENTMORE
PICTON CL.
CHURCH CL.
ALDER CL.
BUNGAY
PONSONBY WY.
MEADOW WY.
Church Fm.
CRITOPH CL.
WELLESLEY CL.
LANSDOWNE
BELLAMY WY.
BAYNES CL.
ROSEBERY BUS. PK.
CARRINGTON DR.
CARR LANE
HOWE LANE
Grove Farm
THE GROVE
Grove Cottage
Brickle Cottages
GLENN RD.
SHOTESHAM ROAD
WEST VW.
Odd Acre
JUBILEE WK.
BARRI CL.
Abbot's Plantation
St. Michaels
LEAFYOAK LANE
Abbot's Cottages
West Poringland
Abbot's Farm
ABBOT'S LANE
West Green
West Green Farm

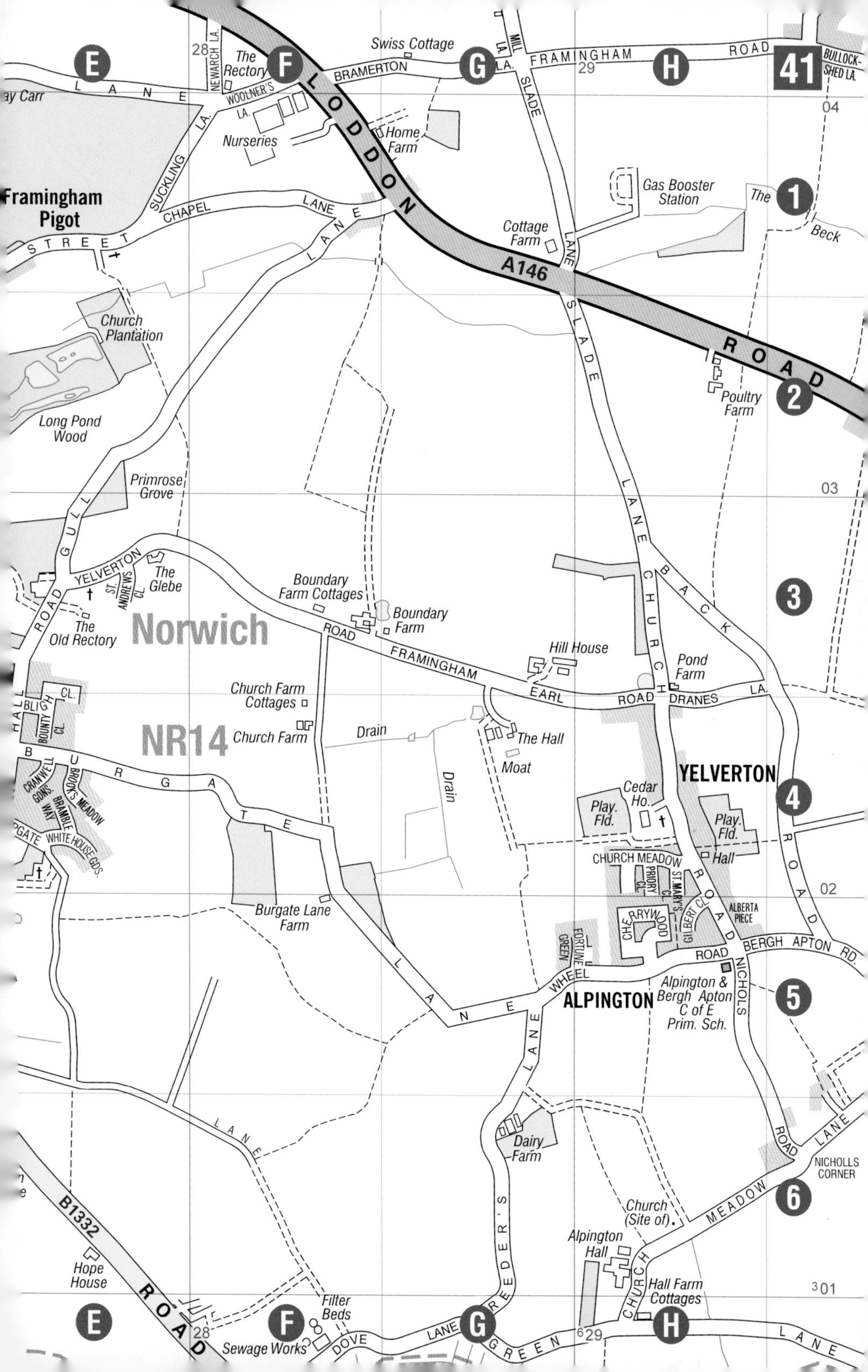
41
E
F
G
H
LANE
BRAMERTON
FRAMINGHAM ROAD
BULLOCKSHED LA.
NEWARCH LA.
MILL LA.
WOOLNER'S LA.
The Rectory
Swiss Cottage
Nurseries
Home Farm
LODDON
A146
ROAD
Framingham Pigot
SUCKLING LA.
CHAPEL LANE
STREET
LANE
SLADE LANE
Gas Booster Station
The Beck
Cottage Farm
Church Plantation
Long Pond Wood
Primrose Grove
Poultry Farm
1
2
3
4
5
6
04
03
02
01
28
29
GULL LANE
YELVERTON ROAD
ST. ANDREWS CL.
The Glebe
The Old Rectory
Norwich
NR14
Boundary Farm Cottages
Boundary Farm
FRAMINGHAM EARL ROAD
Hill House
CHURCH LANE
BACK LANE
Pond Farm
DRANES LA.
Church Farm Cottages
Church Farm
Drain
The Hall
Moat
HALL
BLIGH CL.
BOUNTY CL.
BURGATE LANE
CRANWELL GDNS.
BROOKS MEADOW
BRAMBLE WAY
WHITE HOUSE GDS.
YELVERTON
Cedar Ho.
Play. Fld.
Hall
CHURCH MEADOW
PRIORY CL.
ST. MARY'S CL.
GILBERT CL.
CHERRYWOOD
ALBERTA PIECE
BERGH APTON RD.
ROAD
FORTUNE GREEN
WHEEL ROAD
NICHOLS ROAD
Burgate Lane Farm
ALPINGTON
Alpington & Bergh Apton C of E Prim. Sch.
LANE
Dairy Farm
NICHOLLS CORNER
MEADOW LANE
B1332 ROAD
Hope House
Church (Site of)
Alpington Hall
Hall Farm Cottages
REEDER'S LANE
Filter Beds
Sewage Works
DOVE LANE
GREEN LANE

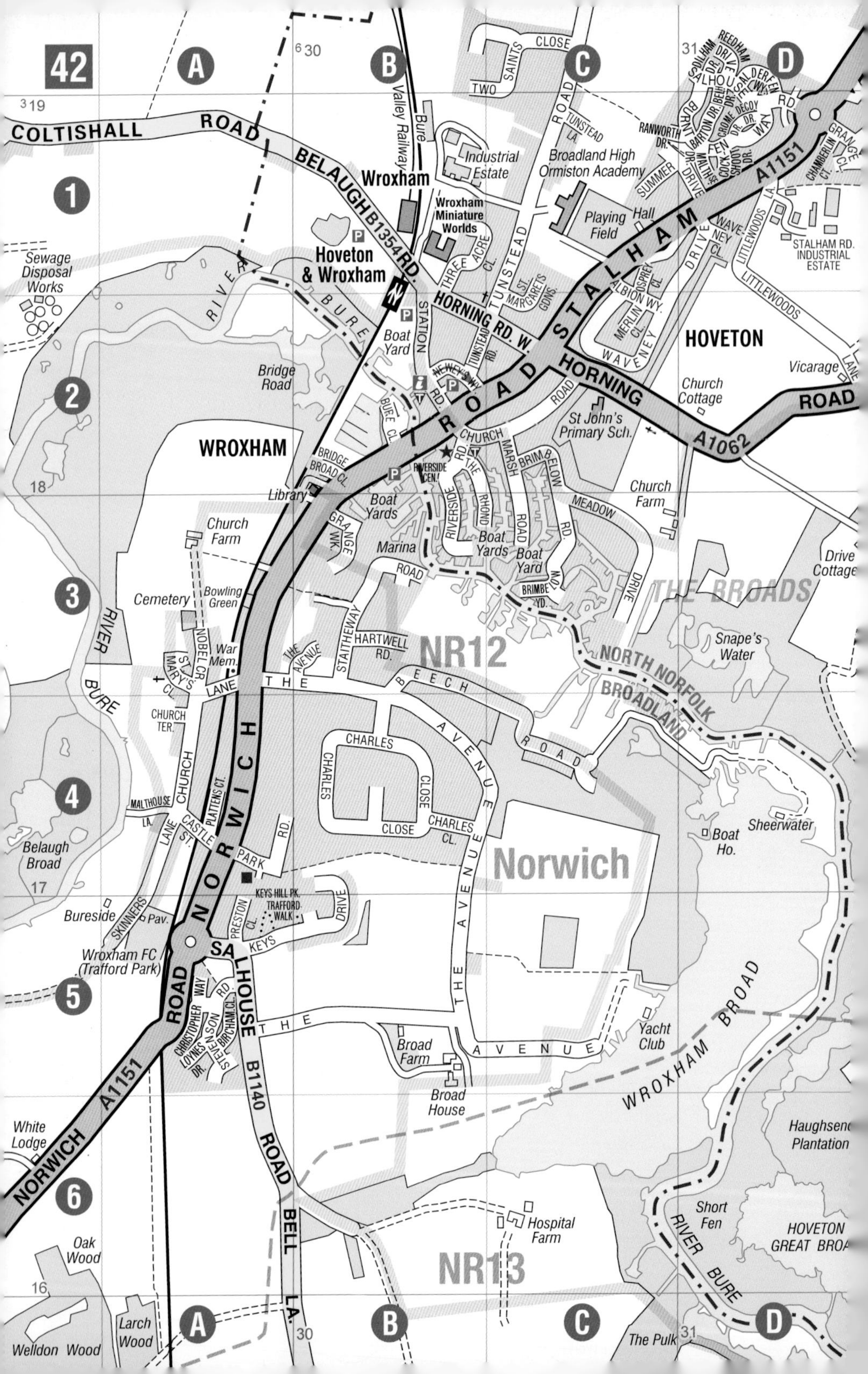
A
B
C
D
1
2
3
4
5
6
COLTISHALL ROAD
BELAUGH B1354 RD.
Valley Railway
Bure
TWO SAINTS CLOSE
Industrial Estate
Wroxham
Wroxham Miniature Worlds
Hoveton & Wroxham
Sewage Disposal Works
RIVER BURE
TUNSTEAD RD.
TUNSTEAD LA.
Broadland High Ormiston Academy
Playing Field
Hall
SUMMER DRIVE
RANWORTH DR.
DILHAM DR.
REEDHAM DRIVE
SALHOUSE DR.
ALDERFEN WAY
BARTON DR.
BURNT FEN DR.
CROME DR.
DECOY DR.
COCKSHOOT DR.
MALTHOUSE DRIVE
A1151
STALHAM ROAD
GRANGE CL.
CHAMBERLIN CT.
LITTLEWOODS LA.
LITTLEWOODS LANE
STALHAM RD. INDUSTRIAL ESTATE
THREE ACRE CL.
TUNSTEAD ROAD
ST. MARGARETS GDNS.
ALBION WY.
OSPREY CL.
MERLIN CL.
WAVENEY DRIVE
WAVENEY CL.
HOVETON
Vicarage
Church Cottage
HORNING ROAD
A1062
HORNING RD. W.
STATION RD.
Boat Yard
NEWEY'S WY
Bridge Road
BURE CL.
CHURCH ROAD
St John's Primary Sch.
WROXHAM
BRIDGE BROAD CL.
Library
RIVERSIDE CEN.
THE RHOND
RIVERSIDE RD.
MARSH ROAD
BRIMBELOW RD.
BRIMBELOW YD.
Church Farm
Boat Yards
Boat Yard
GRANGE WK.
Marina
RIVERSIDE ROAD
MEADOW DRIVE
THE BROADS
Drive Cottage
Cemetery
Bowling Green
NOBEL CR.
ST. MARY'S CL.
War Mem.
THE AVENUE
STAITHEWAY
HARTWELL RD.
NR12
Snape's Water
NORTH NORFOLK
BROADLAND
BEECH ROAD
THE LANE
CHURCH TER.
CHARLES CLOSE
CHARLES CL.
THE AVENUE
NORWICH ROAD
MALTHOUSE LA.
CHURCH LANE
PLATTENS CT.
CASTLE ST.
PARK RD.
Norwich
Boat Ho.
Sheerwater
Belaugh Broad
Bureside
SKINNERS LANE
Pav.
PRESTON CL.
KEYS HILL PK.
TRAFFORD WALK
KEYS DRIVE
Wroxham FC (Trafford Park)
SALHOUSE ROAD
B1140
CHRISTOPHER WAY
LOYNES DR.
STEVENSON RD.
BIRCHAM CL.
THE AVENUE
Broad Farm
Broad House
Yacht Club
WROXHAM BROAD
White Lodge
NORWICH A1151
Haughsend Plantation
Hospital Farm
Short Fen
HOVETON GREAT BROA
RIVER BURE
Oak Wood
NR13
BELL LA.
Larch Wood
Welldon Wood
The Pulk
319
630
31
18
17
16
30
31

INDEX

Including Streets, Places & Areas, Hospitals etc., Industrial Estates, Selected Flats & Walkways, Stations and Selected Places of Interest.

HOW TO USE THIS INDEX

1. Each street name is followed by its Postcode District, then by its Locality abbreviation(s) and then by its map reference; e.g. **Admirals Way** NR9: Hether . . . .4E **33** is in the NR9 Postcode District and the Hethersett Locality and is to be found in square 4E on page **33**. The page number is shown in bold type.

2. A strict alphabetical order is followed in which Av., Rd., St., etc. (though abbreviated) are read in full and as part of the street name; e.g. **Bond St.** appears after **Bonds Rd.** but before **Bone Rd.**

3. Streets and a selection of flats and walkways that cannot be shown on the mapping, appear in the index with the thoroughfare to which they are connected shown in brackets; e.g. **Barn Ter.** *NR13: B'all . . . .3E **31** (off Long Reach)*

4. Addresses that are in more than one part are referred to as not continuous.

5. Places and areas are shown in the index in **BLUE TYPE** and the map reference is to the actual map square in which the town centre or area is located and not to the place name shown on the map; e.g. **BAWBURGH 3E 23**

6. An example of a selected place of interest is **City of Norwich Aviation Mus. 4A 10**

7. Transport hub examples:
   Brundall Gardens Station (Rail) . . . .4D 30; Airport Park & Ride . . . .6H 9; Norwich Airport 6A 10

8. An example of a Hospital, Hospice or selected Healthcare facility is **COLMAN HOSPITAL 5H 25**

9. Map references for entries that appear on large scale pages **4** & **5** are shown first, with small scale map references shown in brackets; e.g. **Abbey Ct.** NR1: Norw 8E **5** (5E **27**)

GENERAL ABBREVIATIONS

All. : Alley
Apts. : Apartments
App. : Approach
Arc. : Arcade
Av. : Avenue
Bk. : Back
Bri. : Bridge
Bldgs. : Buildings
Bus. : Business
Cvn. : Caravan
Cen. : Centre
Cl. : Close
Comn. : Common
Cnr. : Corner
Cott. : Cottage
Cotts. : Cottages
Ct. : Court
Cres. : Crescent
Cft. : Croft
Dr. : Drive
E. : East
Est. : Estate
Fld. : Field
Flds. : Fields
Gdn. : Garden
Gdns. : Gardens
Ga. : Gate
Gt. : Great
Grn. : Green
Gro. : Grove
Hgts. : Heights
Ho. : House
Ind. : Industrial
Info. : Information
La. : Lane
Lit. : Little
Lwr. : Lower
Mnr. : Manor
Mkt. : Market
Mdw. : Meadow
Mdws. : Meadows
M. : Mews
Mt. : Mount
Mus. : Museum
Nth. : North
Pal. : Palace
Pde. : Parade
Pk. : Park
Pl. : Place
Ri. : Rise
Rd. : Road
Sth. : South
Sq. : Square
St. : Street
Ter. : Terrace
Twr. : Tower
Trad. : Trading
Up. : Upper
Va. : Vale
Vw. : View
Vis. : Visitors
Wlk. : Walk
W. : West
Yd. : Yard

LOCALITY ABBREVIATIONS

Alpington: NR14-15 . . . . .Alp
Arminghall: NR1,NR14 . . . . .Arm
Attlebridge: NR9 . . . . .A'bridge
Barford: NR9 . . . . .Barf
Bawburgh: NR5,NR9 . . . . .Baw
Beeston St Andrew: NR12 . . . . .Bee A
Belaugh: NR12 . . . . .Bel
Bergh Apton: NR14 . . . . .Berg A
Bixley: NR14 . . . . .Bix
Blofield: NR13 . . . . .Blof
Bowthorpe: NR5 . . . . .Bow
Bramerton: NR14 . . . . .Bram
Brundall: NR13 . . . . .B'all
Caistor St Edmund: NR14 . . . . .Caist E
Colney: NR4 . . . . .Coln
Costessey: NR8 . . . . .Cost
Cringleford: NR4 . . . . .Cring
Crostwick: NR12 . . . . .Crost
Drayton: NR8 . . . . .Dray
Easton: NR9 . . . . .E'ton
Felthorpe: NR8,NR10 . . . . .Felth
Framingham Earl: NR14 . . . . .Fram E
Framingham Pigot: NR14 . . . . .Fram P
Great Melton: NR9 . . . . .Gt Mel
Great Plumstead: NR13 . . . . .Gt P
Hellesdon: NR6 . . . . .Helle
Hemblington: NR13 . . . . .Hemb
Hethersett: NR9 . . . . .Hether
Horsford: NR10 . . . . .H'ford
Horsham St Faith: NR10 . . . . .Hor F
Hoveton: NR12 . . . . .Hov
Howe: NR14 . . . . .Howe
Intwood: NR4 . . . . .Int
Keswick: NR4 . . . . .Kes
Kirby Bedon: NR14 . . . . .Kir B
Little Melton: NR9 . . . . .Lit Mel
Little Plumstead: NR13 . . . . .Lit P
Lower Hellesdon: NR6 . . . . .Lwr H
Markshall: NR14 . . . . .Mark
Marlingford: NR9 . . . . .Marl
New Costessey: NR5,NR9 . . . . .New C
Norwich: NR1-7 . . . . .Norw
Old Catton: NR6 . . . . .Old C
Panxworth: NR13 . . . . .Panx
Poringland: NR14 . . . . .Por
Postwick: NR7,NR13 . . . . .Post
Rackheath: NR7,NR13 . . . . .Rack
Ringland: NR8 . . . . .R'land
Rockland St Mary: NR14 . . . . .Rock M
Salhouse: NR12-13 . . . . .Sal
Silfield: NR18 . . . . .Silf
Spixworth: NR10 . . . . .Spix
Sprowston: NR6-7 . . . . .Spro
Stanfield: NR18 . . . . .Stanf
Stoke Holy Cross: NR14 . . . . .Stoke X
Strumpshaw: NR13 . . . . .Stru
Surlingham: NR14 . . . . .Surl
Suton: NR18 . . . . .Suton
Swardeston: NR4,NR14 . . . . .Swar
Taverham: NR8,NR10 . . . . .Tav
Thorpe End: NR13 . . . . .Thor E
Thorpe Marriott: NR8 . . . . .Thor Mar
Thorpe St Andrew: NR7 . . . . .Thor And
Trowse: NR14 . . . . .Tro
Wicklewood: NR18 . . . . .Wickle
Witton: NR13 . . . . .Witt
Woodbastwick: NR13 . . . . .W'wick
Wroxham: NR12-13 . . . . .Wrox
Wymondham: NR18 . . . . .Wym
Yelverton: NR14 . . . . .Yelv

24/7 Fitness
Norwich 5E **5** (4E **27**)

A

Abbey Cl. NR10: Hor F 3A **10**
Abbey Ct. NR1: Norw 8E **5** (5E **27**)
Abbey Farm Commercial Pk. NR10: Hor F 2H **9**
Abbey La. NR1: Norw 6E **5** (4E **27**)
Abbey Rd. NR10: Hor F 3A **10**
NR18: Wym 6B **38**
Abbot Cl. NR18: Wym 3D **38**
Abbot Rd. NR1: Norw 1C **36**
Abbot's La. NR14: Por 6A **40**
Aberdare Ct. NR1: Norw 2G **27**
Abinger Way NR4: Norw 3H **35**
Acacia Rd. NR7: Thor And 1C **28**
Achilles Dr. NR5: Baw 6E **13**
Acland M. NR6: Norw 3B **16**
Acorn Ct. NR18: Wym 6D **38**
Acres Way NR8: Thor Mar 3H **7**
Adams Rd. NR7: Spro 2F **17**
Adcock Dr. NR7: Spro 2B **18**
Addey Cl. NR6: Spro 2E **17**
Adelaide St. NR2: Norw 2A **26**
(not continuous)
Admirals Way NR9: Hether 4E **33**
Adshead Ct. NR3: Norw 4A **16**
Aerodrome Cres. NR7: Thor And 1A **28**

Aerodrome Rd. NR7: Thor And ... 1A 28
Afghan Pl. NR3: Norw ... 6D 16
Agricultural Hall Plain NR1: Norw ... 4D 4 (3D 26)
Airedale Cl. NR3: Norw ... 6B 16
Airport Park & Ride ... 6H 9
Aitken Cl. NR7: Spro ... 2G 17
Alan Rd. NR1: Norw ... 8F 5 (5E 27)
Albansfield NR18: Wym ... 3D 38
Albany Rd. NR3: Norw ... 1C 26
Albemarle Rd. NR2: Norw ... 6A 26
Alberta Piece NR14: Alp ... 5H 41
Albertine Cl. NR3: Norw ... 6G 15
Albert Pl. NR1: Norw ... 3F 27
Albert Ter. NR2: Norw ... 5B 26
Albini Way NR18: Wym ... 1G 39
Albion Dr. NR7: Spro ... 4F 17
Albion Way NR1: Norw ... 7F 5 (5E 27)
  NR12: Hov ... 1C 42
Alborough Loke NR9: Hether ... 5C 32
Albury Wlk. NR4: Norw ... 3G 35
Alcathoe Cl. NR9: Hether ... 4C 32
Alder Cl. NR14: Por ... 5D 40
Alder Cotts. NR14: Tro ... 5H 27
Alderfen Way NR12: Hov ... 1D 42
Alderson Pl. NR1: Norw ... 8D 5
Alder Way NR8: Thor Mar ... 4H 7
Aldryche Rd. NR1: Norw ... 1G 27
Aldwick Rd. NR18: Wym ... 2D 38
Alexander Ct. NR4: Kes ... 6G 35
Alexandra NR2: Norw ... 8A 5
Alexandra Rd. NR2: Norw ... 3A 26
Alex Moorhouse Way NR5: New C ... 4D 12
Alford Gro. NR7: Spro ... 4F 17
Alfred Nicholls Ct. NR3: Norw ... 5C 16
Alicante Way NR5: Norw ... 3F 25
Alkmaar Way NR6: Norw ... 1H 15
Allanadale Rd. NR4: Norw ... 2B 36
Allan Bedford Cres. NR8: Cost ... 2D 12
Allenbrooks Way NR18: Wym ... 5D 38
Allens Av. NR7: Spro ... 3F 17
Allens Cl. NR13: Blof ... 3G 21
Allen's La. NR7: Spro ... 3E 17
Allens La. NR2: Norw ... 5B 26
Allerton Cl. NR7: Spro ... 4G 17
Allerton Rd. NR7: Spro ... 4G 17
Allison Bank NR1: Norw ... 8F 5
All Saints Grn. NR1: Norw ... 7C 5 (5D 26)
All Saints Rd. NR14: Por ... 4D 40
All Saints St. NR1: Norw ... 6C 5 (4D 26)
Almary Grn. NR1: Norw ... 4D 4
Alma Ter. NR3: Norw ... 1C 26
Almond Dr. NR4: Cring ... 2C 34
Alms La. NR3: Norw ... 2B 4
Alnwick Ct. NR5: Bow ... 2A 24
ALPINGTON ... 5H 41
Alston Cl. NR14: Fram E ... 3D 40
Alston Rd. NR6: Helle ... 5F 15
Altongate NR13: Thor E ... 4E 19
Ambleside NR9: Hether ... 4E 33
Ambleside Cl. NR5: Norw ... 3D 24
Ambrose Cl. NR5: Bow ... 1B 24
Amderley Dr. NR4: Norw ... 2G 35
Amhirst Cl. NR3: Norw ... 6E 17
Amos Bacon Cl. NR6: Spro ... 3E 17
Ampthill St. NR2: Norw ... 4B 26
Amsterdam Way NR6: Norw ... 1H 15
Anchor Cl. NR3: Norw ... 1E 4 (2E 27)
Anchor Ho. NR2: Norw ... 3B 4
Anchor Quay NR3: Norw ... 3B 4
Anchor St. NR3: Norw ... 1F 4 (1E 27)
Angela Cl. NR10: H'ford ... 1G 9
Angela Cres. NR10: H'ford ... 1G 9
Angela Rd. NR10: H'ford ... 1G 9
Angel Rd. NR3: Norw ... 5C 16
Anglia Dr. NR2: Norw ... 6C 26
Anglia Sq. NR3: Norw ... 1C 4 (2D 26)
Angus Mackay Ct. NR6: Helle ... 3F 15
Anmer Cl. NR3: Norw ... 4E 17
Anna Sewell Dr. NR6: Old C ... 2D 16
Anne Cl. NR7: Thor And ... 1C 28
Annes Wlk. NR3: Norw ... 1C 4
Anson Cl. NR9: Hether ... 4F 33
Anson Rd. NR6: Norw ... 1A 16
Anthony Dr. NR3: Norw ... 5E 17
Antingham Rd. NR7: Norw ... 6A 18
Appleacres NR6: Old C ... 2C 16
Applegarth NR18: Wym ... 4C 38
Applegarth Ct. NR18: Wym ... 4C 38
Appleyard Cres. NR3: Norw ... 4H 15
Apsley Ct. NR5: Norw ... 3G 25
Arcade St. NR2: Norw ... 5C 5 (4D 26)
AR Centre ... 4A 16
Archer Cl. NR6: Spro ... 1F 17
Arden Gro. NR6: Helle ... 6F 9
Arderon Ct. NR2: Norw ... 2A 26
Ardney Ri. NR3: Norw ... 4C 16
Argyle St. NR1: Norw ... 7E 5 (5E 27)
Argyll Cres. NR8: Tav ... 5G 7
Arlington La. NR2: Norw ... 5B 26
Armes Cres. NR2: Norw ... 1H 25
Armes St. NR2: Norw ... 1H 25
ARMINGHALL ... 6H 37
Arminghall Cl. NR3: Norw ... 4B 16
  NR14: Por ... 2A 40
Arminghall La. NR14: Arm ... 4F 37
Armitage Cl. NR4: Cring ... 4D 34
Arms Pk. Rd. NR6: Norw ... 1A 16
Armstrong Rd. NR7: Thor And ... 5B 18
Arneside NR9: Hether ... 4F 33
Arnfield La. NR5: New C ... 1C 24
Arnold Miller Cl. NR1: Norw ... 1E 37
Arnold Miller Rd. NR1: Norw ... 1E 37
Arthurton Rd. NR10: Spix ... 3F 11
Arundel Ct. NR2: Norw ... 8A 5
Arundell Av. NR18: Wym ... 1G 39
Arundel Rd. NR18: Wym ... 2D 38
Ashbourne Ind. Est. NR6: Helle ... 3A 16
Ashbourne Twr. NR7: Norw ... 5A 18
Ashby Ct. NR1: Norw ... 8C 5 (5D 26)
Ashby St. NR1: Norw ... 8C 5 (5D 26)
Ash Cl. NR9: Hether ... 4E 33
  NR18: Wym ... 2E 39
Ashcroft Cl. NR4: Cring ... 2C 34
Ashdown NR8: Thor Mar ... 4H 7
Ash Gro. NR3: Norw ... 5D 16
Ashgrove NR8: Thor Mar ... 3H 7
Ashleigh Gdns. NR18: Wym ... 2F 39
Ashman Bank NR1: Norw ... 8F 5
Ashtree Rd. NR5: New C ... 5B 14
Ashwell Ct. NR5: Bow ... 2A 24
Aslake Cl. NR7: Spro ... 2H 17
Aspen Way NR4: Cring ... 3E 35
Aspland Rd. NR1: Norw ... 4F 4 (3E 27)
Assembly House ... 5B 5
Association Way NR7: Thor And ... 1E 29
Astell Rd. NR1: Norw ... 3D 36
Astley Rd. NR5: Bow ... 1A 24
  NR13: Lit P ... 5C 20
Atkinson Cl. NR5: Bow ... 1H 23
Atlantic Av. NR7: Spro ... 1A 18
Atmere Cl. NR4: Norw ... 2G 35
Attelsey Way NR5: Bow ... 2H 23
Atthill Rd. NR2: Norw ... 2H 25
Attoe Wlk. NR3: Norw ... 5C 16
Audax Rd. NR6: Norw ... 1B 16
Augustus Hare Dr. NR5: Norw ... 3D 24
Aurania Av. NR1: Norw ... 6C 26
Auster Cl. NR6: Norw ... 3B 16
Austin Way NR6: Old C ... 6E 11
Autumn Dr. NR5: New C ... 1C 24
Avebury Rd. NR4: Norw ... 2B 36
The Avenue NR12: Wrox ... 3A 42
Avenue Rd. NR2: Norw ... 4A 26
  NR18: Wym ... 5D 38
The Avenues NR2: Norw ... 5F 25
  NR4: Norw ... 5F 25
Avian Way NR7: Spro ... 5H 17
Aviary Way NR7: Norw ... 6A 18
Avocet Ri. NR7: Spro ... 2B 18
Avocet Way NR18: Wym ... 6E 39
Avonmouth Rd. NR3: Norw ... 6B 16
Aylesbury Cl. NR3: Norw ... 5C 16
Aylmer Twr. NR3: Norw ... 5H 15
Aylsham Cres. NR3: Norw ... 4B 16
Aylsham Rd. NR3: Norw ... 4A 16
Aylsham Rd. Bus. Pk. NR3: Norw ... 5B 16
Aylsham Way NR3: Norw ... 5B 16
Aylsham Way Trade Pk. NR3: Norw ... 5B 16
Ayton Rd. NR18: Wym ... 5D 38

B

Back La. NR8: R'land ... 4A 6
  NR9: Hether ... 4D 32
  NR18: Wym ... 4C 38
Bk. of the Inns NR2: Norw ... 5C 5
Back Rd. NR14: Alp, Yelv ... 3H 41
Back St. NR10: Hor F ... 2A 10
Bacon Rd. NR2: Norw ... 4G 25
Bacton Rd. NR3: Norw ... 5A 16
Badger Rd. NR5: New C ... 6G 13
Badgers Brook Rd. NR8: Thor Mar ... 3H 7
Bagleys Ct. NR2: Norw ... 4B 4 (3C 26)
Bahram Rd. NR8: Cost ... 3D 12
Bailey Cl. NR9: Hether ... 5E 33
Bailey Ct. NR2: Norw ... 2B 26
Baileys Yd. NR3: Norw ... 1C 4
Bainards Cl. NR18: Wym ... 2C 38
Baines Way NR5: Bow ... 1H 23
Baker Dr. NR9: Hether ... 4E 33
Bakers Rd. NR3: Norw ... 1A 4 (1C 26)
Bakery Ct. NR2: Norw ... 2H 25
Balderston Ct. NR3: Norw ... 2C 4 (2D 26)
Baldric Rd. NR8: Tav ... 4G 7
Balfour St. NR3: Norw ... 1E 4 (1E 27)
Baltic Wharf NR1: Norw ... 5E 5 (4E 27)
Banister Way NR18: Wym ... 3B 38
Bank Plain NR2: Norw ... 4C 4 (3D 26)
Bank St. NR2: Norw ... 4D 4 (3D 26)
Bannatyne Health Club
  Norwich ... 3F 29
Barbastelle Cres. NR9: Hether ... 4C 32
Barber Pl. NR7: Thor And ... 4B 28
Barberry Cl. NR8: Tav ... 3E 7
Barclay Grn. NR7: Norw ... 6B 18
Barclay Rd. NR7: Norw ... 5B 18
Bardolphs Ct. NR8: Thor Mar ... 3E 7
Bargate Ct. NR3: Norw ... 1D 4 (2D 26)
Barker's La. NR7: Spro ... 2F 17
Barker St. NR2: Norw ... 1A 4 (1B 26)
Barker Way NR13: Thor E ... 4E 19
Barley Ct. NR5: New C ... 6A 14
Barleyfield Rd. NR10: H'ford ... 2F 9
The Barn NR5: Bow ... 1B 24
Barnard Rd. NR5: Bow ... 1G 23
Barnards Yd. NR3: Norw ... 3B 4
Barnes Cl. NR7: Norw ... 5A 18
Barnesdale Rd. NR4: Norw ... 3B 36
Barnes Yd. NR3: Norw ... 1B 4
Barnham Broom Rd. NR18: Wym ... 1B 38
Barnham Cl. NR5: Bow ... 2H 23
Barn Mdw. NR14: Tro ... 1G 37
Barn Rd. NR2: Norw ... 3A 4 (3B 26)
Barn Ter. *NR13: B'all ... 3C 31*
(off Long Reach)
Barrack Rd. NR1: Norw ... 2G 27
Barrack St. NR3: Norw ... 1D 4 (2D 26)
Barrett-Lennard Rd. NR10: H'ford ... 1F 9
Barrett Rd. NR1: Norw ... 2D 36
Barri Cl. NR14: Por ... 6C 40
Barrow Cl. NR3: Norw ... 6G 15
Barton Dr. NR12: Hov ... 1D 42
Barton Way NR1: Norw ... 4F 27
Bartram Cl. NR18: Wym ... 1G 39
Barwells Ct. NR2: Norw ... 6B 5
Bassingham Rd. NR3: Norw ... 5A 16
Bately Ct. NR2: Norw ... 4H 25
Bateman Cl. NR5: Bow ... 2A 24
Bates Grn. NR5: Norw ... 1D 24
Bathurst Rd. NR2: Norw ... 4A 26
BAWBURGH ... 3E 23
Bawburgh Cl. NR5: New C ... 6G 13
Bawburgh Golf Course ... 1D 22
BAWBURGH HILL ... 5D 22
Bawburgh La. NR5: New C ... 6G 13
Bawburgh Rd. NR9: Baw, Gt Mel ... 5B 22
  NR9: E'ton ... 6A 12
  NR9: E'ton, Marl ... 2A 22
Baxter Ct. NR3: Norw ... 4A 16
Baynes Cl. NR14: Por ... 5C 40
Bay Willow La. NR12: Crost ... 1H 11
Beaconsfield Rd. NR3: Norw ... 1D 26
Bean Goose Row NR7: Spro ... 3B 18
Beatrice Rd. NR1: Norw ... 3F 27
Beatty Rd. NR4: Norw ... 2A 36
Beaufort Cl. NR6: Norw ... 1C 16
Beaumont Pl. NR2: Norw ... 5B 26
Beaumont Rd. NR5: New C ... 6C 14
Beckets Gro. NR18: Wym ... 1G 39
Becketswell Rd. NR18: Wym ... 5C 38
Becketts Ct. NR18: Wym ... 2C 38
Beckham Pl. NR3: Norw ... 1C 4
BECKHITHE ... 2D 32
Beck La. NR10: Hor F ... 1B 10
Becks Fur NR8: Thor Mar ... 3H 7
Beckside NR10: H'ford ... 1C 8
Beckwiths Ct. *NR3: Norw ... 2D 4*
(off Quayside)
Bedding La. NR3: Norw ... 2D 4 (2D 26)
Bedford St. NR2: Norw ... 4C 4 (3D 26)
Bedingfields NR2: Norw ... 5G 25
Beech Av. NR8: Tav ... 4D 6
Beechbank NR2: Norw ... 5A 26
Beechbank Ct. NR2: Norw ... 5A 26
Beechbank Dr. NR13: Thor E ... 4E 19
Beech Cl. NR18: Wym ... 2E 39
Beechcroft NR5: New C ... 6A 14
Beechcroft Ct. NR4: Cring ... 2C 34
Beech Dr. NR1: Norw ... 1F 27
  NR6: Norw ... 3B 16
  NR13: Lit P ... 5B 20
Beecheno Rd. NR5: Norw ... 2C 24
Beeches Cl. NR6: Old C ... 3E 17
Beeching Cl. NR1: Norw ... 2D 36
Beeching Rd. NR1: Norw ... 1D 36
Beechlands NR8: Tav ... 4E 7
Beech Rd. NR2: Norw ... 5A 26
  NR12: Wrox ... 3B 42
Beech Wlk. NR4: Kes ... 5F 35
  NR14: Fram E ... 3D 40

Beech Way NR13: B'all 4E **31**
Beechwood Ct. NR18: Wym 6E **39**
Beechwood Dr. NR7: Thor And 6B **18**
Beechwoods NR6: Old C 2C **16**
Beerlick's Loke NR14: Surl 6E **31**
Beeston La. NR10: Spix 5F **11**
NR12: Bee A 5F **11**
BEESTON ST ANDREW 4H **11**
Begonia Way NR18: Wym 1G **39**
Bek Cl. NR4: Norw 1F **35**
Belaugh Dr. NR12: Hov 1D **42**
Belaugh Rd. NR12: Hov 1B **42**
Bellamy Way NR14: Por 5C **40**
Bell Cl. NR6: Helle 1G **15**
NR8: Tav 5H **7**
Bellingham Ct. NR3: Norw 6E **17**
Bell La. NR13: Sal, Wrox 6A **42**
Bellomonte Cres. NR8: Dray 5A **8**
Bell Rd. NR3: Norw 6D **16**
Bellrope Cl. NR18: Wym 3E **39**
Bellrope La. NR18: Wym 3E **39**
Bells Loke NR13: B'all 4F **31**
Bellville Cres. NR1: Norw 8E **5** (5E **27**)
Belmore Cl. NR7: Thor And 1B **28**
Belmore Rd. NR7: Thor And 1B **28**
Beloe Av. NR5: Bow 2B **24**
Belsize Rd. NR1: Norw 2G **27**
Belt Rd. NR13: Blof 1C **20**
Belvedere Pl. NR4: Norw 6H **25**
Belvoir St. NR2: Norw 3A **26**
(not continuous)
Benbow Cl. NR9: Hether 4F **33**
Bendish Way NR5: Bow 2H **23**
Benjamin Gooch Way NR2: Norw 7A **5** (5C **26**)
Bensley Rd. NR2: Norw 4H **25**
Bentley Way NR6: Norw 3B **16**
Bergh Apton Rd. NR14: Alp 5H **41**
Berkley Cl. NR6: Helle 2G **15**
Bernard Cl. NR13: Rack 2G **19**
Berners Cl. NR3: Norw 6A **16**
Berners Ct. NR3: Norw 6A **16**
Berners St. NR3: Norw 6B **16**
Bernham Rd. NR6: Helle 1F **15**
Berrington Rd. NR6: Helle 1G **15**
Berryfields NR13: B'all 2E **31**
Ber St. NR1: Norw 6C **5** (4D **26**)
Bertie Rd. NR3: Norw 6B **16**
Bertram Way NR1: Norw 3F **4** (3F **27**)
Bessemer Rd. NR4: Norw 3C **36**
Bethel St. NR2: Norw 4A **4** (3C **26**)
Betsy Cl. NR5: Norw 3D **24**
Betts Ct. NR3: Norw 2C **4**
Bevan Cl. NR5: Norw 3C **24**
Beverley Cl. NR5: Norw 3F **25**
Beverley Rd. NR5: Norw 2F **25**
NR13: B'all 3D **30**
Beverley Way NR8: Dray 5A **8**
Bewfeld Rd. NR5: Bow 1H **23**
Bewit Rd. NR7: Spro 3A **18**
Bidewell Cl. NR8: Dray 6C **8**
Bignold Rd. NR3: Norw 5H **15**
Billing Cl. NR6: Old C 2E **17**
Bill Todd Way NR8: Thor Mar 3F **7**
Binyon Gdns. NR8: Tav 5G **7**
Bircham Cl. NR12: Wrox 5A **42**
Birch Cl. NR9: Lit Mel 1G **33**
Birch Ct. NR7: Spro 3A **18**
Birch Rd. NR9: Hether 4E **33**
Birchwood NR7: Thor And 3D **28**
Birkbeck Cl. NR1: Norw 1D **36**
NR14: Stoke X 3A **40**
Birkbeck Rd. NR1: Norw 1D **36**
Birkbeck Way NR7: Thor And 2C **28**
Birkdale NR4: Norw 1H **35**
Bishop Bri. Rd. NR1: Norw 2F **4** (2F **27**)
Bishopgate NR1: Norw 3E **4** (2E **27**)
NR3: Norw 2E **4** (2E **27**)
Bishop Pelham Ct. NR4: Kes 6G **35**
Bishop Ri. NR8: Thor Mar 3H **7**
Bishops Cl. NR7: Thor And 4A **28**
NR9: Hether 4D **32**
Bishop's House
Norwich 2E **4** (2E **27**)
Bishy Barnebee Way NR5: Bow 3A **24**
Bittern Av. NR7: Spro 2B **18**
Bittern Rd. NR8: Cost 2E **13**
Bixley Cl. NR5: Norw 3E **25**
Blackberry Ct. NR6: Norw 5G **15**
Blackburn Rd. NR6: Norw 1B **16**
Blackfriars St. NR3: Norw 2D **4** (2D **26**)
Blackhill Wood La. NR8: Cost 2C **12**
Black Horse Opening NR3: Norw 5E **17**
Blackhorse St. NR2: Norw 2B **26**
Blacksmiths Way NR6: Old C 2D **16**
Blackthorn Cl. NR6: Norw 3C **16**
Blackthorn Rd. NR18: Wym 4E **39**
Blackthorn Way NR14: Por 4C **40**
Black Tower 8F **5**
Blackwell Av. NR7: Spro 5F **17**
Bladewater Rd. NR5: Bow 4A **24**
Blake Dr. NR18: Wym 1G **39**
Blakeney Cl. NR4: Norw 1F **35**
Blakes Ct. NR3: Norw 4E **17**
Blakes La. NR13: B'all 4F **31**
Blakestone Dr. NR7: Thor And 2A **28**
Bland Rd. NR5: Norw 3C **24**
Blaxter Way NR7: Spro 2A **18**
Blazer Ct. NR2: Norw 1A **26**
Blazey Dr. NR18: Wym 1H **39**
Blenheim Cl. NR7: Spro 2G **17**
Blenheim Cres. NR7: Spro 3G **17**
Blenheim Rd. NR7: Spro 2G **17**
Blickling Ct. NR1: Norw 4E **4**
Blickling Rd. NR6: Norw 2B **16**
Bligh Cl. NR14: Fram E 4E **41**
Blind La. NR10: Hor F 3A **10**
Blithemeadow Ct. NR7: Spro 4H **17**
Blithemeadow Dr. NR7: Spro 4H **17**
Blithewood Gdns. NR7: Spro 4H **17**
BLOFIELD 1G **31**
BLOFIELD CORNER 4E **21**
Blofield Cnr. Rd. NR13: Blof 3D **20**
Blofield Hall NR13: Blof 5E **21**
BLOFIELD HEATH 3F **21**
Blofield Rd. NR13: B'all 4G **31**
Blomefield Rd. NR3: Norw 5A **16**
Bluebell Cres. NR4: Norw 1E **35**
Bluebell Rd. NR4: Norw 4E **25**
Blue Boar La. NR7: Spro 2H **17**
(not continuous)
Blue Mill NR1: Norw 8F **5**
Blyth Cl. NR13: Blof 1H **31**
Blythe Way NR10: H'ford 1G **9**
Blyth Rd. NR3: Norw 5C **16**
Blyths Wood Av. NR8: Cost 3C **12**
Boardman Cl. NR3: Norw 4C **16**
Boars Head Yd. NR1: Norw 6C **5**
Bobbin Rd. NR3: Norw 6A **16**
Bob Carter Leisure Cen. 5B **8**
Bobolink Row NR7: Rack 4C **18**
Bodmin Ct. NR7: Thor And 1A **28**
Boileau Cl. NR4: Norw 3B **36**
Bolingbroke Rd. NR3: Norw 4A **16**
Bolton Rd. NR7: Spro 3C **18**
Bonds Rd. NR13: Blof, Hemb 2F **21**
Bond St. NR2: Norw 2H **25**
Bone Rd. NR8: Dray 5C **8**
Boniface Cl. NR4: Norw 2B **36**
Boom Towers 8F **5** (5E **27**)
Boot Binders Rd. NR3: Norw 1B **26**
Booty Rd. NR7: Thor And 6C **18**
Borrowdale Dr. NR1: Norw 1G **27**
Borton Rd. NR13: Blof 4F **21**
Boston St. NR3: Norw 5C **16**
Boswell's Yd. NR3: Norw 2C **4**
Botolph St. NR3: Norw 1B **4** (2C **26**)
Botolph Way NR3: Norw 1C **4**
Bottom Breck Cl. NR5: New C 5A **14**
Boulderside Cl. NR7: Thor And 2B **28**
The Boulevard NR13: Thor E 4F **19**
Boulton Rd. NR7: Thor And 2H **27**
Boulton St. NR1: Norw 5D **5** (4D **26**)
Boundary Av. NR6: Helle 3H **15**
Boundary Cross 4G **15**
Boundary La. NR7: Thor And 3F **29**
Boundary Rd. NR6: Norw 4G **15**
Boundary Way NR14: Por 3B **40**
Bourges Ct. NR7: Rack 4C **18**
Bowers Av. NR3: Norw 4H **15**
Bowers Cl. NR3: Norw 5H **15**
Bowling Grn. Cl. NR10: Spix 2H **11**
Bowman Rd. NR4: Norw 3B **36**
BOWTHORPE 2A **24**
Bowthorpe Care Village NR5: Bow 2C **24**
Bowthorpe Cotts. NR5: Norw 2C **24**
Bowthorpe Employment Area
NR5: Bow 1H **23**
Bowthorpe Hall Rd. NR5: Bow 2A **24**
Bowthorpe Main Cen. 2A **24**
Bowthorpe Rd. NR2: Norw 3G **25**
NR5: Norw 3E **25**
Brabazon Rd. NR6: Helle 2A **16**
Bracey Av. NR6: Spro 2E **17**
Bracken Av. NR6: Helle 3H **15**
Bracken Cl. NR10: H'ford 1D **8**
Bracondale NR1: Norw 8E **5** (5E **27**)
Bracondale Ct. NR1: Norw 8E **5** (6E **27**)
Bracondale Grn. NR1: Norw 8E **5** (5E **27**)
Bracondale Millgate NR1: Norw 1F **37**
Bradbury Ho. *NR2: Norw* *5G **25***
(off Kinghorn Rd.)
Bradecroft NR5: Bow 1C **24**
Bradeham Way NR4: Norw 2H **35**
Bradman's La. NR18: Wym 6A **38**
Bradshaw Rd. NR8: Dray 6D **8**
Braeford Cl. NR6: Lwr H 5F **15**
Braithwait Cl. NR5: Bow 1B **24**
Brakendon Cl. NR1: Norw 8E **5**
Bramble Av. NR6: Helle 2H **15**
Bramble Cl. NR8: Thor Mar 3H **7**
Brambles Cl. NR10: Spix 3F **11**
Bramble Way NR14: Por 4E **41**
NR18: Wym 4E **39**
Brambling La. NR4: Cring 3C **34**
Bramerton La. NR14: Fram P 1F **41**
Bramfield Cl. NR2: Norw 2H **25**
Brampton Ct. NR5: Bow 1B **24**
Brancaster Cl. NR8: Thor Mar 2A **8**
Brandon Cl. NR6: Helle 3F **15**
Brandon Ct. NR13: B'all 4G **31**
Branford Rd. NR3: Norw 6D **16**
Branksome Cl. NR4: Norw 1A **36**
Branksome Rd. NR4: Norw 1H **35**
Brasier Rd. NR3: Norw 4A **16**
Braydeston Av. NR13: B'all 4F **31**
Braydeston Cres. NR13: B'all 4F **31**
Braydeston Dr. NR13: Blof 1H **31**
Braydeston Hall La. NR13: Blof 2H **31**
Bray Dr. NR18: Wym 1G **39**
Brayfield Way NR6: Old C 1E **17**
Braymeadow NR9: Lit Mel 1F **33**
Braymeadow La. NR9: Lit Mel 1F **33**
Brazen Ga. NR1: Norw 7B **5** (5C **26**)
Breck Farm Cl. NR8: Tav 3F **7**
Breck Farm La. NR8: Tav 3F **7**
(not continuous)
Breckland Dr. NR2: Norw 6C **26**
Breckland Rd. NR5: New C 6B **14**
Brecklands Rd. NR13: B'all 5G **31**
Breck Rd. NR7: Spro 5B **18**
Brenda James Cl. NR7: Thor And 2B **28**
Brennewater M. NR5: Bow 1B **24**
Brentwood NR4: Norw 2G **35**
Brereton Cl. NR5: Norw 3D **24**
Brettingham Av. NR4: Cring 4D **34**
Brewers Ct. NR3: Norw 1E **4** (2E **27**)
(not continuous)
Brewery La. NR10: H'ford 3D **8**
NR18: Wym 5D **38**
Brewster Ct. NR13: Blof 1F **31**
Breydon Dr. NR8: Cost 3F **13**
Breydon Dr. Nth. NR8: Cost 2F **13**
Breydon Rd. NR7: Spro 3E **17**
Brian Av. NR1: Norw 6C **26**
Brian McCarter Gdns. NR8: Cost 2E **13**
Briar Ct. NR5: Norw 2G **25**
Briar Rd. NR9: Hether 3C **32**
Brickfield Cl. NR3: Norw 4B **16**
Brickfield Loke NR8: Cost 2E **13**
Brick Kiln Rd. NR13: Lit P 2C **20**
Brickle Loke NR14: Stoke X 4A **40**
Brickle Rd. NR14: Stoke X 4A **40**
Brickle Wood Av. NR14: Por 2A **40**
Bridewell All. NR2: Norw 4C **4**
Bridewell St. NR18: Wym 5D **38**
Bridge Broad Cl. NR12: Wrox 2B **42**
Bridge Ct. NR3: Norw 2D **4** (2D **26**)
Bridge Farm La. NR5: Norw 3D **24**
Bridge Ind. Est. NR18: Wym 6D **38**
Bridge Loke NR18: Wym 5E **39**
Bridgemaster Ct. NR1: Norw 7F **5**
Bridle La. NR4: Kes 6G **35**
Briggs Dr. NR14: Por 3B **40**
Briggs Mead NR18: Wym 1G **39**
Brigg St. NR2: Norw 5B **5** (4C **26**)
Brigham Cl. NR13: B'all 3E **31**
Brightwell Rd. NR3: Norw 4C **16**
Brightys Opening NR2: Norw 2H **25**
Brimbelow Rd. NR12: Hov 2C **42**
Bristol Rd. NR5: New C 6G **13**
Bristol Ter. NR2: Norw 6A **5** (4C **26**)
Britannia Ct. NR5: Norw 1D **24**
Britannia Rd. NR1: Norw 1F **27**
Britannia Way NR5: Baw 6E **13**
Briton Way NR18: Wym 5C **38**
Britten Ho. NR4: Norw 5E **25**
Broadgate NR8: Thor Mar 3E **7**
Broadhurst Rd. NR4: Norw 2A **36**
Broadland Bus. Pk. NR7: Thor And 2F **29**
Broadland Ct. NR1: Norw 6F **5** (4E **27**)
Broadland Dr. NR2: Norw 6C **26**
NR13: Thor E 4E **19**
Broadland Northway NR9: A'bridge 2C **6**
Broadland Way NR7: Thor And 2G **29**
Broad La. NR13: Gt P, Lit P 2G **19**, 4A **20**
Broadmead Grn. NR13: Thor E 4F **19**
The Broads Cen. NR12: Hov 2B **42**
Broads Info. Cen. *5H **27***
(within Whitlingham Country Pk. Vis. Cen.)
Broadsman Cl. NR1: Norw 5F **27**
Broad Vw. NR13: Thor E 4E **19**

Brockwell Ct. NR3: Norw 5E 17
Bronde Cl. NR6: Old C 1D 16
Brooke Pl. NR1: Norw 6C 5 (4D 26)
(not continuous)
Brook Rd. NR7: Thor And 1F 29
Brooks Mdw. NR14: Por 4E 41
Brooks Rd. NR10: H'ford 2G 9
Broom Av. NR6: Helle 2H 15
NR7: Thor And 1B 28
Broom Cl. NR1: Norw 6E 27
NR8: Thor Mar 2F 7
Broom La. NR9: E'ton 6A 12
BROWICK 4G 39
Browick Rd. NR18: Wym 4D 38
Browne Ho. NR4: Norw 5E 25
Browne St. NR2: Norw 2A 26
Browning Cl. NR6: Helle 2F 15
BRUNDALL 4F 31
Brundall Gardens Station (Rail) 4D 30
Brundall Low Rd. NR13: Post 4H 29, 4A 30
Brundall Rd. NR13: Blof 3G 31
Brundall Station (Rail) 5F 31
Brunel Way NR3: Norw 6G 15
Brunswick Ho. NR2: Norw 7A 5
Brunswick Rd. NR2: Norw 7A 5 (5B 26)
Bryony Cl. NR6: Norw 2C 16
Buccaneer Way NR9: Hether 4D 32
Buck Courtney Cres. NR6: Norw 6H 9
Buckingham Dr. NR9: Hether 5B 32
Buckingham Rd. NR4: Norw 6G 25
Buckland Ri. NR4: Norw 3G 35
Bucks Yd. NR3: Norw 2A 4 (3C 26)
Buckthorn Cl. NR8: Tav 3E 7
Buck Yd. NR7: Thor And 4B 28
Bullacebush La. NR13: Blof 6G 21
Bullace Rd. NR5: New C 6A 14
Bullard Rd. NR3: Norw 4B 16
Bullards Spirits 3A 4
Bull Cl. NR3: Norw 1D 4 (2D 26)
Bull Cl. Rd. NR3: Norw 1D 4 (1D 26)
Bullies Way NR13: Blof 3G 21
Bull La. NR1: Norw 7B 5 (5D 26)
Bullock Hill NR10: Hor F 2A 10
Bullockshed La. NR14: Bram 1H 41
Bulmer Rd. NR3: Norw 5H 15
Bulrush Cl. NR10: H'ford 2F 9
Bumpstede Ct. NR5: Bow 1B 24
Bungalow La. NR7: Thor And 3D 28
Bungay Rd. NR14: Bix 3H 37, 1A 40
NR14: Por 5D 40
Bunnett Sq. NR4: Norw 4G 25
Bunns Row NR10: Hor F 3A 10
Bunyan Cl. NR7: Thor And 1E 29
Burdett Cl. NR13: Blof 1H 31
Burdock Cl. NR18: Wym 4F 39
Burdock La. NR9: Gt Mel 1A 32
Bure Cl. NR12: Wrox 2B 42
Bure Valley Railway
Wroxham Station 1B 42
Burgate La. NR14: Alp, Fram E, Por 4E 41
Burges Rd. NR3: Norw 5A 16
Burhill Cl. NR4: Norw 3H 35
Burleigh Twr. NR7: Norw 5A 18
Burma Rd. NR6: Old C 2E 17
Burnet Rd. NR3: Norw 5G 15
Burnt Fen Way NR12: Hov 1D 42
Burnthouse La.
NR9: Hether, Lit Mel 1F 33
NR18: Silf 6G 39
Burroughs Way NR18: Wym 4E 39
Burrow Way NR10: Hor F 1A 10
Burton Cl. NR6: Norw 2B 16
Burton Dr. NR13: Rack 1G 19
Burton Rd. NR6: Norw 2B 16
Burton Rd. Bus. Pk. NR6: Norw 2B 16
Bury St. NR2: Norw 5A 26
Bush Rd. NR6: Helle 6G 9
Bussey Rd. NR6: Norw 3C 16
Butler Gdns. NR18: Wym 1G 39
Buttercup Way NR5: Bow 3A 24
Buttermere Rd. NR5: Norw 3D 24
The Butts NR5: Bow 1A 24
Buxton Cl. NR9: E'ton 5A 12
Buxton Rd. NR3: Norw 1C 26
NR10: Spix 1F 11
Byfield Ct. NR3: Norw 6B 16
Byron Rd. NR8: Tav 5G 7

C

Caddow Rd. NR5: Bow 3A 24
Cadge Cl. NR5: Norw 2E 25
Cadge M. NR5: Norw 3E 25
Cadge Rd. NR5: Norw 3E 25
(not continuous)
Caernarvon Rd. NR2: Norw 3A 26
The Cains NR8: Thor Mar 3F 7
Cairns Ct. NR4: Norw 6A 26
Caistor La.
NR14: Caist E, Por 6E 37, 2A 40
CAISTOR ST EDMUND 6E 37
Caledonian Way NR6: Norw 3B 16
Caley Cl. NR3: Norw 5G 15
Calf Hill NR10: Hor F 2B 10
CALLOW GREEN 6G 21
Calthorpe Rd. NR5: Norw 2C 24
Calvert Ct. NR3: Norw 2C 4
Calvert St. NR3: Norw 2C 4 (2D 26)
Camberley Rd. NR4: Norw 1H 35
Camborne Cl. NR5: Norw 6D 14
Cambridge St. NR2: Norw 5B 26
Camelia Cl. NR9: Hether 4C 32
Cameron Grn. NR8: Tav 5H 7
Campbell Ct. NR3: Norw 1E 27
Camp Gro. NR1: Norw 3F 27
Campion Ho. NR5: Bow 1B 24
Campion Way NR9: Hether 4C 32
Camp Rd. NR8: Tav 4F 7
Canada Goose Ct. NR7: Spro 3B 18
Canaryfields NR1: Norw 5F 27
Canary Way NR1: Norw 5F 27
Canfor Rd. NR13: Rack 1G 19
Cannell Grn. NR3: Norw 1F 4 (2E 27)
Cannerby La. NR7: Spro 3G 17
Cann's La. NR9: Hether 5D 32
Canns Yd. *NR18: Wym* *5D 38*
(off Brewery La.)
Canterbury Pl. NR2: Norw 2B 26
Cantley La. NR4: Cring 6A 34
Capps Rd. NR3: Norw 6D 16
Cardiff Rd. NR2: Norw 4A 26
Cardigan Pl. NR2: Norw 2B 26
Cardinal Cl. NR9: E'ton 5A 12
Cardun Cl. NR13: Blof 4F 21
Carleton Cl. NR7: Spro 4G 17
NR18: Wym 2D 38
Carleton Rd. NR7: Spro 4G 17
Carlton Gdns. NR1: Norw 7C 5
Carlyle Rd. NR1: Norw 8E 5 (6E 27)
Carnoustie NR4: Norw 2H 35
Carol Cl. NR14: Stoke X 3A 40
Caroline Ct. NR4: Norw 5G 25
Carpenter Cl. NR18: Wym 1H 39
Carpenters Ct. *NR4: Norw* *5G 25*
(off Colman Rd.)
Carrefour Health & Beauty 4E 13
Carrington Cl. NR14: Por 6C 40
Carr La. NR14: Por 6C 40
Carrow Abbey 6F 27
Carrowbreck Cl. NR6: Helle 2E 15
Carrowbreck Rd. NR6: Helle 2E 15
Carrow Cl. NR1: Norw 8E 5
Carrow Hill NR1: Norw 8E 5 (5E 27)
Carrow Road 7F 5 (5F 27)
Carrow Rd. NR1: Norw 8F 5 (5E 27)
(not continuous)
Carr's Hill Cl. NR8: Cost 3B 14
Carshalton Rd. NR1: Norw 8E 5 (6E 27)
Carterford Dr. NR3: Norw 4D 16
Carter Rd. NR7: Spro 2B 18
NR8: Dray 5C 8
Cartmel NR9: Hether 4E 33
Castle Hill NR1: Norw 5C 5 (4D 26)
Castle Mall NR1: Norw 5C 5 (4D 26)
Castle Mdw. NR1: Norw 5C 5 (4D 26)
Castle Mus. & Art Gallery 4C 4 (3D 26)
Castle Ri. NR8: Thor Mar 3H 7
Castle St. NR2: Norw 5C 5 (3D 26)
NR12: Wrox 4A 42
Castleton Cl. NR5: Bow 1A 24
Caston Ind. Est. NR7: Spro 5A 18
Caston Rd. NR7: Thor And 6C 18
Cathedral Retail Pk.
Norwich 3A 4 (3B 26)
Cathedral St. NR1: Norw 4E 4 (3E 27)
Catherine Gdns. NR7: Thor And 3D 28
Catherine Wheel Opening NR3: Norw 1C 26
Catkin Cl. NR4: Cring 3D 34
Cator Rd. NR8: Dray 4A 8
Cattle Mkt. St. NR1: Norw 5D 5 (4D 26)
CATTON 2D 16
Catton Chase NR6: Old C 2C 16
Catton Ct. NR6: Old C 1D 16
Catton Gro. Rd. NR3: Norw 5C 16
NR6: Norw 4C 16
Catton Vw. Ct. NR3: Norw 4C 16
Causeway Cl. NR2: Norw 2B 26
Cavalier Cl. NR7: Thor And 2D 28
Cavalry Ride NR3: Norw 1F 4
Cavell Rd. NR1: Norw 1D 36
Cavendish Ct. NR1: Norw 4F 4
Cavendish Ho. NR1: Norw 4F 4 (3E 27)
Cavick Cotts. NR18: Wym 5B 38
Cavick Rd. NR18: Wym 5B 38
Cawstons Mdw. NR14: Por 3C 40
Cecil Gowing Ct. NR7: Spro 3G 17
Cecil Rd. NR1: Norw 6C 26
Cecil Sparkes Wlk. *NR8: Cost* *2D 12*
(off Peter Pulling Dr.)
Cedar Av. NR10: Spix 1G 11
Cedar Ct. NR8: Tav 3F 7
NR18: Wym 2E 39
Cedar Rd. NR1: Norw 4F 27
NR9: Hether 4C 32
NR14: Fram E 2C 40
The Cedars NR2: Norw 5A 26
Cedar Way NR13: B'all 4E 31
Cedarwood Cl. NR4: Cring 2D 34
Cemetery La. NR18: Wym 5C 38
Central Av. NR7: Thor And 3E 29
Central Cl. NR9: Hether 5D 32
Central Cres. NR9: Hether 5D 32
Century Way NR8: Thor Mar 2A 8
Cere Rd. NR7: Spro 3H 17
Chalfont Wlk. NR4: Norw 1F 35
Chalgrove Fld. NR7: Thor And 1E 29
Chalk Hill Rd. NR1: Norw 4F 4 (3E 27)
Chamberlain Ri. NR18: Wym 1G 39
Chamberlin Cl. NR3: Norw 5C 16
Chamberlin Ct. NR12: Hov 1D 42
NR13: Blof 1G 31
Chamberlin Rd. NR3: Norw 6C 16
Chambers Rd. NR3: Norw 4A 16
Chancel Cl. NR13: B'all 4E 31
Chancellors Dr. NR4: Norw 5C 24
Chandler Rd. NR14: Stoke X 3A 40
Chandler's Cl. NR18: Wym 5C 38
Chandlers Ct. NR4: Norw 3G 35
Chandler's Hill NR18: Wym 5C 38
The Chantry NR2: Norw 5B 5 (4C 26)
Chantry Rd. NR2: Norw 5A 5 (4C 26)
Chapel All. NR1: Norw 8D 5
Chapel Break Rd. NR5: Bow 1H 23
Chapel Ct. NR6: Helle 2G 15
NR13: Blof 1G 31
Chapelfield Bus. Cen. NR2: Norw 6B 5
Chapel Fld. E. NR2: Norw 6A 5 (4C 26)
CHAPELFIELD GROVE 5B 5 (4C 26)
Chapel Fld. Nth. NR2: Norw 5A 5 (4C 26)
Chapelfield Plain NR2: Norw 6B 5
Chapel Fld. Rd. NR2: Norw 5A 5 (4B 26)
Chapel La. NR7: Thor And 3B 28
NR14: Fram P 1E 41
NR18: Wym 2A 38
Chapel Loke NR1: Norw 7C 5 (5D 26)
Chapel Rd. NR5: New C 5B 14
Chapel Wlk. NR2: Norw 6A 5
Chapel Yd. *NR10: Hor F* *2A 10*
(off Church St.)
Chaplains Ho. *NR1: Norw* *2E 4*
(off Bishopgate)
Charing Cross NR2: Norw 3B 4 (3C 26)
Charles Av. NR7: Thor And 2B 28
Charles Cl. NR12: Wrox 4B 42
Charles James Ct. *NR3: Norw* *2C 4*
(off Fye Bri. St.)
Charles Jewson Ct. NR3: Norw 5A 16
Charles Sq. NR2: Norw 3B 26
Charles Watling Way NR5: Bow 1H 23
Charles Wesley Ct. *NR2: Norw* *3A 26*
(off Belvoir St.)
Charlotte Dr. NR8: Cost 3D 12
Charlton Rd. NR3: Norw 1D 4 (2D 26)
Charolais Cl. NR14: Tro 1G 37
Chartwell Ct. NR7: Spro 4E 17
Chartwell Rd. NR6: Norw 4C 16
NR7: Norw 4C 16
The Chase NR13: Blof 2H 31
Chase Cl. NR6: Old C 2C 16
Chatham St. NR3: Norw 1A 4 (2C 26)
Cheena Ct. NR8: Cost 2D 12
Chenery Dr. NR7: Spro 2H 17
Cherry Cl. NR1: Norw 8D 5 (6D 26)
Cherry La. NR3: Norw 1B 4 (2D 26)
Cherrywood NR14: Alp 5H 41
Chester Pl. NR2: Norw 3B 26
Chester St. NR2: Norw 5B 26
Chestnut Av. NR10: Spix 1G 11
Chestnut Cl. NR5: New C 5H 13
Chestnut Ct. NR2: Norw 4A 4
Chestnut Dr. NR18: Wym 6B 38
Chestnut Hill NR4: Norw 2F 35
Chestnut Pl. NR4: Cring 2D 34
The Chestnuts NR7: Spro 3G 17
NR18: Wym 3C 38
Cheyham Mt. NR4: Norw 2G 35
Childs Rd. NR9: Hether 4B 32
Childs Ter. NR9: Baw 3E 23
Chipperfield Rd. NR7: Norw 6B 18
Chittock Cl. NR10: Spix 3G 11

Chopyngs Dole Cl. NR7: Spro 2H 17
Choseley Ct. NR18: Wym 4D 38
Christchurch Rd. NR2: Norw 4H 25
Christine Rd. NR10: Spix 3G 11
Christopher Cl. NR1: Norw 1C 36
Christopher Ct. NR5: Norw 2D 24
Christopher Way NR12: Wrox 5A 42
Church All. NR2: Norw 3C 4
NR13: Blof 1G 31
Church Av. NR2: Norw 6A 26
Church Av. E. NR2: Norw 6A 26
Church Cl. NR2: Norw 1A 26
NR14: Arm 6H 37
NR14: Por 5C 40
Churchfield NR4: Cring 3E 35
Churchfield Grn. NR7: Thor And 1A 28
Churchfields NR9: Hether 4E 33
Church Grn. NR7: Spro 2G 17
Churchill Rd. NR3: Norw 1D 26
Church La. NR4: Norw 2F 35
NR7: Spro 2G 17
NR9: E'ton 4A 12
NR10: Spix 2D 10
NR12: Bee A 2G 17
NR12: Wrox 4A 42
NR13: B'all 4E 31
Churchman Rd. NR7: Norw 5H 17
Church Mdw. NR14: Alp 4H 41
Church Mdw. La. NR14: Alp 6H 41
NR15: Alp 6H 41
Church Rd. NR12: Hov 2B 42
NR13: Blof 2G 31
NR13: Gt P 6A 20
NR13: Post 4H 29
NR14: Alp, Yelv 3H 41
Church St. NR6: Old C 2D 16
NR9: Baw 3D 22
NR10: H'ford 2E 9
NR10: Hor F 2A 10
NR18: Wym 4C 38
Church Ter. NR12: Wrox 4A 42
Church Vw. Cl. NR7: Spro 2G 17
Church Vw. Ct. NR7: Spro 2G 17
Churston Cl. NR1: Norw 6E 27
Cinema City 4C 4 (3D 26)
Cintra Rd. NR1: Norw 3G 27
Cirrus Way NR7: Spro 5H 17
City Hgts. *NR1: Norw* *4G 27*
(off Telegraph La. E.)
City of Norwich Aviation Mus. 4A 10
City Rd. NR1: Norw 8D 5 (6D 26)
City Vw. Rd. NR6: Helle 3H 15
Civic Gdns. NR3: Norw 4H 15
Clabon First Cl. NR3: Norw 4D 16
Clabon Rd. NR3: Norw 5E 17
Clabon Second Cl. NR3: Norw 4E 17
Clabon Third Cl. NR3: Norw 4E 17
Clancy Rd. NR7: Norw 6H 17
Clare Cl. NR3: Norw 6D 16
Claremont Rd. NR4: Norw 1H 35
Clarence Rd. NR1: Norw 4F 27
Clarendon Rd. NR2: Norw 4B 26
Clarendon Steps NR2: Norw 4A 26
Clarke Rd. NR3: Norw 1D 26
Clark's Loke NR13: Blof 4G 21
Clarkson Rd. NR5: Norw 2D 24
Clearview Dr. NR14: Por 3B 40
Clematis Way NR18: Wym 2G 39
Clement Ct. NR2: Norw 4C 4
Clere Cl. NR18: Wym 3D 38
Cleveland Rd. NR2: Norw 4A 4 (3C 26)
Cleves Way NR8: Cost 3H 13
Clickers Rd. NR3: Norw 1B 26
Cliffe Cotts. NR1: Norw 8E 5
Clifton Cl. NR2: Norw 2B 26
Clifton Rd. NR18: Wym 2D 38
Clifton St. NR2: Norw 2A 26
THE CLOSE 3E 4 (3E 27)
The Close NR9: Lit Mel 6G 23
NR13: B'all 3E 31
Clovelly Dr. NR6: Lwr H 5F 15
Clover Ct. NR7: Spro 4E 17
CLOVER HILL 2B 24
Clover Hill Rd. NR5: Bow 1B 24
Clover Rd. NR7: Spro 4E 17
Coach & Horses Row NR2: Norw 6A 5 (4C 26)
Coach Ho. Ct. NR4: Norw 6H 25
Coach Ho. M. NR4: Kes 6G 35
Coachmaker Way NR9: Hether 3E 33
Coachmans Ct. NR7: Spro 3E 17
Cobham Way NR7: Spro 5H 17
Coburg St. NR1: Norw 6B 5
Cock St. NR18: Wym 4C 38
The Coigncroft NR13: B'all 4G 31
Coke Rd. NR1: Norw 1D 36
Coldershaw Rd. NR6: Helle 3A 16
Coldham Hall Carnser NR14: Surl 6D 30
Coleburn Rd. NR1: Norw 3C 36
Colegate NR3: Norw 3B 4 (3C 26)
(not continuous)
Coleman Cl. NR8: Thor Mar 3A 8
Coleridge Cl. NR8: Tav 5G 7
Colindeep La. NR7: Spro 3F 17
Colkett Dr. NR6: Old C 4D 16
College Dr. NR9: E'ton 1A 22
College La. NR4: Kes 6G 35
College Rd. NR2: Norw 4H 25
Collingwood Cl. NR9: Hether 5E 33
NR14: Por 5C 40
Collins Ct. NR3: Norw 5C 16
Colls Rd. NR7: Norw 6A 18
Colls Wlk. NR7: Norw 6A 18
COLMAN HOSPITAL 5H 25
Colman Ho. NR2: Norw 4A 4 (3C 26)
NR4: Norw 5E 25
Colman Rd. NR4: Norw 4G 25
COLNEY 5B 24
Colney Dr. NR4: Cring 3E 35
Colney La. NR4: Coln, Cring 5B 24
NR9: Hether 4G 33
Colney Wood Burial Pk. 4G 23
Colossus Way NR5: New C 6E 13
Coltishall La. NR10: Hor F 2B 10
Coltishall Rd. NR12: Bel 1A 42
Coltsfoot Rd. NR10: H'ford 1C 8
The Columbine NR5: Bow 2H 23
Columbine Rd. NR10: H'ford 1D 8
Combined Court
Norwich 2E 4 (2E 27)
The Common NR8: R'land 5B 6
NR14: Surl 6C 30
Common La. NR7: Thor And 4C 28
Common Loke NR12: Crost 1H 11
Common Rd. NR14: Surl 6D 30
Commonwealth Way NR7: Thor And 1D 28
Compass Twr. NR7: Norw 5A 18
Concorde Rd. NR6: Norw 3B 16
Conesford Dr. NR1: Norw 6E 27
Coniston Cl. NR5: Norw 3D 24
NR9: Hether 4F 33
Connaught Rd. NR2: Norw 3A 26
Connells M. *NR7: Thor And* *3F 29*
(off St Andrews Pk.)
Conroy Cl. NR7: Spro 2A 18
Constable Rd. NR4: Norw 3A 36
Constable Ter. NR4: Norw 5C 24
Constitution Hill NR3: Norw 6D 16
NR6: Spro 6D 16
Constitution Opening NR3: Norw 5D 16
Convent Rd. NR2: Norw 4B 26
Conyers NR18: Wym 2D 38
Cooke Cl. NR5: Bow 2H 23
Cookes Ct. NR3: Norw 2C 4
Cooper La. NR1: Norw 3D 36
Cooper Row NR13: B'all 2D 30
Coopers Cl. NR8: Thor Mar 2H 7
Coot Dr. NR7: Spro 2B 18
Copeman Rd. NR13: Lit P 5B 20
Copeman St. NR2: Norw 4A 4 (3B 26)
Copenhagen Way NR3: Norw 5B 16
Copper Smith Way NR18: Wym 3G 39
Coppice Av. NR6: Helle 2F 15
The Copse *NR7: Thor And* *3F 29*
(off St Andrews Pk.)
Coralie Ct. NR4: Norw 2F 35
Corbet Av. NR7: Spro 5G 17
Cordwainer Cl. NR7: Spro 3C 18
Corie Rd. NR4: Norw 4G 25
Corncutters Cl. NR3: Norw 3C 4 (3D 26)
Corner La. NR10: H'ford 2G 9
Cornet Cl. NR7: Thor And 6F 19
Cornwall Cl. NR13: Rack 1G 19
Cornwallis Cl. NR5: Bow 2B 24
Coronach Cl. NR8: Cost 3D 12
Coronation Cl. NR6: Helle 3H 15
Coronation Rd. NR6: Helle 4H 15
Corton Ho. NR1: Norw 8E 5
Corton Rd. NR1: Norw 8E 5 (6E 27)
Coslany Sq. NR3: Norw 3B 4
Coslany St. NR3: Norw 3B 4 (3C 26)
(not continuous)
Cossgrove Cl. NR3: Norw 4A 16
COSTESSEY 3H 13
Costessey La. NR8: Cost, R'land 6A 6
NR8: Dray 1H 13
Costessey Park & Ride 6E 13
Costessey Pk. Golf Course 4F 13
Costessey Rd. NR8: Tav 5F 7
Cotman Flds. NR1: Norw 2F 4 (2E 27)
Cotman Rd. NR1: Norw 4G 27
The Cottage Dr. NR7: Thor And 1B 28
Cotterall Ct. NR5: Bow 1C 24
Cottinghams Dr. NR6: Helle 1F 15
Coughtrey Cl. NR7: Spro 3G 17
The County Arts Bowl Club 1A 28
Courtenay Cl. NR5: Bow 1A 24
The Courtyard NR5: Norw 4D 24
The Covey NR8: Thor Mar 3G 7
Cowdewell M. NR8: Thor Mar 3G 7
Cowgate NR3: Norw 1C 4 (2D 26)
Cow Hill NR2: Norw 4A 4 (3C 26)
Cow Tower 2F 4 (2E 27)
Cow Yd. NR2: Norw 4A 4
Cozens-Hardy Rd. NR7: Spro 2G 17
Cozens Rd. NR1: Norw 5F 27
Cozens-Wiley Rd. NR13: Lit P 5B 20
Crabapple Cl. NR18: Wym 4F 39
Cranage Rd. NR1: Norw 2D 36
Cranes Cft. Rd. NR7: Spro 2H 17
Cranleigh Ri. NR4: Norw 2G 35
Cranley Rd. NR7: Thor And 2F 29
Cranwell Gdns. NR14: Por 4E 41
Cranworth Gdns. NR1: Norw 8B 5 (5C 26)
Craske Dr. NR13: Rack 1G 19
Craske M. NR5: Bow 1G 23
Craven Ct. NR3: Norw 6E 17
Crawshay Ct. NR3: Norw 5B 16
Creance Rd. NR7: Spro 3H 17
Cremorne La. NR1: Norw 4G 27
The Crescent NR2: Norw 6A 5 (4C 26)
NR8: Dray 5A 8
NR9: Hether 6C 32
Cressener Cl. NR6: Helle 2F 15
Cresswell Cl. NR5: Norw 3C 24
Cricket Cl. NR8: Thor Mar 2H 7
Cricket Fld. Vw. NR13: B'all 5G 31
Cricket Ground Rd. NR1: Norw 6E 27
CRINGLEFORD 3E 35
Cringleford Bus. Cen. NR4: Cring 3E 35
Cringleford Chase NR4: Cring 2D 34
Critoph Cl. NR14: Por 5D 40
Crocodile Ct. *NR2: Norw* *2B 26*
(off Ely St.)
Crocus St. NR18: Wym 2G 39
The Croft NR8: Cost 2A 14
NR9: Gt Mel 3A 32
Croftholme Way NR1: Norw 1H 27
The Crofts NR5: Bow 2A 24
Crome Dr. NR12: Hov 1D 42
Crome Rd. NR3: Norw 6E 17
Cromer Rd. NR6: Helle 1H 15
NR10: H'ford, Hor F 4G 9
Cromes Oak Cl. NR14: Por 5C 40
Cromwell Cl. NR9: Hether 4D 32
Cromwell Rd. NR7: Spro 4G 17
Crooks Pl. NR1: Norw 7A 5 (5C 26)
Crossbill Cl. NR8: Cost 1E 13
Cross Keys Cl. NR10: Hor F 2A 10
Cross Keys Yd. NR3: Norw 1C 4
Cross La. NR3: Norw 2C 4 (2D 26)
CROSTWICK 1H 11
Crostwick La. NR10: Spix 2F 11
Crowes Loke NR13: Lit P 2C 20
Crown Hill NR10: H'ford 1D 8
Crown Rd. NR1: Norw 4D 4 (3D 26)
NR5: New C 6C 14
NR10: Hor F 2A 10
Crownthorpe Rd.
NR18: Wickle, Wym 2A 38
Crummock Rd. NR5: Norw 3D 24
Cubitt Rd. NR1: Norw 2H 27
Cuckoo La. NR13: Stru 5H 31
Cucumber La. NR13: B'all 2D 30
Culling's Hill NR13: Post 5H 29
Culloden Av. NR5: New C 6F 13
Culverin Cl. NR7: Thor And 1E 29
Culyers Cl. NR14: Por 2A 40
Cunningham Rd. NR5: Norw 4D 24
Curson Cl. NR9: Hether 5C 32
Cursons M. NR18: Wym 2C 38
Curtis Rd. NR6: Norw 3A 16
Custance Ct. NR4: Norw 6F 25
Cuthbert Cl. NR7: Spro 3G 17
Cutler Way NR5: Bow 1G 23
Cutters Row *NR3: Norw* *6A 16*
(off Hemming Way)
Cuttons Cnr. NR13: Blof, Hemb 3H 21
Cypress Cl. NR8: Tav 5H 7
Cyprus St. NR1: Norw 8D 5 (6D 26)
Cyril Rd. NR7: Thor And 2C 28

D

Dacre Cl. NR4: Norw 2F 35
Daffodil Cl. NR4: Cring 2C 34
NR18: Wym 1G 39
Daisy Hill Ct. NR4: Norw 2E 35
Daisy St. NR18: Wym 2G 39
Dakin Rd. NR3: Norw 6C 16
Dakota Dr. NR6: Norw 1C 16

Dalbier Cl. NR7: Thor And 1F 29
The Dales NR13: B'all 4F 31
Dales Loke NR7: Thor And 4A 28
Dales Pl. NR7: Thor And 4C 28
Dalrymple Way NR6: Norw 3B 16
Dalymond Ct. NR3: Norw 1C 4 (1D 26)
Damgate Ct. NR18: Wym 5C 38
Damgate St. NR18: Wym 5C 38
Damocles Ct. NR2: Norw 4A 4 (3C 26)
Danby Cl. NR4: Norw 3A 36
Danesbower Cl. NR13: Blof 1H 31
Danesbower La. NR13: Blof 1H 31
Daniels Rd. NR4: Norw 6A 26
Darlington M. NR3: Norw 6A 16
Darrell Pl. NR5: Norw 2E 25
Davey Pl. NR2: Norw 4C 4
David Lloyd Leisure
Norwich 4G 15
Davidson Cl. NR7: Thor And 2C 28
Davidson Gdns. NR8: Tav 4G 7
Davidson Rd. NR7: Thor And 2C 28
Dawson Ct. NR1: Norw 8B 5 (5C 26)
The Daynes Sports Cen. 4D 4 (3D 26)
Deacon Cl. NR13: B'all 3F 31
Deacon Dr. NR9: Hether 4E 33
De Berney Cl. NR1: Norw 3D 36
De Caux Rd. NR3: Norw 6D 16
Decoy Dr. NR12: Hov 1D 42
Deepdale NR13: B'all 4F 31
Deep Rd. NR18: Wym 1C 38
Defiant Rd. NR6: Norw 2C 16
De Grey Cl. NR5: New C 6C 14
De Hague Rd. NR4: Norw 5G 25
De Havilland Pl. NR7: Norw 6B 18
Delane Rd. NR8: Dray 6D 8
Delft Way NR6: Norw 1H 15
The Dell NR14: Tro 1G 37
Dell Cres. NR5: Norw 2F 25
Dell Loke NR14: Tro 1G 37
Dell Rose Ct. NR4: Norw 5F 25
Deloney Rd. NR7: Norw 5H 17
Delta Cl. NR6: Norw 3B 16
Denbigh Ho. NR2: Norw 3A 26
Denbigh Rd. NR2: Norw 4A 26
The Denes NR7: Thor And 4H 27
Denmark Opening NR3: Norw 6D 16
Denmark Rd. NR3: Norw 6D 16
Denmead Cl. NR4: Norw 3H 35
Dennis Rd. NR6: Helle 6G 9
Denton Rd. NR3: Norw 4E 17
Derby St. NR2: Norw 2B 26
Dereham Rd. NR2: Norw 2G 25
NR5: Bow, New C 5E 13
(not continuous)
NR9: E'ton, New C 5A 12
Dersley Ct. NR5: Bow 2H 23
Desborough Way NR7: Thor And 1E 29
Desmond Dr. NR6: Old C 1E 17
Devlin Dr. NR14: Por 4C 40
Devon Av. NR6: Helle 3F 15
Devonshire Pl. *NR2: Norw 2B 26*
(off Devonshire St.)
Devonshire St. NR2: Norw 2A 26
Devon Way NR14: Tro 1H 37
Dial Ho. NR2: Norw 8A 5
Diamond Rd. NR6: Norw 2A 16
Dian Rd. NR13: B'all 4G 31
Dibden Rd. NR3: Norw 1E 27
Dilham Dr. NR12: Hov 1D 42
The Dining Ter. NR2: Norw 6B 5
Distillery Sq. NR2: Norw 3B 26
Dixon Rd. NR7: Spro 3F 17
Dixons Fold NR6: Old C 3E 17
Doctors Mdw. NR10: Hor F 1A 10
Doctors Rd. NR13: Blof 1G 31
Dr Torrens Way NR5: New C 6G 13
Dodderman Way NR5: Bow 4B 24
Dog La. NR10: H'ford 1A 8
Dogwood Cl. NR18: Wym 4F 39
Dogwood Rd. NR6: Norw 3C 16
Dolphin Gro. NR2: Norw 1A 26
Dolphin Path NR2: Norw 1A 26
Dolphin Rd. NR5: New C 6F 13
Doman Rd. NR1: Norw 8E 5 (5E 27)
Donchurch Cl. NR5: Bow 2B 24
Donkey La. NR4: Norw 2G 35
Don Pratt Ct. NR3: Norw 1E 4
Doris Rd. NR2: Norw 4A 26
Doughty's Hospital NR3: Norw 2C 4
Douglas Cl. NR6: Norw 6C 10
Douglas Haig Rd. NR5: Norw 3D 24
Douglas Rd. NR10: Spix 3F 11
Douro Pl. NR2: Norw 3B 26
Dove Av. NR18: Wym 1G 39
Dovedales NR6: Spro 3E 17
Dovedales Ct. NR6: Spro 3E 17
Dove La. NR14: Howe 6F 41
Dover St. NR2: Norw 4A 26
Dove St. NR2: Norw 4B 4
Dow Cl. NR5: Bow 4A 24
Dowding Rd. NR6: Norw 1C 16
DOWNHAM 1D 38
Downham Cres. NR18: Wym 2D 38
Downham Gro. NR18: Wym 1G 39
Downing M. NR5: Bow 1G 23
Dowsing Ct. NR7: Thor And 6E 19
Dowson Rd. NR3: Norw 6A 16
Dragonfly La. NR4: Cring 2C 34
Dragon Hall 6E 5 (4E 27)
Dragoon Cl. NR7: Thor And 2E 29
Dragoon St. NR3: Norw 1F 4 (1E 27)
Drake Cl. NR9: Hether 4E 33
Dranes La. NR14: Yelv 4H 41
Draper Way NR5: Bow 1G 23
Drays Yd. NR1: Norw 6E 5 (4E 27)
DRAYTON 5B 8
Drayton Gro. NR8: Dray 5A 8
Drayton Hall Pk. NR8: Dray 5C 8
Drayton Hall Pk. Rd. NR8: Dray 5C 8
Drayton High Rd. NR6: Helle 6B 8
NR8: Dray 6B 8
Drayton Ind. Est. NR8: Dray 5A 8
Drayton La. NR10: H'ford 2D 8
Drayton Lodge Pk. NR8: Dray 6C 8
Drayton Rd. NR3: Norw 5G 15
Drayton Wood Rd. NR6: Helle 1E 15
Drewray Dr. NR8: Thor Mar 2H 7
The Drive NR5: New C 1C 24
NR14: Bix 1H 37
NR18: Wym 1H 39
Driving Test Cen. 2F 29
The Drove NR8: Thor Mar 3F 7
Drury Cl. NR5: Bow 1C 24
Dryden Rd. NR8: Tav 5G 7
Duckett Cl. NR1: Norw 2D 36
Duff Rd. NR3: Norw 5C 16
Dugard Av. NR1: Norw 1G 27
Dukes Ct. NR2: Norw 4A 4
Dukes Pal. Wharf NR3: Norw 3B 4
Duke St. NR3: Norw 2B 4 (2C 26)
Dunch Cres. NR13: Hemb 4H 21
Dungar Rd. NR7: Spro 2A 18
Dunham Rd. NR9: E'ton 1B 22
Dunlin Dr. NR4: Cring 2C 34
Dunnock Ct. *NR8: Cost 2E 13*
(off Dunnock Dr.)
Dunnock Dr. NR8: Cost 2D 12
Dunston Cotts. NR1: Norw 8F 5
Dunwood Dr. NR6: Old C 6E 11
Durham St. NR2: Norw 5A 26
Dussindale NR18: Wym 2D 38
Dussindale Dr. NR7: Thor And 5E 19
(not continuous)
DUSSINDALE PARK 1E 29
Duverlin Cl. NR4: Norw 2H 35
Dyer Cl. NR10: H'ford 1G 9
Dyers Yd. NR3: Norw 3B 4 (3C 26)
Dye's Rd. NR13: Blof 2D 20
Dykebeck NR18: Wickle, Wym 5A 38

E

Eade Rd. NR3: Norw 1C 26
Eagle Wlk. NR2: Norw 5B 26
Earles Gdns. NR4: Norw 4F 25
EARLHAM 4E 25
Earlham Ct. NR2: Norw 3B 26
Earlham Crematorium 3H 25
EARLHAM FIVE WAYS 4E 25
Earlham Grn. La. NR4: Norw 2C 24
NR5: Bow, Norw 2B 24
Earlham Gro. NR5: Norw 3E 25
Earlham Ho. NR2: Norw 4H 25
Earlham Ho. Shops *NR2: Norw 4H 25*
(off Earlham Rd.)
EARLHAM RISE 3F 25
Earlham Rd. NR2: Norw 3G 25
NR4: Norw 4D 24
Earlham W. Cen. NR5: Norw 3D 24
Earnshaw Ct. NR7: Thor And 3B 28
East Av. NR13: B'all 4G 31
East Bank NR1: Norw 6F 5
Eastbourne Pl. NR1: Norw 4E 4 (3E 27)
Eastern Av. NR7: Thor And 2D 28
Eastern Cl. NR7: Thor And 2D 28
Eastern Cres. NR7: Thor And 2D 28
Eastern Rd. NR7: Thor And 2D 28
East Farm La. NR10: Hor F 1C 10
Eastfield NR8: Tav 5G 7
Eastgate Ho. NR1: Norw 4F 27
East Hills Rd. NR5: New C 6G 13
Eastlodge NR1: Norw 3H 27
EASTON 5A 12
Easton Sports & Conference Cen. 1A 22
Easton Tennis Cen. 1A 22
East Wing NR7: Thor And 3F 29
Eastwood M. NR6: Old C 4D 16
EATON 2F 35
Eaton Cen. 2F 35
Eaton Chase NR4: Norw 1F 35
Eaton Ga. NR4: Kes 5G 35
Eaton Golf Course
Norwich 2H 35
Eatonhill NR4: Norw 2F 35
Eaton Rd. NR4: Norw 1A 36
Eaton St. NR4: Norw 3E 35
Eaton Vale Activity Cen. 4G 35
Ebbisham Dr. NR4: Norw 3G 35
Ebenezer Pl. NR3: Norw 1A 4 (1C 26)
Ecton Wlk. NR6: Old C 2E 17
Eddington Way NR9: E'ton 5A 12
Eden Cl. NR7: Norw 3H 27
Edenhurst Cl. NR4: Norw 6G 25
Edgefield Cl. NR6: Old C 6E 11
Edgehill NR7: Thor And 1E 29
Edgeworth Rd. NR5: Norw 3D 24
Edinburgh Rd. NR2: Norw 3H 25
Edith Cavell Cl. NR18: Wym 2G 39
Edmund Bacon Ct. NR3: Norw 6C 16
Edrich Cl. NR13: Blof 1G 31
Edrich Way NR5: Bow 2H 23
Edward Gambling Ct. NR2: Norw 1A 26
Edward Jodrell Plain
NR2: Norw 7A 5 (5B 26)
Edwards Ct. NR7: Spro 2F 17
Edwards Rd. NR7: Spro 2F 17
Edward St. NR3: Norw 1B 4 (1D 26)
Edwin Cl. NR18: Wym 3C 38
Egyptian Goose Rd. NR7: Spro 2B 18
Eider Cft. NR7: Spro 2B 18
Elan Cl. NR18: Wym 5E 39
Elder Cl. NR5: New C 5C 14
Elderflower M. NR5: Bow 3A 24
Eleanor Rd. NR1: Norw 8B 5 (6C 26)
Elise Way NR18: Wym 6E 39
Elizabeth Av. NR7: Thor And 2C 28
Elizabeth Cl. NR7: Spro 2G 17
NR10: Spix 1F 11
Elizabeth Fry Rd. NR2: Norw 4G 25
Elizabeth Rd. NR14: Por 5C 40
Elizabeth Way NR8: Cost 3C 12
Elkins Rd. NR18: Wym 3C 38
Ella Rd. NR1: Norw 3F 27
Ellcar Ri. NR4: Norw 2H 35
Ellis Cl. NR7: Spro 3B 18
Ellis Gdns. NR4: Kes 6G 35
Elm Cl. NR5: New C 5A 14
NR9: Lit Mel 1G 33
Elmdon Ct. NR1: Norw 3F 27
Elm Gro. La. NR3: Norw 5C 16
Elm Hill 3C 4
Elm Hill NR3: Norw 3C 4 (3D 26)
The Elms NR2: Norw 4A 26
NR6: Old C 1D 16
Elm Ter. NR18: Wym 4D 38
Elstead Cl. NR4: Norw 3G 35
Elveden Cl. NR4: Norw 2G 35
Elvina Rd. NR10: Spix 2F 11
Elvin Way NR3: Norw 6G 15
Elwyn Rd. NR1: Norw 1D 36
Ely St. NR2: Norw 2B 26
Embry Cres. NR6: Norw 1C 16
Emmas Way NR13: Lit P 2C 20
Enfield Rd. NR5: Norw 3D 24
Enfield Row NR18: Wym 2G 39
English Rd. NR6: Old C 3D 16
Epic Studios 1C 4
The Erins NR3: Norw 6D 16
Ernest Dr. NR6: Old C 6E 11
Ernest Gage Av. NR5: New C 5E 13
Erpingham Gateway 3D 4
Esdelle St. NR3: Norw 1B 4 (1C 26)
Esprit Cl. NR18: Wym 6E 39
Essex St. NR2: Norw 4B 26
Estelle Way NR18: Wym 2F 39
Ethel Gooch Rd. NR18: Wym 3C 38
Ethel Rd. NR1: Norw 4F 27
Europa Way NR1: Norw 1F 37
Europa Way Ind. Est. NR1: Norw 1F 37
Eustace Rd. NR3: Norw 4H 15
Eva Cl. NR10: H'ford 1F 9
Evans Way NR6: Old C 6C 10
Eva Rd. NR13: Rack 1G 19
Everett Cl. NR7: Spro 2A 18
Eversley Rd. NR6: Helle 3A 16
Everson Cl. NR5: New C 6D 14
Evora Rd. NR18: Wym 6E 39
Exchange Cl. NR8: Tav 4G 7
Exchange St. NR2: Norw 4B 4 (3C 26)
Exeter St. NR2: Norw 2B 26

Exige Way NR18: Wym .6E 39
Exmouth Cl. NR9: Hether .4E 33

F

Fairfax Dr. NR7: Thor And .6E 19
Fairfax Rd. NR4: Norw .5G 25
Fairfield Cl. NR13: Lit P .2C 20
Fairfield Rd. NR2: Norw .6B 26
Fairhaven Ct. NR2: Norw .3H 25
Fairland Ct. *NR18: Wym .5D 38*
(off Fairland St.)
Fairland St. NR18: Wym .5D 38
Fair La. NR13: Post .6H 29
Fairmile Cl. NR2: Norw .6A 26
Fairstead Ct. NR7: Spro .4F 17
Fairstead Rd. NR7: Spro .4F 17
Fairview Cl. NR8: Dray .6B 8
Fairway NR8: Cost .2C 12
Fairway Ct. NR8: Cost .2D 12
Fairways NR6: Helle .2E 15
Fakenham Rd. NR8: Dray, Tav .1A 6
Falcon Cres. NR8: Cost .2E 13
Falconers Chase NR18: Wym .3G 39
Falcon M. NR7: Spro .3H 17
Falcon Rd. E. NR7: Spro .4H 17
Falcon Rd. W. NR7: Spro .3G 17
Falkland Cl. NR6: Helle .2E 15
Fallowfield NR14: Fram E, Por .4D 40
Fallowfield Cl. NR1: Norw .1H 27
The Fallows NR8: Thor Mar .3G 7
Farman Way NR13: Blof .1H 31
Farmers Av. NR1: Norw .5C 5 (4D 26)
Farmland Rd. NR5: New C .5A 14
Farrier Cl. NR18: Wym .3G 39
Farrow Rd. NR5: Norw .3G 25
Fastolf Cl. NR6: Helle .2F 15
The FDC Norwich .1B 24
Fellowes Cl. NR5: Norw .3E 25
Felsham Way NR8: Thor Mar .2H 7
Fen Ct. *NR2: Norw .2B 26*
(off Ely St.)
Fenn Cres. NR3: Norw .6A 16
Fern Ct. NR18: Wym .4C 38
Ferndale Cl. NR6: Helle .3F 15
Fern Dr. NR4: Cring .3D 34
Fernhill NR1: Norw .4G 27
FERRY CORNER .6C 30
Ferry La. NR1: Norw .3E 4 (3E 27)
NR13: Post .5H 29, 5A 30
Ferrymans Ct. NR7: Thor And .4A 28
Ferry Rd. NR1: Norw .4F 4 (3E 27)
NR14: Surl .5B 30
Fiddlers Loke NR12: Crost .1H 11
Fiddle Wood Rd. NR6: Norw .3C 16
Fiddy's Yd. NR1: Norw .7D 5
Fieldfare Cl. NR10: Spix .3G 11
Fieldfare Way NR8: Cost .2D 12
Fielding Ct. NR1: Norw .8C 5
Field La. NR13: Blof .5G 21
Field Rd. NR8: R'land .5A 6
Fieldview NR5: Norw .3F 25
Fiennes Rd. NR7: Thor And .6E 19
Fifers La. NR6: Norw .1H 15
Fifers La. Trad. Est. NR6: Norw .1A 16
Filby Cl. NR5: Norw .3F 25
Finch Cl. NR7: Norw .5A 18
Finchley Ct. NR2: Norw .2A 26
Finch Way NR13: B'all .4E 31
Finderne Dr. NR18: Wym .2E 39
Finishers Rd. NR3: Norw .6B 16
Finkelgate NR1: Norw .8D 5 (5D 26)
Fiona Cl. NR18: Wym .2F 39
Firbanks Cl. NR8: Dray .5B 8
Fir Covert Rd. NR8: Felth, Tav .2E 7
NR10: Felth .2E 7
Firecrest Cl. NR18: Wym .6E 39
Firethorn Cl. NR8: Tav .3E 7
Fir Hill NR4: Kes .5F 35
Firman Ct. NR7: Thor And .1C 28
Firs Rd. NR6: Helle .1G 15
NR9: Hether .5D 32
Fir Tree Cl. NR13: B'all .3D 30
Firtree Rd. NR7: Thor And .6B 18
Firwood Cl. NR1: Norw .1H 27
Fishergate NR3: Norw .2C 4 (2D 26)
Fisher's Cl. NR5: New C .6H 13
Fishers La. NR2: Norw .4A 4 (3C 26)
Fish Mkt. NR1: Norw .5E 5 (4E 27)
Fitzgerald Rd. NR1: Norw .2D 36
NR14: Fram E .3D 40
Fitzhenry M. NR5: Bow .1C 24
Flanders Ri. NR18: Wym .2G 39
Fleet Rd. NR8: Cost .1D 12
Fleetwood Dr. NR7: Thor And .1E 29
Fletcher Way NR3: Norw .4B 16
Flint Ho. Gdns. NR9: Hether .5C 32
Florence Rd. NR1: Norw .3F 27
Flowerdew Cl. NR9: Hether .5C 32
Folgate Cl. NR8: Cost .2A 14
Folgate La. NR8: Cost .2A 14
Folly Cl. NR18: Wym .3D 38
Folly Gdns. NR18: Wym .3D 38
Folly Rd. NR18: Wym .3D 38
Folwell Rd. NR5: New C .6H 13
The Footpath NR14: Por .4C 40
Foregate Cl. NR8: Thor Mar .3G 7
Forester Cl. NR4: Norw .2B 36
Forest Way NR5: New C .5D 12
Forge Cl. NR14: Por .5D 40
Fortune Grn. NR14: Alp .5H 41
Foster Cl. NR13: B'all .3D 30
Foster Rd. NR3: Norw .4C 16
Foulgers Ho. NR1: Norw .7E 5
Foulgers Opening NR1: Norw .8E 5 (5E 27)
Foundry Ct. NR1: Norw .4E 4
Fountain Ct. NR1: Norw .8A 5
Fountains Rd. NR4: Norw .3B 36
Fowell Cl. NR5: Norw .3C 24
Foxburrow Rd. NR7: Spro .2F 17
Foxcotte Cl. NR6: Helle .6F 9
Foxes Cl. NR14: Por .2A 40
Foxes Ct. NR5: New C .5C 14
Foxhouse Rd. NR8: Cost .2C 12
Fox La. NR13: Blof .1H 31
NR14: Fram P .1D 40
Foxley Cl. NR5: Norw .3E 25
Fox Rd. NR14: Fram P .1D 40
Fox Wood NR13: Hemb .4H 21
Foxwood Cl. NR8: Thor Mar .2H 7
Framingham Cres. NR14: Por .2B 40
FRAMINGHAM EARL .3D 40
Framingham Earl Community Sports Cen. .2B 40
Framingham Earl Rd. NR14: Yelv .3G 41
FRAMINGHAM PIGOT .1E 41
Framingham Rd. NR14: Bram .1G 41
Frances Ct. NR2: Norw .3A 26
Francis La. NR13: Blof .3F 21
Francis Stone Ct. NR7: Thor And .3E 29
Francis Way NR5: Bow .6H 13
Freeland Cl. NR8: Thor Mar .2H 7
Freeman Sq. NR2: Norw .1B 26
Freesia Way NR4: Cring .3D 34
Frenbury Est. NR6: Helle .4G 15
Frensham Rd. NR3: Norw .6G 15
Frere Rd. NR7: Norw .6A 18
Fresher M. NR5: Bow .3A 24
Freshfield Cl. NR5: Norw .2D 24
Freshwater Way NR8: Thor Mar .2A 8
Friarscroft La. NR18: Wym .5C 38
Friars Quay NR3: Norw .2C 4 (3D 26)
Friar Tuck Rd. NR4: Norw .2B 36
Friendship Rd. NR6: Norw .1C 16
Friends Rd. NR5: Norw .4D 24
Fritillary Dr. NR18: Wym .4F 39
Frogs Hall La. NR1: Norw .4G 27
Frogshall La. NR18: Wym .3B 38
Frogs Hole NR13: Blof .1F 31
Frost Cl. NR7: Thor And .1C 28
Frost Ind. Pk. NR8: Dray .6C 8
Fuchsia Ct. NR18: Wym .2F 39
Fuggles Yd. NR1: Norw .6D 5 (4D 26)
Fugill Grn. NR7: Norw .6A 18
Fugill Rd. NR7: Norw .5A 18
Fulford Cl. NR4: Norw .1H 35
Fuller Cl. NR13: Rack .1F 19
Fuller M. NR5: Bow .1H 23
Fullers Loke NR8: Thor Mar .3A 8
Fulton Cl. NR4: Norw .2H 35
Furze Av. NR7: Thor And .1B 28
Furze La. NR10: Tav .1G 7
Furze Rd. NR7: Thor And .1B 28
Fye Bri. St. NR3: Norw .2C 4 (2D 26)

G

Gable M. NR6: Helle .2G 15
Gaffers Ct. NR2: Norw .4A 4
Gage Rd. NR7: Spro .3H 17
Galley Hill NR3: Norw .5H 15
Gambling Cl. NR6: Norw .6H 9
Gamecock Cl. NR6: Norw .1B 16
Gamewell Cl. NR1: Norw .1D 36
Ganners Hill NR8: Thor Mar .2H 7
Gaol Hill NR2: Norw .4B 4 (3C 26)
Gardeners Ter. NR7: Spro .3E 17
Garden Pl. NR3: Norw .1D 26
Garden Rd. NR13: Blof .1G 31
Garden St. NR1: Norw .6D 5 (4D 26)
Gardyn Cft. NR8: Thor Mar .3G 7
Gargle Hill NR7: Thor And .2C 28
Garnett Dr. NR9: E'ton .5A 12
Garrett Ct. NR3: Norw .6E 17
Garrick Grn. NR6: Old C .2D 16
Gas Hill NR1: Norw .3F 4 (3F 27)
Gatekeeper Cl. NR18: Wym .4F 39
Gateley Gdns. NR3: Norw .4B 16
Gateway 11 Bus. Pk. NR18: Wym .3G 39
Gawdy Rd. NR7: Norw .6H 17
Gaynor Cl. NR18: Wym .2B 38
Gayton Wlk. NR6: Old C .1E 17
Gentleman's Wlk. NR2: Norw .4B 4 (4C 26)
Gentry Pl. NR5: Norw .1D 24
Geoffrey Rd. NR1: Norw .6E 27
Geoffrey Watling Way NR1: Norw .7F 5 (5F 27)
George Borrow Rd. NR4: Norw .4F 25
George Cl. NR8: Dray .5C 8
George Dance Pl. NR5: Norw .2D 24
George Dr. NR8: Dray .6C 8
George Fox Way NR5: Norw .4D 24
George Gdns. NR8: Cost .2D 12
GEORGE HILL .3E 17
George Hill NR6: Old C .3D 16
George Lowe Cl. NR5: New C .6B 14
George Pope Cl. NR3: Norw .5B 16
George Pope Rd. NR3: Norw .5B 16
George Winter Ct. NR3: Norw .5B 16
Gerald Cl. NR1: Norw .1H 27
Gerard Hudson Gdns. NR4: Kes .6G 35
Gertrude Rd. NR3: Norw .6E 17
Gibbs Cl. NR9: Lit Mel .1E 33
Gilbard Rd. NR5: Norw .2D 24
Gilbert Cl. NR14: Alp .5H 41
Gilbert Way NR4: Cring .2E 35
Gilchrist Cl. NR4: Norw .3C 36
Gildencroft NR3: Norw .1B 4 (2C 26)
Gilders Way NR3: Norw .1E 4 (2E 27)
Giles Rd. NR10: Spix .3G 11
Gilman Rd. NR3: Norw .6E 17
Gipsy Cl. NR5: Norw .3E 25
Gipsy La. NR5: Norw .4E 25
(not continuous)
Girlings La. NR7: Thor And .4B 28
Girton Rd. NR2: Norw .5A 26
The Glade NR8: Cost .3A 14
Gladstone St. NR2: Norw .3A 26
The Glebe NR13: Post .5H 29
Glebe Cl. NR8: Dray .4A 8
Glebe Rd. NR2: Norw .5H 25
Glenalmond NR4: Norw .1H 35
Glenburn Av. NR7: Spro .3F 17
Glenburn Ct. NR7: Spro .3F 17
Glenda Cl. NR5: New C .6C 14
Glenda Ct. NR5: New C .5D 14
Glenda Cres. NR5: New C .5D 14
Glenda Rd. NR5: New C .6D 14
Glendenning Rd. NR1: Norw .4G 27
Glengarry Cl. NR9: Hether .4C 32
Glenmore Gdns. NR3: Norw .5A 16
Glenn Rd. NR14: Por .6C 40
Globe Ct. NR13: Blof .1G 31
Globe La. NR13: Blof .1G 31
Globe Pl. NR2: Norw .6A 5 (4B 26)
Gloucester St. NR2: Norw .5A 26
Goals Soccer Cen.
Norwich .1C 36
Godfrey Rd. NR10: Spix .2G 11
Godric Pl. NR2: Norw .3G 25
Golden Ball St. NR1: Norw .5C 5 (4D 26)
Golden Dog La. NR3: Norw .2C 4 (2D 26)
GOLDEN TRIANGLE .5A 26
Golding Pl. NR2: Norw .3B 26
Goldsmith St. NR2: Norw .2B 26
Goldwell Rd. NR1: Norw .8C 5 (5D 26)
Golf Links Rd. NR13: B'all .3F 31
Goodhale Rd. NR5: Bow .2C 24
Goodman Sq. NR2: Norw .2A 26
Goodson Rd. NR7: Spro .2A 18
Goodwood Cl. NR7: Thor And .6B 18
Gooseberry Gdn. Wlk. NR1: Norw .3E 4
Goose La. NR3: Norw .6D 16
Gordon Av. NR7: Thor And .2H 27
Gordon Godfrey Way NR10: H'ford .2F 9
Gordon Sq. NR1: Norw .8D 5 (5D 26)
Gorse Av. NR6: Helle .2H 15
Gorse Rd. NR7: Thor And .1A 28
Goulburn Rd. NR7: Norw .6A 18
Gould Rd. NR2: Norw .5G 25
Governors Ct. NR1: Norw .8F 5 (5E 27)
Gowing Cl. NR6: Helle .6G 9
Gowing Ct. NR3: Norw .4A 16
Gowing Rd. NR6: Helle .6G 9
Grace Edwards Cl. NR8: Thor Mar .3A 8
Grace Jarrold Ct. NR3: Norw .2C 4
Graham Sq. NR7: Norw .6A 18
Granary Vw. NR1: Norw .8F 5
Grange Cl. NR6: Old C .3D 16
NR12: Hov .1D 42

Grange Rd. NR2: Norw 5H **25**
Grange Wlk. NR12: Wrox 3B **42**
Grant Rd. NR10: Spix 2H **11**
Grant St. NR2: Norw 2H **25**
Grapes Hill NR2: Norw 3B **26**
Grasmere NR9: Hether 4E **33**
Grasmere Cl. NR5: Norw 3D **24**
Gravelfield Cl. NR1: Norw 1G **27**
Gray Cl. NR13: B'all 2D **30**
Grays Fair NR5: New C 6A **14**
Gt. Eastern Ct. NR1: Norw 5F **5**
Gt. Melton Cl. NR9: Hether 4D **32**
Gt. Melton Rd. NR9: Hether 4C **32**
NR9: Lit Mel 1D **32**
GREAT PLUMSTEAD 6A **20**
Grebe Ct. NR8: Cost 2E **13**
Grebe Dr. NR7: Spro 2B **18**
The Green NR8: Dray 5B **8**
Greenacre Cl. NR13: B'all 3E **31**
Greenacres NR9: Lit Mel 1G **33**
Greenacres Dr. NR14: Por 3B **40**
Greenborough Cl. NR7: Spro 5B **18**
Greenborough Rd. NR7: Spro 5B **18**
Green Cl. NR5: New C 6H **13**
Green Ct. NR7: Thor And 2A **28**
Green Fall NR14: Por 5D **40**
Greenfields NR5: New C 6G **13**
Greenfield Way NR13: Rack 1G **19**
Green Hills Cl. NR8: Cost 4A **14**
Green Hills Rd. NR3: Norw 1C **26**
Greenland Av. NR18: Wym 2F **39**
Green La. NR9: Lit Mel 5F **23**
NR14: Alp 6G **41**
Green La. E. NR13: Rack 2F **19**
Green La. Nth. NR13: Thor E 5E **19**
Green La. Sth. NR7: Thor And 6F **19**
Green La. W. NR13: Rack 1F **19**
Green Pk. Rd. NR10: H'ford 2G **9**
Greenways NR4: Norw 2G **35**
Greenwood Rd. NR4: Norw 2C **36**
Greenwood Way NR7: Spro 5C **18**
Grenville Cl. NR9: Hether 4F **33**
Gresham Rd. NR3: Norw 5H **15**
Greyfriars Cl. NR6: Old C 2D **16**
Greyfriars Rd. NR1: Norw 4D **4** (3D **26**)
Greyhound Opening NR2: Norw 2B **26**
Greylag Cl. NR7: Spro 3B **18**
Griffin Ct. NR18: Wym 5C **38**
Griffin La. NR7: Thor And 3E **29**
Gristock Pl. NR5: Norw 1D **24**
Grosvenor Rd. NR2: Norw 4B **26**
Grouts Thoroughfare NR1: Norw 5C **5**
The Grove NR3: Norw 4C **16**
NR14: Por 6A **40**
Grove Av. NR1: Norw 8A **5** (5C **26**)
NR5: New C 6A **14**
Grovebury Cl. NR13: B'all 3E **31**
Grovedale Cl. NR5: New C 6B **14**
Grove Rd. NR1: Norw 8A **5** (5C **26**)
NR9: Hether 4D **32**
Grove Wlk. NR1: Norw 8B **5** (6C **26**)
Guardian Rd. NR5: Norw 2G **25**
Guardian Rd. Ind. Est. NR5: Norw 2F **25**
Guelph Rd. NR1: Norw 3F **27**
Guernsey Rd. NR3: Norw 1D **26**
Guildhall *4B 4*
(off Guildhall Hill)
Guildhall Hill NR2: Norw 4B **4** (3C **26**)
Gull La. NR14: Fram E 3E **41**
Gunner Cl. NR7: Thor And 6D **18**
Gunn Rd. NR7: Norw 6H **17**
Gunns Cl. NR13: Blof 1H **31**
Gunns Ct. NR2: Norw 4A **4** (3B **26**)
Gunton La. NR5: New C 5C **14**
Gunton Rd. NR2: Norw 4G **25**
NR18: Wym 4E **39**
Gurney Cl. NR5: New C 1C **24**
Gurney Ct. NR3: Norw 2C **4**
NR5: New C 1B **24**
Gurney Dr. NR7: Spro 3A **18**
Gurney La. NR4: Cring 1D **34**
Gurney Rd. NR1: Norw 1F **4** (2F **27**)
NR5: New C 6B **14**
Gwendoline Ct. *NR1: Norw 3F 27*
(off Florence Rd.)

H

Haconsfield NR9: Hether 5E **33**
Hadden Cl. NR14: Por 4D **40**
Hadley Dr. NR2: Norw 3G **25**
Halcombe Ct. NR3: Norw 6D **16**
Halden Av. NR6: Helle 1G **15**
Hale Ct. NR13: Gt P 1A **30**
Half Mile Cl. NR3: Norw 5A **16**
Half Mile Rd. NR3: Norw 5A **16**
Half Moon Way NR2: Norw 1A **26**
Hall Bk. La. NR14: Arm 6G **37**
Hall Cl. NR9: Hether 5E **33**
Hall Dr. NR5: New C 4G **13**
NR6: Old C 2D **16**
Hall Farm Pl. NR9: Baw 3E **23**
Hallgate NR13: Thor E 4E **19**
Hall La. NR8: Dray 5B **8**
NR13: Post 6H **29**
Hall Rd. NR1: Norw 8D **5** (1C **36**)
NR4: Norw 4B **36**
NR5: New C 5B **14**
NR9: E'ton 6A **12**
NR9: Gt Mel 2A **32**
NR13: Blof 5D **20**
NR13: Witt 1C **30**
NR14: Fram E 4E **41**
Hall Wood Rd. NR7: Spro 2A **18**
Hamlin Ct. NR3: Norw 5B **16**
Hammond Cl. NR7: Spro 4B **18**
Hammond Ct. NR3: Norw 1C **4**
Hammond Way NR7: Spro 4B **18**
Hamond Rd. NR6: Helle 2E **15**
Hampden Dr. NR7: Thor And 1D **28**
Hanbury Cl. NR5: Norw 4E **25**
Hancock Ct. NR5: Bow 2H **23**
Hankin Ct. NR5: Norw 4D **24**
Hanly Cl. NR7: Norw 5H **17**
Hanover Ct. NR2: Norw 8A **5** (5B **26**)
Hanover Rd. NR2: Norw 8A **5** (5B **26**)
Hansard Cl. NR3: Norw 6A **16**
Hansard La. NR3: Norw 2D **4** (2D **26**)
Hansard Rd. NR3: Norw 5A **16**
Hansell Rd. NR7: Thor And 1C **28**
Hanson Cl. NR7: Spro 3C **18**
Harbord Rd. NR4: Norw 4G **25**
Harbour Rd. NR1: Norw 4F **27**
Harcourt Cl. NR3: Norw 1E **4** (1E **27**)
Hardesty Cl. NR14: Por 4C **40**
Hardley Rd. NR14: Por 3B **40**
Hardwick Cl. NR4: Norw 3H **35**
Hardwick Ho. NR1: Norw 4D **4**
Hardy Dr. NR14: Por 5C **40**
Hardy Rd. NR1: Norw 5F **27**
Hare Rd. NR13: Gt P 4H **19**, 6A **20**
Harewood Dr. NR8: Thor Mar 2H **7**
Harford Hill NR4: Norw 4B **36**
Harford Mnr. Cl. NR2: Norw 1B **36**
Harford Park & Ride 6A **36**
Harford St. NR1: Norw 6D **26**
Harker Way NR13: Blof 3G **21**
Harlington Av. NR6: Helle 3H **15**
Harman Cl. NR9: Hether 4E **33**
Harmer Cl. NR4: Cring 2E **35**
Harmer Cres. NR4: Cring 2D **34**
Harmer La. NR4: Cring 2D **34**
Harmer Rd. NR3: Norw 4B **16**
Harness Maker Way NR9: Lit Mel 3E **33**
Harold Mackintosh Ho. *NR2: Norw 4A 26*
(off Grosvenor Rd.)
Harpsfield NR5: Bow 1H **23**
Harrier Cl. NR9: Hether 4E **33**
Harrier Way NR6: Norw 6C **10**
Harriet Ct. NR1: Norw 6E **27**
Harris M. NR5: Bow 2B **24**
Harrisons Dr. NR7: Spro 4B **18**
Harrold Cl. NR8: Thor Mar 3H **7**
Harry Barber Cl. NR5: Bow 1B **24**
Harry Daniels Cl. NR18: Wym 6E **39**
Harry Perry Cl. NR4: Norw 1B **36**
Harry Watson Ct. *NR3: Norw 4B 16*
(off Weston Rd.)
Harsnett Cl. NR5: Bow 1A **24**
Hartbee Rd. NR6: Norw 1B **16**
Hart Ct. NR7: Spro 2B **18**
Hartleys Ct. NR3: Norw 1C **4**
Harts Farm Rd. NR18: Wym 5D **38**
Harts La. NR4: Cring 2D **34**
NR9: Baw 2D **22**
Hartwell Rd. NR12: Wrox 3B **42**
Harvey Cl. NR7: Thor And 2H **27**
NR9: Hether 5C **32**
NR18: Wym 1G **39**
Harvey La. NR7: Norw 3H **27**
Harwood Rd. NR1: Norw 2D **36**
Haslips Cl. NR2: Norw 2B **26**
Hassett Cl. NR3: Norw 1F **4** (1E **27**)
Hastings Av. NR6: Helle 3H **15**
Hatton Rd. NR1: Norw 6D **26**
Hauteyn Ct. NR3: Norw 5B **16**
Havant Cl. NR4: Norw 2F **35**
Havelock Rd. NR2: Norw 3A **26**
Haverscroft Cl. NR8: Thor Mar 3G **7**
Havers Rd. NR3: Norw 6A **16**
Hawk Cl. NR9: Hether 4D **32**
Hawthorn Cl. NR10: Spix 3F **11**
NR18: Wym 2E **39**
Hawthorne Av. NR6: Helle 2H **15**
Hawthorn Rd. NR5: New C 5B **14**
Hawthorn Row NR2: Norw 2A **26**
Hayden Ct. NR1: Norw 8C **5** (6D **26**)
Hay Hill NR2: Norw 5B **5**
Haymarket NR2: Norw 5B **5** (4C **26**)
Hazel Cl. NR8: Thor Mar 4H **7**
NR18: Wym 4E **39**
Hazel Rd. NR5: New C 5A **14**
Hearne Ct. NR5: Bow 1H **23**
Heartsease La. NR7: Norw 6G **17**
The Heath NR13: Blof 2E **21**
Heath Cl. NR6: Helle 1A **16**
NR10: H'ford 2F **9**
Heath Cres. NR6: Helle 2H **15**
(not continuous)
Heather Av. NR6: Helle 3H **15**
Heather Cl. NR9: Hether 3C **32**
Heatherwood Cl. NR13: Thor E 4E **19**
Heathgate NR3: Norw 1F **4** (2F **27**)
Heath Loke NR14: Por 4B **40**
Heath Rd. NR3: Norw 1C **26**
NR13: Thor E 5E **19**
Heathside Rd. NR1: Norw 4G **27**
Heath Way NR13: Blof 4E **21**
(not continuous)
Hedgemere NR8: Thor Mar 3F **7**
The Hedgerows NR5: Bow 2B **24**
HEIGHAM GROVE 3B **26**
Heigham Gro. NR2: Norw 3B **26**
Heigham Rd. NR2: Norw 3A **26**
Heigham St. NR2: Norw 2A **4** (1A **26**)
Heigham Watering NR2: Norw 1A **26**
The Heights NR1: Norw 4F **27**
Helena Rd. NR2: Norw 3H **25**
Helford St. NR2: Norw 1A **26**
Helgate Ct. NR2: Norw 3A **4**
HELLESDON 2F **15**
Hellesdon Cl. NR6: Norw 1E **25**
Hellesdon Hall Rd.
NR6: Lwr H, Norw 6F **15**
HELLESDON HOSPITAL 3E **15**
Hellesdon M. NR6: Lwr H 5E **15**
Hellesdon Mill La. NR6: Lwr H 6E **15**
Hellesdon Pk. Ind. Est. NR6: Helle 4F **15**
Hellesdon Pk. Rd. NR6: Helle 4F **15**
Hellesdon Rd. NR6: Lwr H, Norw 1E **25**
HEMBLINGTON CORNER 3H **21**
Hemblington Hall Rd. NR13: Hemb 3H **21**
Hemlin Cl. NR5: Norw 3D **24**
Hemmings Cl. NR5: Bow 2A **24**
Hemming Way NR3: Norw 6A **16**
Hempsted M. NR5: Bow 2H **23**
Henby Way NR7: Thor And 2A **28**
Henderson Rd. NR4: Norw 4G **25**
Hendon Cl. NR5: New C 6C **14**
Hendry Gdns. NR18: Wym 1G **39**
Henley Rd. NR2: Norw 5H **25**
Henstead Rd. NR9: Hether 4D **32**
Herbert Nursey Cl. NR8: Dray 6D **8**
Herb Robert Glade NR18: Wym 4F **39**
Hercules Cl. NR6: Helle 3G **15**
Hercules Rd. NR6: Helle 3G **15**
Heron Cl. NR7: Spro 2B **18**
Heron Ri. NR18: Wym 6E **39**
Heron Rd. NR8: Cost 2E **13**
Herrick Rd. NR8: Tav 5G **7**
HETHERSETT 5D **32**
Hethersett Bus. Cen. *NR9: Hether 5E 33*
(off Queen's Rd.)
Hethersett Ho. NR9: Hether 4D **32**
Hethersett La. NR4: Coln 2H **33**
Hethersett Rd. NR9: Gt Mel 3A **32**
Hewett Yd. NR1: Norw 1C **36**
Hewitt Cl. NR14: Por 4B **40**
Hewitts La. NR18: Wym 3D **38**
Heyford Rd. NR6: Norw 1B **16**
Higham Cl. NR7: Spro 4F **17**
High Banks NR18: Wym 5E **39**
Highefield NR13: Lit P 3C **20**
Highfield Av. NR13: B'all 4F **31**
Highfield Cl. NR7: Thor And 3D **28**
Highfield Rd. NR8: Dray 4A **8**
Highfields NR5: New C 6G **13**
HIGH GREEN 4A **32**
High Green NR1: Norw 4G **27**
NR9: Gt Mel 4A **32**
Highgrove Ct. NR14: Por 2B **40**
High Ho. Av. NR18: Wym 3E **39**
High Ho. Cl. NR18: Wym 3E **39**
High Ho. La. NR13: Blof 4G **21**
Highland NR14: Por 1A **40**
Highland Av. NR2: Norw 5H **25**
Highland Cres. NR14: Tro 1G **37**
Highland Rd. NR2: Norw 5H **25**
NR8: Tav 4G **7**
Highlands NR8: Cost 3A **14**

Highlow Rd. NR5: New C 6B 14
Highview Cl. NR13: Blof 1G 31
Hilary Av. NR1: Norw 1G 27
Hilda Brookes Way NR5: New C 5C 14
The Hill NR10: Hor F 3A 10
Hill Crest NR5: New C 5B 14
Hillcrest Rd. NR7: Thor And 2A 28
Hill Farm Cl. NR4: Cring 3E 35
Hill Ho. Gdns. NR4: Cring 3D 34
Hill Ho. Rd. NR1: Norw 4F 27
Hillmead NR3: Norw 4C 16
Hill Rd. NR5: New C 5B 14
Hillside NR14: Por 3B 40
Hillside Av. NR7: Thor And 3C 28
Hillside Cl. NR7: Thor And 3C 28
Hillside Rd. NR7: Thor And 3C 28
Hill St. NR2: Norw 5B 26
Hill Top Dr. NR8: Cost 4A 14
Hillvue Cl. NR5: New C 5B 14
Hilly Plantation NR7: Thor And 2B 28
Hinks Cl. NR8: Thor Mar 2F 7
Hinshalwood Way NR8: Cost 3H 13
HMP & YOI Norwich 1F 27
Hobart Cl. NR18: Wym 2E 39
Hobart Dr. NR13: Lit P 5B 20
Hobart La. NR1: Norw 8D 5 (6D 26)
Hobart Sq. NR1: Norw 8D 5 (5D 26)
Hobby Dr. NR18: Wym 6E 39
Hobrough La. NR1: Norw 6E 5 (4E 27)
Hockering La. NR9: Baw 3E 23
Hodgson Rd. NR4: Norw 4G 25
Holls La. NR1: Norw 8D 5 (5D 26)
Holly Bank NR7: Spro 5F 17
Holly Blue M. NR8: Cost 1E 13
Holly Blue Rd. NR18: Wym 4E 39
Holly Cl. NR8: Thor Mar 4G 7
Holly Ct. NR18: Wym 2F 39
Holly Dr. NR2: Norw 2H 25
Holly La. NR10: H'ford 4E 9
NR13: Blof 5F 21
Holly Wlk. NR4: Cring 2C 34
Hollywood Bowl
Norwich 6F 5 (4E 27)
Holme Cotts. NR1: Norw 2E 4
Holmes Cl. NR7: Norw 1A 28
Holmesdale Rd. NR13: B'all 3D 30
Holmwood Ri. NR7: Norw 3H 27
Holt Rd. NR6: Norw 5G 9
NR10: Felth, H'ford, Hor F 1F 9
Holworthy Rd. NR5: Bow 1C 24
Homecroft NR9: Lit Mel 6E 23
The Homestead *NR7: Thor And* *3E 29*
(off St Andrews Pk.)
Home St. NR2: Norw 1B 26
Honey Cl. NR1: Norw 2G 27
HONEYCOMBE 1C 20
Honeycombe Rd. NR13: Lit P, Sal 1C 20
Honeysuckle Cl. NR4: Cring 2C 34
Honeysuckle Sq. NR18: Wym 2G 39
Honingham La. NR8: R'land 5A 6
Hooker Rd. NR7: Norw 6A 18
Hooks Wlk. NR1: Norw 3E 4 (3E 27)
Hooper La. NR3: Norw 5E 17
Hopton Cl. NR7: Thor And 1E 29
Horatio Ct. NR2: Norw 1A 26
Horizon Bus. Cen. NR7: Thor And 3G 29
Hornbeam Cl. NR7: Spro 3A 18
Hornbeam Dr. NR14: Por 4C 40
Horning Cl. NR5: Norw 2E 25
Horning Rd. NR12: Hov 2C 42
(not continuous)
Horning Rd. W. NR12: Hov 2B 42
Hornor Cl. NR2: Norw 6B 26
Horn-Pie Rd. NR5: Bow 3A 24
Horns La. NR1: Norw 6D 5 (4D 26)
Horsbeck Ind. Est. NR10: H'ford 1D 8
Horsbeck Way NR10: H'ford 2F 9
Horsefair Loke NR1: Norw 3E 4
Horseshoe Cl. NR5: New C 6H 13
Horseshoe Rd. NR9: Hether 4C 32
HORSFORD 2G 9
Horsford St. NR2: Norw 1A 26
HORSHAM ST FAITH 2A 10
Hospital La. NR1: Norw 6D 26
NR6: Helle 4E 15
Hospital Rd. NR13: Lit P 5B 20
The Hostry 3D 4 (3D 26)
Hotblack Rd. NR2: Norw 2H 25
Houghton Cl. NR5: Bow 1C 24
HOVETON 2C 42
Hoveton & Wroxham Station (Rail) 1B 42
Hoveton Visitor Cen. 2B 42
Howard Cl. NR7: Thor And 2A 28
Howard M. NR3: Norw 6D 16
Howard St. NR1: Norw 8B 5 (5C 26)
Howard Ter. NR3: Norw 1B 4
Howe La. NR14: Por 6D 40
Howell Rd. NR8: Dray 6D 8
Howes Cl. NR9: Hether 5D 32
Howe Way NR10: H'ford 1D 8
Howlett Dr. NR5: Bow 1B 24
Hubbard Cl. NR18: Wym 2B 38
Hubbards Loke NR9: Hether 5C 32
Hudson Av. NR14: Tro 1G 37
Hudson Way NR5: Bow 2H 23
Hughenden Rd. NR1: Norw 6D 26
Hughes Ct. NR9: Hether 4E 33
Humbleyard NR5: Bow 1B 24
Hunt Cl. NR6: Old C 6D 10
Hunter Rd. NR3: Norw 4B 16
Hunters Cl. NR13: Blof 2H 31
Hunting Fld. NR5: New C 6A 14
Huntingfield Cl. NR5: New C 6A 14
Hurd Rd. NR4: Norw 6G 25
Hurn Rd. NR8: Dray 1D 14
Hurricane Way NR6: Norw 1B 16
Husenbeth Cl. NR8: Cost 3H 13
Hutchinson Rd. NR5: Norw 3E 25
Huxley Cl. NR1: Norw 1E 37
Huxley Rd. NR1: Norw 1E 37
Hyde Ct. NR7: Thor And 6F 19

I

Ice Ho. La. NR1: Norw 8F 5 (5E 27)
Ilex Ct. NR7: Spro 3A 18
Impala Cl. NR6: Spro 1F 17
Imperial Way NR10: Hor F 3B 10
Independent Way NR7: Thor And 1E 29
Indigo Yd. NR3: Norw 3A 4 (3C 26)
Ingleby Rd. NR1: Norw 4G 27
Ingram Ct. NR1: Norw 6D 26
Inman Rd. NR7: Spro 3A 18
Intu Chapelfield NR2: Norw 6A 5 (4C 26)
INTWOOD 6E 35
Intwood La. NR14: Swar 6E 35
Intwood Rd. NR4: Cring, Int 4E 35
Ipswich Gro. NR2: Norw 8A 5 (5C 26)
Ipswich Rd. NR1: Norw 8A 5 (6A 36)
NR2: Norw 8A 5 (6A 36)
NR4: Norw 6A 36
Ireton Cl. NR7: Thor And 2E 29
Irstead Rd. NR5: Norw 3F 25
Irving Rd. NR4: Norw 2A 36
Isbets Dale NR8: Thor Mar 3G 7
Isidore Ter. *NR3: Norw* *6H 15*
(off Wheeler Rd.)
Ives Rd. NR6: Norw 2B 16
Ivory NR2: Norw 7A 5 (5C 26)
Ivory Rd. NR4: Norw 5F 25
Ivy Cl. NR14: Por 4D 40
Ivy Rd. NR5: Norw 3F 25
NR10: Spix 2F 11

J

Jaguar Rd. NR9: Hether 4E 33
James Alexander M. *NR5: Norw* *4E 25*
(off Gipsy La.)
James Grn. Cl. NR10: Spix 2G 11
James Watson Rd. NR4: Coln 6A 24
Jamieson Pl. NR5: Norw 1D 24
Janet Smith Cl. NR7: Thor And 1C 28
Jarrold Way NR5: Bow 1A 24
Jarrold Way Ind. Est. NR5: Bow 1A 24
Jasmine Cl. NR4: Norw 4F 25
Jasmine Wlk. NR4: Cring 3C 34
Javelin Rd. NR6: Norw 6B 10
Jay Gdns. NR5: Bow 1H 23
Jeckyll Rd. NR18: Wym 1G 39
Jenkins La. NR3: Norw 1A 4
Jenny Rd. NR10: Spix 2G 11
Jerningham Rd. NR5: New C 6B 14
Jessica Ct. *NR2: Norw* *2B 26*
(off Orchard St.)
Jessopp Rd. NR2: Norw 5G 25
Jewson Rd. NR3: Norw 5B 16
Jex Av. NR5: Norw 1E 25
Jex La. NR5: Norw 1E 25
Jex Rd. NR5: Norw 1E 25
Jobie Wood Cl. NR7: Spro 2A 18
Joe Ellis Ct. NR5: Bow 1C 24
John Drewry Cl. NR14: Fram E 3D 40
John Gale Ct. NR8: Thor Mar 2A 8
John Grooms Ct. NR3: Norw 6E 17
John Howes Cl. NR9: E'ton 5A 12
John Hyrne Way NR5: New C 4D 12
John Jarrold Printing Mus. 1D 4 (2E 27)
Johnson Cl. NR5: New C 6H 13
Johnson Pl. NR2: Norw 4B 26
John Stephenson Ct. *NR3: Norw* *6E 17*
(off Violet Rd.)
Jolly Butchers Yd. NR1: Norw 7D 5
Jolly Gardeners Ct. *NR3: Norw* *1C 26*
(off Heath Rd.)
Jordan Cl. NR5: Norw 3C 24
NR8: Thor Mar 1H 7
Josephine Cl. NR1: Norw 6C 26
Joseph Lancaster Way NR3: Norw 3D 4
Joyce Way NR7: Thor And 6E 19
Jubilee Rd. NR7: Spro 3F 17
Jubilee Ter. NR1: Norw 6D 26
Jubilee Wlk. NR14: Por 6C 40
Judges Dr. NR4: Norw 6G 25
Judges Gdns. NR8: Thor Mar 3H 7
Judges Wlk. NR4: Norw 1G 35
The Julian Cen. 6D 5 (4D 26)
Julian Dr. NR14: Tro 1H 37
JULIAN HOSPITAL 3G 25
Julian Rd. NR10: Spix 2F 11
Junction Rd. NR3: Norw 6B 16
Juniper Cl. NR4: Cring 2D 34
Juniper Way NR8: Tav 3E 7
Jupiter Rd. NR6: Helle 3B 16

K

Kabin Rd. NR5: New C 5C 14
Karen Cl. NR9: Hether 6C 32
Keable Cl. NR5: Norw 3D 24
Keats Rd. NR8: Tav 5G 7
Kedleston Dr. NR4: Cring 4D 34
Keelan Cl. NR6: Norw 3A 16
Kempe Cl. NR7: Norw 6H 17
Kendal Cl. NR9: Hether 4E 33
Kennedy Cl. NR9: E'ton 5A 12
Kenneth McKee Plain
NR2: Norw 7A 5 (5B 26)
Kennett Cl. NR4: Norw 5G 25
Kensington Pl. NR1: Norw 8D 5 (5D 26)
Kered Cl. NR6: Helle 1G 15
Kered Rd. NR6: Helle 1G 15
The Kerridges NR5: New C 6A 14
Kerrison Rd. NR1: Norw 5F 27
Kerrison Rd. Ind. Est. NR1: Norw 5F 27
Kerville St. NR5: Bow 2B 24
Kestrel Av. NR8: Cost 2D 12
Kestrel Rd. NR7: Spro 3H 17
KESWICK 5F 35
Keswick Cl. NR4: Cring 4E 35
Keswick Hall NR4: Kes 6G 35
Keswick Hall Rd. NR4: Int, Kes 6E 35
(not continuous)
Keswick Rd. NR4: Cring, Kes 3D 34
NR7: Spro 3F 17
Ketteringham La. NR9: Hether 6D 32
Ketteringham Rd. NR18: Wym 5G 39
Kett Ho. NR4: Norw 5E 25
Kett's Av. NR18: Wym 3D 38
Kett's Cl. NR9: Hether 5D 32
NR18: Wym 3D 38
Kett's Hill NR1: Norw 2F 27
Kett's Oak NR9: Hether 6C 32
Kevill Davis Dr. NR13: Lit P 5B 20
Key & Castle Yd. NR3: Norw 1A 4 (2C 26)
Keyes Cl. NR1: Norw 1D 36
Keyes Rd. NR1: Norw 1D 36
Keys Dr. NR12: Wrox 5A 42
Keys Hill Pk. NR12: Wrox 4A 42
KIDD'S MOOR 1E 39
Kilderkin Way NR1: Norw 6D 5
Kiln Cl. NR6: Old C 6D 10
NR14: Por 2B 40
Kiln Rd. NR10: H'ford 1F 9
Kimberley St. NR2: Norw 4B 26
NR18: Wym 4D 38
Kingfisher Cl. NR4: Cring 3C 34
NR8: Cost 2D 12
Kinghorn Rd. NR2: Norw 5G 25
Kingsgate Ct. NR2: Norw 4A 4 (3C 26)
Kings La. NR1: Norw 8C 5 (5D 26)
Kingsley Rd. NR1: Norw 7A 5 (5C 26)
Kingston Sq. NR4: Norw 1H 35
King St. NR1: Norw 4D 4 (3D 26)
Kingsway NR2: Norw 1B 26
Kingsway Trad. Est. *NR2: Norw* *1B 26*
(off Kingsway)
Kingswood Av. NR8: Thor Mar 3E 7
Kingswood Cl. NR4: Norw 3G 35
Kingswood Ct. NR8: Thor Mar 3G 7
Kinsale Av. NR6: Helle 2F 15
Kinver Cl. NR4: Norw 6A 26
Kirby Bedon Rd. NR14: Bix 2H 37
Kirby Rd.
NR14: Bix, Bram, Kir B, Tro 1H 37
(not continuous)
Kirklands NR8: Cost 3H 13
Kirklees NR4: Norw 3B 36

Kirkpatrick Rd. NR3: Norw 5A 16
Kitchener Cl. NR18: Wym 2G 39
Knappers Way NR8: Cost 2C 12
Knights Rd. NR3: Norw 5A 16
Knowland Gro. NR5: Norw 1D 24
Knowsley Rd. NR3: Norw 1D 26
Knox Av. NR1: Norw 1G 27
Knox Cl. NR1: Norw 1G 27
Knox Rd. NR1: Norw 2G 27
Koblenz Av. NR1: Norw 5F 5, 7F 5 (4E 27)
Kost Rd. NR8: Cost 4B 14

L

Labour in Vain Yd. NR2: Norw 4B 4
Laburnum Av. NR8: Tav 4E 7
Laburnum Cl. NR10: H'ford 1F 9
NR18: Wym 2G 39
Laburnum Dr. NR13: Blof 1G 31
Lacey Rd. NR8: Tav 4G 7
Lackford Cl. NR13: B'all 3E 31
Ladbrooke Pl. NR1: Norw 2F 27
Lady Betty Rd. NR1: Norw 6C 26
Lady Mary Rd. NR1: Norw 6C 26
Lady's La. NR18: Wym 5B 38
Ladysmith Rd. NR3: Norw 6E 17
Ladysmock Way NR5: Bow 2B 24
Lakeland Cl. NR13: Lit P 5B 20
Lakeland Way NR9: Hether 4F 33
Lakenfields NR1: Norw 1E 37
LAKENHAM 6D 26
Lakenham Rd. NR4: Norw 1B 36
Lakenham Way NR1: Norw 8C 5 (6D 26)
NR4: Norw 2D 36
Lake Vw. Dr. NR13: B'all 3D 30
Lambert Ho. NR5: Bow 1B 24
(off Humbleyard)
Lambert Rd. NR7: Spro 4F 17
Lancaster Cl. NR6: Old C 1C 16
Lanchester Ct. NR2: Norw 2A 26
Landlow La. NR9: Gt Mel 6A 22
The Lane NR3: Norw 5A 16
THE LANES 4B 4 (3C 26)
Lanes Yd. NR1: Norw 5D 5
Langham Grn. NR13: Blof 3G 31
Langham Pl. NR1: Norw 8B 5 (5C 26)
Langley Cl. NR4: Cring 4D 34
Langley Wlk. NR2: Norw 2A 26
Langton Cl. NR5: Norw 2C 24
Lansdowne Dr. NR14: Por 6C 40
Lansdowne Rd. NR6: Norw 1A 16
Lapwing Dr. NR8: Cost 2E 13
Larch Cl. NR7: Spro 3A 18
NR9: Lit Mel 1G 33
Larkman La. NR5: Norw 3D 24
Larkman Rd. NR5: Norw 2D 24
Larners Way NR3: Norw 6H 15
(off Wheeler Rd.)
Larwood Way NR10: H'ford 1G 9
The Lathes NR3: Norw 1B 4 (2C 26)
Latimer Rd. NR1: Norw 1D 36
Laud Cl. NR7: Thor And 2E 29
Launceston Ter. NR2: Norw 8A 5
Laundry Cl. NR7: Thor And 2B 28
Laundry La. NR7: Spro 3A 18
NR7: Thor And 2C 28
NR13: Blof 4D 20
Laurel Ct. NR7: Thor And 6B 18
Laurel Dr. NR13: B'all 4C 30
Laurel Gro. NR13: B'all 4F 31
Laurel Rd. NR7: Thor And 6C 18
Lavare Ct. NR6: Old C 1D 16
Lavender Cl. NR10: H'ford 1F 9
Lavender Dr. NR4: Cring 2C 34
Lavender Rd. NR18: Wym 2F 39
Lavengro Rd. NR3: Norw 1E 27
Lawn Cl. NR10: H'ford 2G 9
Lawn Cres. NR13: Thor E 4F 19
Lawson Rd. NR3: Norw 6D 16
Layer Cl. NR5: Bow 2A 24
Layson Dr. NR3: Norw 6D 16
Layton Cl. NR8: Dray 6C 8
Leach's Turn NR14: Surl 6D 30
Leafyoak La. NR14: Por 6C 40
Leander Ct. NR4: Norw 2F 35
Leas Ct. NR6: Norw 1E 25
Leeder Hill NR13: Post 5H 29
Leewood Cres. NR5: Norw 6D 14
Lefroy Rd. NR3: Norw 4H 15
Legarda Ct. NR3: Norw 5E 17
Leicester NR2: Norw 7A 5
Leicester St. NR2: Norw 5B 26
Lemon Av. NR2: Norw 3G 25
Leng Cres. NR4: Norw 1F 35
Lenthall Cl. NR7: Thor And 1E 29
Leonards St. NR3: Norw 1B 4 (1C 26)
Leopard Ct. NR3: Norw 1D 4 (2D 26)
Leopold Cl. NR4: Norw 6H 25
Leopold Rd. NR4: Norw 6H 25
Le Safferne Gdns. NR3: Norw 5E 17
Le Strange Cl. NR2: Norw 4G 25
Le Tunder Cl. NR7: Thor And 2B 28
Leven Cl. NR7: Thor And 6E 19
Leveson Rd. NR7: Spro 4G 17
Levine Cl. NR13: B'all 3D 30
Leyham Ct. NR5: Bow 1B 24
Liberator Rd. NR6: Norw 1B 16
Libra Ct. NR7: Spro 3H 17
Library Cl. NR13: Blof 1G 31
Lilac Cl. NR10: H'ford 1F 9
Lilburne Av. NR3: Norw 5C 16
Lilian Cl. NR6: Helle 3A 16
Lilian Rd. NR10: Spix 1F 11
Lilly Ter. NR1: Norw 7D 5 (5D 26)
Lime Kiln M. NR3: Norw 1B 26
Limes Cl. NR9: Lit Mel 1E 33
Lime Tree Av. NR7: Thor And 2H 27
NR8: Cost 3A 14
NR18: Wym 2D 38
Lime Tree Cl. NR10: H'ford 2G 9
NR14: Fram E 2B 40
NR18: Wym 3E 39
Limetree Ct. NR8: Tav 4E 7
Lime Tree Rd. NR2: Norw 6A 26
Linacre Av. NR7: Spro 4H 17
Linacre Cl. NR7: Spro 4H 17
Linalls Dr. NR8: Cost 3F 13
Lincoln Ho. *NR7: Thor And 5B 18*
(off Racecourse Rd.)
Lincoln St. NR2: Norw 4A 26
Linden Dr. NR9: Hether 5C 32
Linden Rd. NR5: New C 6D 14
Lindford Dr. NR4: Norw 3G 35
Lindley Cl. NR6: Old C 1D 16
Lindley Rd. NR9: Hether 5C 32
Lindley St. NR1: Norw 6D 26
Lindsay Rd. NR7: Spro 3H 17
Lings Cl. NR10: H'ford 2G 9
Lingwood Rd. NR13: Blof 1H 31
Links Av. NR6: Helle 2G 15
NR13: B'all 3E 31
Links Cl. NR6: Helle 2G 15
Linnet Rd. NR8: Cost 2D 12
The Linnets NR5: New C 6A 14
Lintock Rd. NR3: Norw 4C 16
Linton Cl. NR7: Spro 4G 17
Linton Cres. NR7: Spro 3G 17
Lion & Castle Yd. NR1: Norw 5C 5
Lion Cl. NR5: New C 6F 13
Lion Wood Rd. NR1: Norw 2G 27
Lishman Rd. NR7: Norw 5B 18
Lisle Rd. NR5: Bow 2A 24
Lit. Armes St. NR2: Norw 1H 25
Lit. Bethel Ct. NR2: Norw 5A 5
Lit. Bethel St. NR2: Norw 5A 5 (4C 26)
Lit. Bull Cl. NR3: Norw 1C 4 (2D 26)
Lit. John Rd. NR4: Norw 2B 36
Little La. NR10: H'ford 2G 9
Lit. London St. NR2: Norw 4C 4 (3D 26)
LITTLE MELTON 1F 33
Lit. Melton La. NR4: Coln 6H 23
Lit. Melton Rd.
NR9: Hether, Lit Mel 3D 32
LITTLE PLUMSTEAD 2C 20
Lit. Water La. NR3: Norw 3C 4 (3C 26)
Littlewood NR8: Thor Mar 3H 7
Littlewoods La. NR12: Hov 1D 42
Livingstone St. NR2: Norw 2H 25
The Lizard NR18: Wym 5E 39
Lloyd Rd. NR1: Norw 2G 27
NR8: Tav 4E 7
The Loaning NR1: Norw 6E 27
Lobelia Cl. NR18: Wym 2G 39
Lobelia La. NR4: Cring 3D 34
Lobster La. NR2: Norw 4B 4 (3C 26)
Locksley Rd. NR4: Norw 3B 36
Loddon Rd.
NR14: Bix, Fram P, Yelv 2H 37, 1F 41
Lodge Breck NR8: Dray 6B 8
Lodge Cl. NR5: Norw 4D 24
Lodge Farm Dr. NR6: Old C 6C 10
Lodge La. NR6: Old C 6D 10
Lodge Pl. NR7: Thor And 3B 28
Lodge Rd. NR9: E'ton 3A 12
Lodore Av. NR6: Helle 1H 15
The Loke NR4: Cring 3F 35
NR5: New C 4H 13
NR5: Norw 2F 25
NR13: Blof 1H 31
NR18: Wym 3F 39
Lollards Rd. NR1: Norw 3F 4 (3E 27)
London Rd. NR18: Suton, Wym 6A 38
London St. NR2: Norw 4C 4 (3D 26)
Lone Barn Rd. NR7: Spro 4G 17
Longbow Cl. NR4: Norw 2B 36
Long Dale NR8: Thor Mar 3A 8
Longdell Hills NR5: New C 5H 13
Longe Rd. NR6: Old C 1E 17
Longfields Rd. NR7: Thor And 6D 18
Long John Hill NR1: Norw 1D 36
LONG JOHN'S HILL 1E 37
Longland Cl. NR6: Old C 1D 16
Longlands Dr. NR18: Wym 2B 38
Long La. NR9: Baw 2E 23
(not continuous)
NR13: Stru 5H 31
NR14: Stoke X 4A 40
Longmead NR1: Norw 1D 36
Long Mdw. NR13: B'all 4D 30
Long Reach NR13: B'all 3E 31
Long Rd. NR14: Fram E 3C 40
Long Row NR3: Norw 6C 16
Longs Bus. Cen. NR8: Tav 3G 7
Long's Cres. NR13: Rack 1E 19
Longview NR9: Hether 3D 32
Longwater La. NR5: New C 4G 13
NR8: Cost 4G 13
Lonsdale Rd. NR13: Rack 1G 19
Looses Yd. NR3: Norw 2C 4
Lord Nelson Dr. NR5: New C 6F 13
Lord Rosebery M. *NR7: Thor And 3E 29*
(off St Andrews Pk.)
Lords Hill NR8: Cost 2C 12
Lorraine Gdns. NR3: Norw 4D 16
Losinga Cres. NR3: Norw 4A 16
Lothian St. NR2: Norw 2B 26
Louis Cl. NR6: Old C 1C 16
Lound Rd. NR4: Norw 4G 25
Lovelace Rd. NR4: Norw 5F 25
Lovelstaithe NR1: Norw 4F 4 (3E 27)
Lovett Cl. NR6: Old C 1E 17
LOW COMMON 6D 22
Lwr. Clarence Rd.
NR1: Norw 5F 5 (4E 27)
Lower Cl. NR1: Norw 3E 4 (3E 27)
LOWER EASTON 4A 12
Lower Farm Ct. NR6: Norw 1E 25
Lwr. Globe La. NR13: Blof 6G 21
Lwr. Goat La. NR2: Norw 4B 4
LOWER HELLESDON 5F 15
Lwr. Spink's La. NR18: Wym 3H 39
Loweswater Gdns. *NR5: Norw 3E 25*
(off Douglas Haig Rd.)
Lowes Yd. NR3: Norw 2C 4
Low Rd. NR4: Kes 4F 35
NR6: Helle, Lwr H 3E 15
NR8: Dray 6B 8
NR9: E'ton 4A 12
NR13: Gt P 6F 19, 6A 20
(not continuous)
NR13: Stru 6H 31
Lowry Cole Rd. NR6: Spro 2E 17
Lowther Rd. NR4: Norw 2A 36
Loxwood NR6: Helle 6F 9
Loynes Dr. NR12: Wrox 5A 42
Lubbock Cl. NR2: Norw 4G 25
Lucas Ct. NR7: Thor And 6D 18
Lucerne Cl. NR6: Old C 3E 17
Luke Cl. NR5: New C 6A 14
Lupin Cl. NR18: Wym 2G 39
Lurkins Cres. NR7: Spro 2A 18
Luscombe Way NR13: Rack 1G 19
Lusher Ri. NR6: Norw 1E 25
Lusher's Loke NR7: Spro 3E 17
Lushington Cl. NR5: Bow 1C 24
Lyhart Rd. NR4: Norw 2A 36
LYNCH GREEN 4D 32
Lynch Grn. NR9: Hether 4C 32
Lynes Cl. NR13: Blof 1H 31
Lyngate Cl. NR9: Hether 5B 32
Lynn Cl. NR7: Thor And 6E 19
Lytton Rd. NR8: Tav 5G 7

M

McCarney Ct. NR6: Helle 2E 15
Mackintosh Cl. NR13: Blof 1H 31
Mack's La. NR8: Dray, Tav 6G 7
Macmillan Way NR13: Lit P 5B 20
Maddermarket Theatre 4B 4
Maden Cl. NR18: Wym 3C 38
Magdalen Cl. NR3: Norw 1C 4 (1D 26)
Magdalen Rd. NR3: Norw 1D 26
Magdalen St. NR3: Norw 1C 4 (1D 26)
Magistrates' Court
Norwich 2D 4 (2D 26)
Magnay Rd. NR8: Dray 6D 8
Magnolia Cl. NR10: H'ford 1F 9
Magnolia Way NR8: Cost 3D 12

Magpie Cl. NR8: Cost 2D 12
Magpie Rd. NR3: Norw 1C 26
Mahoney Grn. NR13: Rack 1E 19
Maida Va. NR2: Norw 4A 26
Maidens Cl. NR7: Thor And 6F 19
Maid Marian Rd. NR4: Norw 2B 36
Maidstone Rd. NR1: Norw 4D 4 (3D 26)
Malbrook Rd. NR5: Norw 3C 24
Mallard Cl. NR13: B'all 5G 31
Mallard Way NR7: Spro 3A 18
Mallet Cl. NR7: Spro 3C 18
Mallory Rd. NR6: Norw 1C 16
Mallow Way NR18: Wym 4E 39
Maltby Ct. NR3: Norw 6E 17
Malten Cl. NR14: Por 5D 40
Malthouse Cl. NR9: Hether 5C 32
Malthouse Dr. NR12: Hov 1D 42
Malthouse La. NR2: Norw 6B 5
NR12: Wrox 4A 42
Malthouse Rd. NR2: Norw 6B 5 (4C 26)
(not continuous)
NR9: Hether 4C 32
Maltsters Yd. NR1: Norw 6D 5 (4D 26)
Malvern Rd. NR1: Norw 3F 27
Malzy Ct. NR3: Norw 1B 4
Manby Rd. NR7: Norw 6H 17
Manchester Pl. NR2: Norw 4B 26
Mancroft St. *NR2: Norw 2B 26*
(off Exeter St.)
Mancroft Wlk. NR2: Norw 2B 26
Mandela Cl. NR3: Norw 2A 4 (2C 26)
Mandells Ct. NR3: Norw 3C 4
Mangreen La. NR4: Kes, Swar 6A 36
Mann Cl. NR18: Wym 1G 39
Manor Chase NR8: Tav 5H 7
Manor Cl. NR10: Hor F 1A 10
Manor Cotts. NR13: Blof 1F 31
Mnr. Farm Cl. NR8: Dray 4B 8
Manor Ridge NR13: Blof 1H 31
Manor Rd. NR10: Hor F 1A 10
Mansel Dr. NR6: Old C 4D 16
Mansfield La. NR1: Norw 1D 36
Manthorpe Cl. NR1: Norw 2D 36
Mantle Cl. NR7: Spro 3A 18
Maple Cl. NR18: Wym 2E 39
Maple Dr. NR2: Norw 2G 25
NR8: Tav 3E 7
Mapletree Cl. NR4: Cring 2D 34
Marauder Rd. NR6: Norw 1C 16
Mardle St. NR5: Bow 4A 24
Margaret Cl. NR6: Helle 2E 15
Margaret Cres. NR7: Thor And 2C 28
Margaret Dewing Cl. NR10: Spix 2H 11
Margaret Paston Av. NR3: Norw 5H 15
Margaret Reeve Cl. NR18: Wym 3E 39
Margaret Rd. NR5: New C 5C 14
Margetson Av. NR7: Thor And 2H 27
Marigold Cl. NR10: H'ford 2F 9
Marilyn Welch Ct. NR4: Cring 3D 34
Mariners La. NR1: Norw 7D 5 (5D 26)
Marion Cl. NR18: Wym 3D 38
Marion Rd. NR1: Norw 3F 27
Marion Roberts Ct. NR9: Hether 5C 32
Marionville Rd. NR3: Norw 4D 16
Marjorie Hinde Ct. NR2: Norw 5A 5
Market Av. NR1: Norw 4D 4 (3D 26)
Marketfield La. NR10: Hor F 1C 10
Market La. NR9: Gt Mel, Lit Mel 2A 32
Market Pl. NR2: Norw 4B 4 (4C 26)
NR18: Wym 5D 38
Market St. NR18: Wym 4C 38
Markham Twr. NR3: Norw 5H 15
Mark Lemmon Cl. NR4: Cring 4F 35
MARKSHALL 6D 36
Markshall Farm Rd. NR14: Mark 6B 36
(not continuous)
Markshall La.
NR14: Caist E, Mark 6D 36
Marland Rd. NR8: Thor Mar 3G 7
Marlborough Ct. NR1: Norw 4F 27
NR7: Spro 3G 17
Marlborough Ho. NR1: Norw 8A 5
Marlborough Rd. NR3: Norw 1D 26
MARLINGFORD 2A 22
Marlingford Rd. NR9: Baw 2D 22
NR9: E'ton, Marl 1A 22
Marlingford Way NR9: E'ton 5A 12
Marlow Ct. NR3: Norw 4D 16
Marl Pit La. NR5: Norw 1D 24
Marriott Chase NR8: Thor Mar 4H 7
Marriott Cl. NR2: Norw 2B 26
Marryat Rd. NR7: Norw 6H 17
Marshall Cl. NR5: New C 1C 24
NR10: Spix 2G 11
Marshall Rd. NR3: Norw 4A 16
Marsh Rd. NR12: Hov 2C 42
Marston La. NR4: Norw 3G 35
Marston Moor NR7: Thor And 1E 29
Martin Cl. NR7: Spro 3G 17
Martineau La. NR1: Norw 2E 37
Marvell Grn. NR7: Thor And 6E 19
Marwood Cl. NR18: Wym 5C 38
Mary Chapman Cl. NR7: Thor And 2E 29
Mary Chapman Ct. NR3: Norw 3B 4
Mary Conner Ho. *NR2: Norw 5G 25*
(off Elizabeth Fry Rd.)
Mason Rd. NR6: Norw 4B 16
Massingham Rd. NR3: Norw 6D 16
Matlock Rd. NR1: Norw 4G 27
Maude Gray Ct. *NR2: Norw 3A 4*
(off St Benedicts St.)
Maud St. NR2: Norw 3A 26
Maurecourt Dr. NR13: B'all 2D 30
Maurice Raes Cl. NR3: Norw 6D 16
Mavish Cl. NR5: Bow 3A 24
Mawkin Cl. NR5: Bow 3A 24
May Cl. NR18: Wym 3C 38
Mayes Cl. NR5: Bow 1C 24
Mayfield Av. NR6: Helle 3A 16
Mayflower Ct. NR5: Bow 2C 24
Maze Av. NR8: Cost 2C 12
Meadowbrook Cl. NR1: Norw 6D 26
Meadow Brown Way NR18: Wym 4F 39
Meadow Cl. NR5: New C 5B 14
NR6: Helle 2H 15
NR9: Hether 5C 32
NR14: Tro 1G 37
Meadow Dr. NR12: Hov 3C 42
Meadow Farm Dr. NR4: Cring 5D 34
Meadow Farm La. NR10: Hor F 1B 10
Meadow Gdns. NR6: Spro 3E 17
Meadow La. NR7: Thor And 3C 28
Meadow Ri. Av. NR2: Norw 5H 25
Meadow Ri. Cl. NR2: Norw 5H 25
Meadow Ri. Rd. NR2: Norw 5H 25
Meadow Rd. NR5: New C 5B 14
The Meadows NR5: Bow 2C 24
Meadowsweet NR10: H'ford 2F 9
Meadowsweet Rd. NR18: Wym 4F 39
Meadowvale NR5: New C 4B 14
Meadow Vw. NR13: B'all 3F 31
Meadow Way NR6: Helle 2G 15
NR10: H'ford 2G 9
NR14: Por 5C 40
Meadway NR4: Cring 4D 34
Mecca Bingo
Norwich 5B 16
Medeswell Cl. NR13: B'all 2E 31
Melbourne Cotts. *NR2: Norw 5B 26*
(off Union St.)
Melrose Rd. NR4: Norw 6H 25
Melton Cl. NR18: Wym 2C 38
Melton Ct. NR9: Hether 4C 32
Melton Dr. NR8: Thor Mar 4H 7
Melton Ga. NR18: Wym 3C 38
Melton Rd. NR18: Wym 3C 38
Memorial Rd. NR10: H'ford 1G 9
Memorial Way NR7: Thor And 2F 29
Mendham Cl. NR1: Norw 1D 36
Mentmore Way NR14: Por 5C 40
Merchants Ct. NR3: Norw 3C 4
Merchants Hall NR2: Norw 6A 5
Merchant Way NR6: Helle 3H 15
Meredith Rd. NR6: Helle 1F 15
Meridian Bus. Pk. NR7: Thor And 4F 29
Meridian Way NR7: Thor And 3F 29
Merlin Av. NR7: Spro 3H 17
Merlin Cl. NR12: Hov 2C 42
Merlin M. NR7: Spro 3H 17
Merrow Gdns. NR4: Norw 3G 35
Merton Rd. NR2: Norw 2H 25
Metcalf Cl. NR3: Norw 6G 15
Meteor Cl. NR6: Norw 6C 10
The Mews NR2: Norw 5B 26
Mews Ct. NR13: Blof 1G 31
Middle Rd. NR13: Gt P 6F 19, 6A 20
Middleton Cl. NR3: Norw 4B 16
Middleton Ct. NR18: Wym 4C 38
Middleton Cres. NR5: New C 5A 14
Middleton's Cl. NR6: Helle 3F 15
Middleton's La. NR6: Helle 3F 15
Middleton St. NR18: Wym 4C 38
Midland St. NR2: Norw 2B 26
Midland Wlk. NR2: Norw 2B 26
Mid Norfolk Railway
Wymondham Abbey Station 5B 38
MILE CROSS 6H 15
Mile Cross La. NR6: Norw 3A 16
Mile Cross Rd. NR2: Norw 1A 26
NR3: Norw 6A 16
Mile End Cl. NR4: Norw 6H 25
Mile End Rd. NR4: Norw 6H 25
Milestone Cl. NR5: New C 5A 14
Milford Rd. NR2: Norw 4A 26
Millbrooks Cl. NR18: Wym 6E 39
Mill Cl. NR1: Norw 8C 5 (6D 26)
NR9: Hether 5C 32
NR13: Blof 3G 21
NR14: Por 3B 40
Millcroft NR3: Norw 6D 16
Mill Cft. Cl. NR5: New C 6G 13
Millennium Av. NR6: Helle 2F 15
Millennium Plain NR2: Norw 5B 5
Miller Cl. NR9: Hether 3E 33
Miller's Breck NR8: Tav 4G 7
Millers Ct. NR18: Wym 4D 38
Millers La. NR3: Norw 6C 16
Millers Way NR10: H'ford 1G 9
Millfield Cl. NR13: Blof 4G 21
Mill Gdns. NR10: H'ford 1G 9
MILL HILL 6D 16
Mill Hill Rd. NR2: Norw 4A 26
Mill La. NR3: Norw 1D 26
NR4: Kes 5H 35
NR10: H'ford 1G 9
NR10: Hor F 1B 10
NR13: Witt 3B 30
NR14: Bram, Fram P 1G 41
Mill Rd. NR9: Hether 5C 32
NR9: Lit Mel 1D 32
NR13: Blof 3F 21
Mills Cl. NR8: Tav 4F 7
Mill St. NR10: Hor F 2B 10
Millway NR18: Wym 2C 38
Millwrights Way NR3: Norw 5E 17
Milton Cl. NR1: Norw 6D 26
Milverton Rd. NR1: Norw 8E 5 (6E 27)
Minion Cl. NR7: Thor And 1E 29
Minns Cres. NR14: Por 4B 40
Minotaur Way NR5: New C 6F 13
Mitchell Ct. NR5: Bow 1A 24
Mitre Ct. NR3: Norw 4H 15
Module Bus. Cen. NR6: Norw 2B 16
Mokyll Cft. NR8: Thor Mar 3G 7
Monarch Cl. NR18: Wym 4F 39
The Monastery NR3: Norw 3C 4 (3D 26)
The Monastery Ct. *NR3: Norw 3C 4*
(off The Monastery)
Mons Av. NR1: Norw 1F 27
Montcalm Rd. NR1: Norw 3G 27
Mont Cross NR8: Thor Mar 4G 7
Montgomery Cl. NR5: Bow 2A 24
Montrose Ct. NR7: Thor And 1D 28
Moore Av. NR6: Spro 3E 17
Moore Cl. NR10: H'ford 1G 9
Moorhen Cl. NR7: Spro 2A 18
The Moorings NR3: Norw 2A 4
Moorland Cl. NR7: Norw 5F 17
The Moors NR8: Thor Mar 3A 8
Morello Cl. NR4: Norw 4F 25
Morgan Ho. NR1: Norw 6D 5
Morgan Way NR5: Bow 1A 24
Morley St. NR3: Norw 1E 4 (1E 27)
Mornington Rd. NR2: Norw 5H 25
Morris Cl. NR5: Bow 1B 24
Morris Dr. NR13: Lit P 5C 20
Morse Av. NR1: Norw 2H 27
Morse Cl. NR13: B'all 4F 31
Morse Rd. NR1: Norw 2H 27
Mosely Ct. NR5: Bow 1H 23
Mossfield Cl. NR1: Norw 1G 27
Mottram Cl. NR5: Norw 3E 25
Motum Rd. NR5: Norw 2D 24
Mountbatten Dr. NR6: Spro 1F 17
Mounteney Cl. NR6: Spro 3E 17
Mountergate NR1: Norw 5E 5 (4E 27)
Mountfield Av. NR6: Helle 3G 15
MOUNT PLEASANT 6H 25
Mt. Pleasant NR2: Norw 5A 26
Mt. Surrey NR18: Wym 2D 38
Mousehold Av. NR3: Norw 1E 27
Mousehold Ho. NR1: Norw 3G 27
Mousehold La. NR7: Norw 4F 17
Mousehold St. NR3: Norw 1E 4 (1E 27)
Mulbarton Rd. NR4: Kes 6H 35
Mulberry Cl. NR3: Norw 3A 4
NR14: Por 4C 40
Mulberry Ct. NR8: Tav 3E 7
Munnings Rd. NR7: Norw 5A 18
Muriel Kenny Ct. NR9: Hether 5C 32
Muriel Rd. NR2: Norw 5H 25
Murrayfield Rd. NR6: Norw 2A 16
Murrells Ct. NR1: Norw 5D 5
Mus. of Norwich at the Bridewell 4C 4
Music Ho. La. NR1: Norw 6E 5 (4E 27)
Musketeer Way NR7: Thor And 2E 29
Musley Ct. NR2: Norw 6A 26
Muspole St. NR3: Norw 2B 4 (2C 26)
Mustard Mill NR1: Norw 8F 5
Mustard Way NR14: Tro 1G 37
Mute Cres. NR7: Spro 2A 18

Myrtle Av. NR8: Cost 4A 14
Myrtle Rd. NR9: Hether 4C 32

N

Naber Furlong NR8: Thor Mar 3G 7
Namco Funscape
 Norwich 1A 24
Napier Pl. NR2: Norw 2B 26
Naseby Way NR7: Thor And 2E 29
Nasmith Rd. NR4: Norw 1F 35
Natterers Rd. NR9: Hether 4C 32
Naylor Rd. NR3: Norw 6G 15
Neale Av. NR14: Por 3B 40
Neatmarket NR4: Norw 4B 36
Needham Pl. NR1: Norw 7A 5
Nelonde Dr. NR18: Wym 3D 38
Nelson Cl. NR9: Hether 4F 33
 NR14: Por 4C 40
Nelson Ct. NR4: Norw 5E 25
Nelson Dr. NR13: Lit P 5C 20
Nelson St. NR2: Norw 2A 26
Neptune Loke NR5: New C 6E 13
The Nest NR1: Norw 3F 4 (3F 27)
Netherconesford *NR1: Norw* *5D 5*
 (off King St.)
Netherwood Grn. NR1: Norw 1E 37
Neville Cl. NR7: Spro 4E 17
Neville Rd. NR7: Spro 4E 17
Neville St. NR2: Norw 4B 26
Newarch La. NR14: Fram P 1F 41
Newark Cl. NR7: Thor And 2E 29
Newbegin Cl. NR1: Norw 2H 27
Newbegin Rd. NR1: Norw 2G 27
New Botolph St. NR3: Norw 1B 4 (2C 26)
Newbury Way NR7: Thor And 1E 29
Newcastle Cl. NR7: Thor And 1E 29
NEW CATTON 6C 16
NEW COSTESSEY 6A 14
Newey's Way NR12: Hov 2B 42
Newfound Dr. NR4: Cring 2D 34
Newman Rd. NR13: Rack 1E 19
Newmarket Dr. NR4: Cring 3E 35
Newmarket Rd. NR2: Norw 8A 5 (6A 26)
 NR4: Cring 3C 34
 (not continuous)
Newmarket St. NR2: Norw 5B 26
New Mills Yd. NR3: Norw 2A 4 (2C 26)
NEW RACKHEATH 2G 19
New Rd. NR9: Baw 3E 23
 (not continuous)
 NR9: Hether 5B 32
NEW SPROWSTON 4E 17
Newstead Gdns. NR13: Blof 2G 31
Newton Cl. NR4: Norw 2A 36
 NR14: Tro 1G 37
Neylond Cres. NR6: Helle 1F 15
NHS WALK-IN CENTRE (NORWICH) 5D 5
Nicholas Ct. *NR3: Norw* *6D 16*
 (off Magdalen Rd.)
Nicholas M. NR2: Norw 2A 26
Nicholls Cnr. NR14: Alp 6H 41
Nichols Rd. NR14: Alp 5H 41
Nightingale Cl. NR8: Tav 4E 7
Nightingale Cotts. NR1: Norw 6E 27
Nightingale Dr. NR4: Cring 3C 34
 NR8: Tav 4E 7
Nightingale La. NR3: Norw 1D 4 (1D 26)
Nightingale M. *NR8: Cost* *2E 13*
 (off Heron Rd.)
Nile St. NR2: Norw 2A 26
Nimrod Cl. NR9: Hether 4D 32
Ninhams Ct. NR2: Norw 5A 5
Ninham St. NR1: Norw 8D 5 (6D 26)
Nobel Cres. NR12: Wrox 3A 42
Noble Cl. NR7: Norw 6A 18
Noctule Gro. NR9: Hether 4C 32
Noot All. NR5: Bow 2C 24
NORFOLK & NORWICH UNIVERSITY HOSPITAL
 6B 24
Norfolk Bowling Club 1G 35
Norfolk Heritage Cen. 5B 5
Norfolk Ho. *NR2: Norw* *4B 4*
 (off Exchange St.)
Norfolk Premier Golf Course 2F 31
Norfolk Retail Pk. 5D 12
Norfolk Rd. NR4: Norw 6D 24
Norfolk Showground 6D 12
Norfolk Snowsports Club 6G 27
Norfolk St. NR2: Norw 6A 5 (4B 26)
Norfolk Ter. NR4: Norw 6D 24
Norgate Rd. NR4: Norw 6F 25
Norgate Way NR8: Tav 5H 7
Normandie Twr. NR1: Norw 7E 5
Norman Dr. NR6: Old C 6D 10
Norman Recreation Cen. 5A 16
Norman Rd. NR3: Norw 6D 16
Normans Bldgs. NR1: Norw 5D 5 (4D 26)
Norris Ct. NR3: Norw 3C 4
Northampton Ct. NR1: Norw 2F 27
Northcote Rd. NR3: Norw 1D 26
NORTH EARLHAM 1D 24
Northfield Cl. NR18: Wym 2C 38
Northfield Gdns. NR18: Wym 3C 38
Northfield Loke NR18: Wym 2C 38
Northfields NR4: Norw 5F 25
Nth. Gage Cl. NR7: Spro 3H 17
Northgate NR6: Helle 2G 15
 NR13: Thor E 4E 19
North Pk. Av. NR4: Norw 6E 25
North Pk. Dr. NR4: Norw 5G 25
Northside NR7: Thor And 3E 29
North St. NR13: Blof 6G 21
North Ter. NR2: Norw 6B 5
Northumberland Ct. *NR2: Norw* *2A 26*
 (off Northumberland St.)
Northumberland St. NR2: Norw 2A 26
Northview Rd. NR5: New C 6D 14
Nth. Walsham Rd. NR6: Spro 3E 17
 NR12: Bee A, Crost 3E 17
Norton Dr. NR4: Norw 2H 35
Norvic Dr. NR4: Norw 1F 35
NORWICH 4C 4 (3D 26)
Norwich Airport 6A 10
Norwich Airport Ind. Est. NR6: Norw 1A 16
 (Anson Rd.)
 NR6: Norw 6B 10
 (Javelin Rd.)
Norwich Arts Cen. 3A 4
Norwich Bus. Pk. NR4: Norw 2C 36
Norwich Bus Station 6B 5 (4C 26)
Norwich Cathedral 3D 4 (3E 27)
Norwich City FC 7F 5 (5F 27)
Norwich Comn. NR18: Wym 2H 39
NORWICH COMMUNITY HOSPITAL 2G 25
Norwich Family Golf Cen. 6B 12
Norwich Livestock Mkt. NR4: Norw 4C 36
Norwich Register Office 1E 37
Norwich Research Pk. NR4: Coln 5B 24
Norwich Rd. NR5: New C 4C 14
 NR9: Hether 6C 32
 NR10: Hor F 2A 10
 NR12: Sal, Wrox 6A 42
 NR13: Lit P 2H 19, 2A 20
 NR13: Rack, Sal 1H 19
 NR14: Fram E, Por 1B 40
 NR18: Wym 4D 38
Norwich St John the Baptist RC Cathedral
 3B 26
Norwich St Peter Mancroft Church 5B 5
Norwich Southern By-Pass
 NR9: E'ton 4A 12
Norwich Station (Rail) 5F 5 (4E 27)
Norwich Tourist Info. Cen. 5B 5 (4C 26)
Notridge Rd. NR5: Bow 2B 24
Notykin St. NR5: Bow 1B 24
NOVI SAD FRIENDSHIP BRIDGE 7E 5 (5E 27)
Nuffield Heath
 Norwich 1F 4 (2E 27)
Nurseries Av. NR13: B'all 3G 31
Nursery Cl. NR6: Helle 2F 15
Nursery Gdns. NR13: Blof 1H 31
Nursery La. NR8: Cost 3A 14
Nutfield Cl. NR4: Norw 2F 35
Nutwood Cl. NR8: Thor Mar 3G 7

O

Oak Av. NR7: Thor And 1C 28
 NR14: Por 4C 40
Oak Cl. NR5: New C 5A 14
 NR9: Hether 4D 32
Oakcroft Dr. NR14: Fram E 3B 40
Oakdale Rd. NR13: B'all 4F 31
Oakfields Cl. NR4: Cring 3F 35
Oakfields Rd. NR4: Cring 3E 35
Oak Gro. NR10: H'ford 2G 9
Oakhill NR13: B'all 4F 31
Oak Ho. NR5: Bow 1H 23
Oaklands NR8: Tav 3E 7
 NR14: Fram E 2B 40
Oaklands Dr. NR4: Cring 2D 34
Oak La. NR3: Norw 4C 16
 NR6: Old C 4C 16
Oak Lodge NR7: Norw 4H 27
Oak Lodge Cotts. NR6: Spro 6G 11
Oak's La. NR13: Post 4H 29
Oak St. NR3: Norw 1A 4 (2C 26)
Oaktree Dr. NR7: Spro 5G 17
Oak Wood NR13: Blof 2G 31
Oakwood Cl. NR9: E'ton 5A 12
Oakwood Dr. NR18: Wym 2F 39
Oatfield Cl. NR10: H'ford 2F 9
Octagon Chapel 2C 4
Octagon Ct. NR3: Norw 2C 4
Odeon Cinema 6F 5 (4E 27)
Offley Ct. NR5: Bow 1B 24
Ogden Cl. NR18: Wym 4D 38
Old Allotment Ct. *NR3: Norw* *1E 27*
 (off Balfour St.)
Old Bank of England Ct. NR2: Norw 3C 4
Old Barge Yd. NR1: Norw 6E 5 (4E 27)
The Old Barley Mkt. NR2: Norw 4B 4
Old Blenheim Way NR6: Norw 1C 16
OLD CATTON 3D 16
Old Chapel Way NR7: Thor And 3F 29
The Old Church NR1: Norw 4F 4
Old Church Cl. NR14: Caist E 6E 37
Old Farm La. NR3: Norw 6A 16
Old Grove Ct. NR3: Norw 5C 16
Old Hall Cl. NR14: Tro 1G 37
Old Hall La. NR10: Spix 2E 11
Old Hall Rd. NR13: Lit P 5B 20
Oldhall Rd. NR4: Norw 4B 36
OLD LAKENHAM 3D 36
Old Lakenham Hall Dr. NR1: Norw 2D 36
Old Laundry Ct. NR2: Norw 1A 26
Old Library M. NR1: Norw 5F 5 (4F 27)
Old Meeting Ho. All. *NR3: Norw* *2C 4*
 (off Colegate)
Old Meeting Ho. Yd. *NR3. Norw* *2C 4*
 (off Colegate)
Old Millers Wharf NR3: Norw 2D 4 (2D 26)
Old Mill Rd. NR14: Por 3B 40
Old Mint Yd. NR3: Norw 2C 4
Old Norwich Rd. NR10: Hor F 4A 10
Old Oak Cl. NR18: Wym 1G 39
The Old Orchard NR9: Hether 5E 33
Old Palace Rd. NR2: Norw 1A 26
Old Post Office Ct. NR2: Norw 4C 4
Old Post Office Yd. NR2: Norw 4C 4 (3D 26)
Old Rectory Cl. NR7: Thor And 3B 28
Old School Cl. NR5: Norw 3F 25
Old School Ct. NR1: Norw 8E 5 (5E 27)
Old Stoke Rd. NR14: Arm 3E 37
Old Tram Yd. NR2: Norw 2H 25
Old Warren NR8: Thor Mar 3F 7
Old Watton Rd. NR4: Coln 5B 24
Olive Cl. NR5: New C 6D 14
Olive Cres. NR10: H'ford 1F 9
Olive Rd. NR5: New C 5C 14
Ollett Ct. NR18: Wym 1H 39
One Post All. NR2: Norw 6B 5
Onley St. NR2: Norw 5A 26
Opie St. NR1: Norw 4C 4 (3D 26)
Orchard Bank NR8: Dray 5H 7
Orchard Cl. NR7: Norw 1H 27
 NR13: Blof 4F 21
Orchard Dr. NR6: Helle 4E 15
Orchard Rd. NR10: Spix 1G 11
Orchard St. NR2: Norw 2B 26
Orchard Way NR9: Hether 4D 32
 NR18: Wym 4C 38
Orford Hill NR1: Norw 5C 5 (4D 26)
Orford Pl. NR1: Norw 5C 5 (4D 26)
Orford St. NR1: Norw 5C 5 (4D 26)
Orford Yd. NR1: Norw 5C 5 (4D 26)
Oriole Dr. NR4: Cring 3C 34
Orion Dr. NR5: New C 6F 13
Orwell Cl. NR4: Norw 5E 25
 NR18: Wym 3E 39
Orwell Rd. NR2: Norw 6B 26
Osbert Cl. NR1: Norw 2D 36
Osborne Ct. NR2: Norw 6B 26
Osborne Rd. NR4: Norw 1F 35
Osprey Cl. NR12: Hov 1C 42
Osprey Loke NR7: Spro 3H 17
Ottaway Cl. NR5: New C 4B 14
Oulton Rd. NR6: Norw 2B 16
Oval Av. NR5: New C 6D 14
Oval Rd. NR5: New C 6D 14
Overbury Rd. NR6: Helle 3H 15
Overstone Ct. NR6: Old C 2E 17
Overstrand Way NR7: Spro 3B 18
OVER THE WATER 2C 4
Overtons Way NR14: Por 4C 40
Owen Ct. NR7: Thor And 3F 29
Oxford St. NR2: Norw 4B 26
Oxnead Rd. NR3: Norw 5A 16

P

The Paddock NR6: Old C 6E 11
 NR14: Tro 1F 37
The Paddocks NR6: Old C 1D 16
Paddock St. NR2: Norw 1B 26
Padgate NR13: Thor E 4E 19
Page Cl. NR14: Por 5C 40

Page Rd. NR3: Norw 6G 15
NR13: B'all 3E 31
Pages Cl. NR18: Wym 5C 38
Paine Rd. NR7: Norw 1A 28
Palace St. NR3: Norw 3D 4 (3D 26)
Palgrave Cl. NR8: Tav 4E 7
Palgrave Ho. NR6: Helle 6F 9
Palm Cl. NR18: Wym 3C 38
Palmer Cl. NR3: Norw 5B 16
Palmer Rd. NR3: Norw 5B 16
NR13: Rack 1G 19
Palmers Yd. NR1: Norw 5C 5
Paper Mill Yd. NR1: Norw 8F 5 (5E 27)
Papillon Rd. NR18: Wym 4E 39
Papplewick Cl. NR4: Norw 2B 36
Paradise Pl. NR1: Norw 6D 5 (4D 26)
Paragon Pl. NR2: Norw 3B 26
Parana Cl. NR7: Spro 2H 17
Parana Ct. NR7: Spro 2H 17
Parana Rd. NR7: Spro 2H 17
Park & Ride
Airport 6H 9
Costessey 6E 13
Harford 6A 36
Postwick 4G 29
Sprowston 1A 18
Thickthorn 4B 34
Park Cl. NR6: Old C 2D 16
NR9: Hether 5D 32
Park Dr. NR9: Hether 5C 32
Parker Cl. NR13: B'all 3D 30
Parker Rd. NR2: Norw 4A 26
Parkers Cl. NR9: E'ton 5B 12
NR18: Wym 2C 38
Park Grn. NR9: Hether 5D 32
Park Ho. NR7: Thor And 3E 29
Park Ho. Ct. *NR3: Norw 4C 16*
(off Catton Gro. Rd.)
Parkland Cres. NR6: Spro 4E 17
Parkland Rd. NR6: Spro 4E 17
Parklands NR8: Cost 3G 13
Park La. NR2: Norw 3A 26
NR13: Blof 5D 20
NR18: Silf, Wym 6D 38
Park Rd. NR10: Spix 3F 11
NR12: Wrox 4A 42
Parkside Dr. NR6: Old C 2D 16
Park Vw. NR10: H'ford 1F 9
Park Way NR6: Helle 2F 15
Parliament Ct. NR7: Thor And 1E 29
Parmentergate Ct. NR1: Norw 5D 5 (4D 26)
Parmenter Rd. NR4: Norw 6G 25
Parr Rd. NR3: Norw 6H 15
Parsonage Sq. NR2: Norw 4C 4
Parsons Mead NR4: Norw 2G 35
Partridge Way NR6: Norw 3C 16
Paston Ct. NR3: Norw 5A 16
Paston Ho. NR4: Norw 5E 25
Paston Way NR7: Thor And 5B 18
PATCHEY'S CORNER 1F 4 (2E 27)
Patricia Rd. NR1: Norw 6C 26
Patteson Cl. NR4: Cring 4D 34
Patteson Rd. NR3: Norw 1C 26
The Pavilion NR2: Norw 7A 5 (5C 26)
Pavilion M. NR7: Thor And 3E 29
Paxton Pl. NR2: Norw 5B 26
Peachman Way NR7: Thor And 2F 29
Peacock Chase NR18: Wym 4E 39
Peacock Cl. NR9: E'ton 5A 12
Peacock Gro. NR8: Cost 1D 12
Peacock St. NR3: Norw 1C 4 (2D 26)
Peakwell Cl. NR8: Thor Mar 3F 7
Pearcefield NR3: Norw 5D 16
Peck Cl. NR5: Bow 1H 23
Peckover Rd. NR4: Norw 1F 35
Peddars Way NR8: Thor Mar 3G 7
PEDHAM 2H 21
Pedham Rd. NR13: Hemb, Panx 3G 21
Peel M. NR3: Norw 3A 4
Pegg Cl. NR9: E'ton 5A 12
Pelargonium Dr. NR18: Wym 1G 39
Pelham Rd. NR3: Norw 6C 16
Pembrey Cl. NR3: Norw 4C 16
Pembroke Rd. NR2: Norw 4A 26
Pendlesham Ri. NR8: Thor Mar 3H 7
Pendleton Ga. NR3: Norw 2C 4
Penfold Dr. NR18: Wym 3F 39
Penn Cl. NR8: Tav 5G 7
Penn Gro. NR3: Norw 6B 16
Penn Rd. NR8: Tav 5G 7
Pennycress Dr. NR18: Wym 4F 39
Pennyroyal NR6: Norw 2C 16
Penrice Rd. NR13: Lit P 5B 20
Penryn Cl. NR4: Norw 4F 25
Penshurst M. NR4: Norw 2G 35
Percival Cl. NR4: Norw 5F 25
Percy Howes Cl. NR13: Thor E 4E 19
Peregrine Cl. NR7: Spro 3H 17
Peregrine M. NR4: Cring 3C 34
NR7: Spro 3H 17
Peregrine Rd. NR7: Spro 3H 17
Perrings NR18: Wym 2C 38
Peterkin Rd. NR4: Norw 3B 36
Peter Pulling Dr. NR8: Cost 1D 12
Peterson Rd. NR3: Norw 5H 15
Peto Ct. NR5: Norw 2D 24
Pettus Rd. NR4: Norw 6F 25
Petty Spurge Sq. NR18: Wym 4F 39
Petunia Ct. NR18: Wym 1G 39
Peverell Rd. NR5: Bow 2B 24
Phelps Rd. NR7: Thor And 2C 28
Philadelphia La. NR3: Norw 5C 16
Philip Ford Way NR18: Wym 6D 38
Phillipa Ct. NR3: Norw 2C 4
Phillipa Flowerday Plain NR2: Norw 7A 5
Phoenix Yd. *NR3: Norw 1D 4*
(off Leopard Ct.)
Piccoli Cl. NR8: Cost 3B 14
Picton Cl. NR14: Por 5C 40
Picturehouse Ct. NR5: Norw 1D 24
Pigg La. NR3: Norw 2D 4 (3D 26)
Pigot La. NR14: Fram E, Fram P 3C 40
Pikeman Pl. NR7: Thor And 6F 19
Pilch Cl. NR1: Norw 6E 27
Pilling Pk. Rd. NR1: Norw 2G 27
Pilling Rd. NR7: Thor And 2A 28
Pimpernel Rd. NR10: H'ford 1D 8
Pinder Cl. NR3: Norw 6H 15
Pinder Rd. NR3: Norw 6H 15
Pine Cl. NR4: Norw 6H 25
Pine Ct. NR7: Spro 4A 18
Pine Gro. NR14: Fram E 2C 40
Pinelands Ind. Est. NR10: H'ford 1F 9
Pinelands Rd. NR10: H'ford 1F 9
The Pinelodges NR1: Norw 3H 27
Pine Loke NR14: Stoke X 3A 40
Pine Rd. NR7: Thor And 6B 18
The Pines NR4: Cring 2C 34
Pinetrees Bus. Pk. NR7: Spro 4A 18
Pinetrees Rd. NR7: Spro 4A 18
Pinewood Cl. NR6: Helle 3G 15
Pioneer Rd. NR6: Spro 1F 17
Piper Rd. NR7: Thor And 6B 18
Pipistrelle St. NR9: Hether 4C 32
Pippin Grn. NR4: Norw 4F 25
Pishmire Cl. NR5: Bow 3A 24
Pitchford Rd. NR5: Norw 3D 24
Pitt Farm Grn. NR8: R'land 5B 6
Pitt St. NR3: Norw 1B 4 (2C 26)
Plaford Rd. NR7: Norw 5F 17
The Plantation NR2: Norw 5A 26
Plantation Dr. NR7: Spro 4A 18
The Plantation Garden 3B 26
Plantation Rd. NR6: Helle 1F 15
NR13: Blof 1G 31
Plantsman Cl. NR2: Norw 6A 26
Plashet Ct. NR5: Norw 3C 24
Plattens Ct. NR12: Wrox 4A 42
Players Way NR6: Old C 1D 16
Playhouse Theatre 3C 4
Pleasant Cl. NR6: Helle 2E 15
Plough Yd. NR2: Norw 3A 4
PLUMSTEAD GREEN 4A 20
Plumstead Rd. NR1: Norw 2G 27
NR7: Norw 2G 27
NR13: Gt P, Thor E 5E 19
NR13: Panx 1G 21
Plumstead Rd. E.
NR7: Norw, Thor And 1H 27
Pochard St. NR8: Cost 2E 13
Pockthorpe Ga. NR3: Norw 1F 4 (2E 27)
Poethlyn Dr. NR8: Cost 2D 12
Pointer Way NR5: Norw 2G 25
Poll Cl. NR18: Wym 1G 39
Pollywiggle Cl. NR5: Bow 3A 24
Polypin Yd. NR1: Norw 5D 5 (4D 26)
Pond Cl. NR9: Hether 5C 32
Pond La. NR8: Dray 5A 8
Pond Rd. NR10: H'ford 2F 9
Pond Way NR7: Spro 2B 18
NR18: Wym 1G 39
Ponsonby Way NR14: Por 5C 40
Poplar Av. NR4: Norw 2F 35
Poplar Cl. NR5: New C 5H 13
NR10: H'ford 2G 9
Pople St. NR18: Wym 4C 38
Poppy Cl. NR4: Cring 3D 34
Poppyfields NR10: H'ford 2F 9
Poppy St. NR18: Wym 2G 39
Poppy Way NR7: Thor And 2G 29
PORINGLAND 5D 40
Poringland Library 4C 40
Poringland Rd. NR14: Stoke X 4A 40
Porson Rd. NR7: Norw 6H 17
Portersfield Rd. NR2: Norw 4A 26
Porters Loke NR7: Spro 4F 17
Portland St. NR2: Norw 4A 26
Portway Pl. NR2: Norw 2A 26
Portway Sq. NR2: Norw 2B 26
Postle M. NR3: Norw 6H 15
Post Mill Cl. NR7: Spro 4E 17
Postmill Cl. NR18: Wym 4D 38
Post Office Rd. NR13: Lit P 2C 20
POSTWICK 5H 29
Postwick La. NR13: B'all, Witt 4C 30
Postwick Park & Ride 4G 29
Pottergate NR2: Norw 4A 4 (3C 26)
Potters Way NR14: Por 4B 40
Pound La. NR7: Thor And 5D 18
NR13: Blof 2H 31
Poynt Cl. NR18: Wym 3C 38
Press Dr. NR14: Por 4C 40
Press La. NR3: Norw 6B 16
Preston Av. NR18: Wym 6B 38
Preston Cl. NR12: Wrox 5A 42
Pride Way NR7: Thor And 6F 19
Primrose Cres. NR7: Thor And 3D 28
Primrose Pl. NR2: Norw 5A 26
Primrose Rd. NR1: Norw 3F 27
Primrose Way NR10: H'ford 2F 9
Primula Dr. NR4: Norw 4F 25
Prince Andrew's Cl. NR6: Helle 2A 16
Prince Andrew's Rd. NR6: Helle 2A 16
Prince Cl. NR5: New C 5E 13
Prince Edward Cl. NR7: Thor And 2C 28
Prince of Wales Rd. NR1: Norw 4D 4 (3D 26)
Prince Rupert Way NR7: Thor And 5E 19
Princess Beatrice Cl. NR6: Helle 5E 15
Princes St. NR3: Norw 3C 4 (3D 26)
Prior Ct. NR1: Norw 2F 4 (2E 27)
Prior Rd. NR7: Thor And 6D 18
Priors Dr. NR6: Old C 1D 16
Priorswood NR8: Thor Mar 2H 7
The Priory NR7: Thor And 3E 29
Priory Cl. NR9: Hether 6D 32
NR14: Alp 4H 41
Priory Rd. NR9: Hether 5D 32
Priory Vw. NR1: Norw 8F 5
PRISCILLA BACON CENTRE (HOSPICE) *5H 25*
(within Colman Hospital)
Priscilla Cl. NR5: Norw 3E 25
Proctor Rd. NR6: Old C, Spro 1E 17
Prospect Ter. *NR1: Norw 4F 27*
(off Carrow Rd.)
Providence Pl. NR1: Norw 3F 27
Pudding La. NR2: Norw 5B 5
Pull's Ferry 3F 4 (3E 27)
Pump Ho. Cl. NR8: Cost 3C 12
Puppet Theatre 1D 4 (2D 26)
Purdance Cl. NR5: Bow 1G 23
Purland Rd. NR7: Norw 5A 18
Purtingay Cl. NR4: Norw 2H 35
Pyehurn Cl. NR10: H'ford 1F 9
Pyehurn La. NR10: H'ford 2F 9
Pyehurn M. NR8: Thor Mar 2H 7
Pye's Yd. NR3: Norw 2D 4 (2D 26)
Pym Cl. NR7: Thor And 6F 19
Pyrford Dr. NR4: Norw 2G 35

Q

Quaker La. NR10: Spix 4D 10
Quakers La. NR3: Norw 1B 4
Quarry Rd. NR8: Cost 2D 12
Quayside NR3: Norw 3D 4 (2D 26)
Quebec Cl. NR4: Cring 4D 34
Quebec Rd. NR1: Norw 3F 27
Queen Elizabeth Cl. NR3: Norw 2E 4
Queens Cl. NR4: Norw 6H 25
QUEEN'S HILLS 2D 12
Queen's Rd. NR1: Norw 7B 5 (5C 26)
NR9: Hether 4D 32
Queen St. NR2: Norw 4D 4 (3D 26)
NR18: Wym 5D 38
Queensway NR18: Wym 3C 38
Quintain M. NR3: Norw 1A 4 (1C 26)
Quinton Gurney Ho. NR4: Kes 6G 35

R

Racecourse Rd. NR7: Thor And 6B 18
Rachel Cl. NR5: Norw 4D 24
Rackham Rd. NR3: Norw 5C 16
Rackheath La. NR12: Crost 2H 11
RACKHEATH PARK 1D 18
Radcliffe Rd. NR8: Thor Mar 3H 7
Rafeman Cl. NR5: Bow 2H 23
Raglan St. NR2: Norw 3B 26
Railway Cotts. NR1: Norw 5F 27

Rainsborough Ri. NR7: Thor And 6E 19
Raleigh Ct. NR1: Norw 5D 5
The Ramblers NR14: Por 1A 40
Rampant Horse St. NR2: Norw 5B 5 (4C 26)
Ramsey Cl. NR4: Norw 6F 25
Randall Rd. NR7: Spro 3F 17
Randle Grn. NR5: Norw 1D 24
Randolf Rd. NR1: Norw 1D 36
Rangoon Cl. NR7: Spro 2H 17
Ranson Rd. NR1: Norw 4G 27
Ranworth Dr. NR12: Hov 1C 42
Ranworth Rd. NR5: Norw 2E 25
NR13: Blof 4H 21
Rattle Row NR18: Wym 4C 38
Raven Cft. NR4: Cring 3C 34
Raven Yd. NR1: Norw 5D 5
Rawley Rd. NR5: Bow 1B 24
Raymond Cl. NR6: Helle 6F 9
Raymond Rd. NR6: Helle 1G 15
Raynham St. NR2: Norw 1B 26
Rayns Cl. NR6: Spro 2E 17
Recorder Rd. NR1: Norw 4E 4 (3E 27)
Recreation Ground Rd. NR7: Spro 3F 17
Recreation Rd. NR2: Norw 4H 25
NR9: Hether 5C 32
Recreation Road Sports Cen. 4H 25
Rectory Ct. NR3: Norw 5C 16
Rectory La. NR9: Lit Mel 1D 32
NR14: Por 5D 40
Red Admiral Cl. NR8: Cost 2D 12
NR18: Wym 4F 39
Red Bri. La. NR5: New C 5D 14
Redcliffe Way NR13: B'all 3D 30
Red Cott. Cl. NR3: Norw 5H 15
Redfern Cl. NR7: Norw 6B 18
Redfern Rd. NR7: Norw 6A 18
Red Lion St. NR1: Norw 5C 5 (4D 26)
Red Lion Yd. NR3: Norw 3C 4
Redmayne Vw. NR6: Spro 1F 17
Redpoll Rd. NR8: Cost 1E 13
Red Poll Ter. *NR2: Norw* *4A 4*
(off Cow Hill)
Redwell St. NR2: Norw 3C 4 (3D 26)
Redwing Gdns. NR10: Spix 3G 11
Reeder's La. NR14: Alp 6G 41
Reedham Dr. NR12: Hov 1D 42
Reepham Rd. NR6: Helle 1F 15
NR10: Felth, H'ford 1G 7
Reeve's Cnr. NR13: Gt P 3H 19
Reeve Way NR18: Wym 1G 39
Regency Ct. NR1: Norw 5F 5
Regency Cres. *NR7: Thor And* *3F 29*
(off St Andrews Pk.)
Regina Rd. NR1: Norw 8B 5 (5C 26)
Renson Cl. NR6: Norw 3B 16
Repton Av. NR6: Old C 6C 10
Reve Cres. NR13: Blof 4F 21
Revel Burroughs Way NR14: Por 3B 40
Reydon Cl. NR5: Bow 2B 24
Reynolds M. NR18: Wym 3C 38
Rhombus Bus. Pk. NR6: Norw 2A 16
The Rhond NR12: Hov 2B 42
Rice Way NR7: Spro 5H 17
Richardson Cres. NR9: Hether 4B 32
Richenda Cl. NR5: Norw 4D 24
Richmond Ct. NR7: Thor And 4B 28
RICHMOND HILL 8D 5 (5E 27)
Richmond Rd. NR5: New C 6H 13
Riddlings Ct. NR3: Norw 5C 16
Rider Haggard Rd. NR7: Norw 6H 17
The Ridgeway NR1: Norw 1G 27
The Ridings NR4: Cring 3E 35
NR14: Por 3B 40
Rigby Cl. NR14: Fram E 3D 40
Rigby's Ct. NR2: Norw 4A 4
Rightup La. NR18: Wym 5E 39
Riley Cl. NR7: Norw 6A 18
Rimer Cl. NR5: Bow 3A 24
Rimington Rd. NR7: Spro 3F 17
Ringers Cl. NR18: Wym 3E 39
RINGLAND 5A 6
Ringland La. NR8: Cost 1C 12
NR8: R'land 4A 6
NR9: E'ton 5A 12
Ringland Rd. NR8: R'land, Tav 5B 6
NR9: E'ton 3A 12
Ring Rd. NR7: Thor And 2B 28
Ringwood Cl. NR9: Lit Mel 1E 33
Ripley Cl. NR2: Norw 4G 25
Riseway Cl. NR1: Norw 1G 27
Riverdale Ct. NR13: B'all 4F 31
Riverdene M. NR8: Thor Mar 2H 7
River Green Ct. NR7: Thor And 3B 28
River Hgts. NR1: Norw 6E 5
River La. NR3: Norw 1E 4 (2E 27)
Riverside NR1: Norw 5F 5 (4E 27)
Riverside Cl. NR6: Lwr H 5E 15
RIVERSIDE ESTATE 5F 31
Riverside Leisure Cen.
Norwich 7F 5 (5E 27)
Riverside Retail Pk.
Norwich 6F 5 (4E 27)
Riverside Rd. NR1: Norw 4F 4 (3E 27)
NR12: Hov 3B 42
Riverside Wlk. NR1: Norw 6E 5 (4E 27)
NR2: Norw 1A 4 (1B 26)
NR3: Norw 3A 4
Riverway Ct. NR1: Norw 4F 4
Roaches Ct. NR3: Norw 3C 4 (3D 26)
Robberds Way NR5: Bow 1H 23
Robert Cl. NR18: Wym 2D 38
Robert Gybson Way NR2: Norw 3A 4 (3C 26)
NR3: Norw 3C 26
Robert Kett Ct. NR1: Norw 2F 4
Robin Cl. NR8: Cost 2D 12
Robin Ct. NR8: Cost 2D 12
Robin Hood Rd. NR4: Norw 2B 36
Robson Rd. NR5: Norw 3C 24
Rocelin Cl. NR3: Norw 4D 16
Rochester Ct. *NR5: Norw* *3D 24*
(off Edgeworth Rd.)
Rockingham Rd. NR5: Norw 3D 24
Rockland Dr. NR7: Thor And 3H 27
Roedich Dr. NR8: Tav 4F 7
Roe Dr. NR5: Norw 3F 25
Rogers Cl. NR5: Norw 2C 24
Rolleston Cl. NR5: Norw 2C 24
Roman Dr. NR13: B'all 3D 30
Romany Rd. NR3: Norw 6E 17
Romany Wlk. NR14: Por 3C 40
Ron Hill Rd. NR8: Cost 2D 12
Rook Dr. NR8: Thor Mar 3H 7
Ropemakers Row NR3: Norw 6B 16
Ropes Wlk. NR13: Blof 1G 31
Rosa Cl. NR10: Spix 3H 11
Rosalie Cl. NR6: Helle 3A 16
Rosary Rd. NR1: Norw 3F 4 (3F 27)
Roseacre Cl. NR2: Norw 1B 36
Rose Av. NR1: Norw 5D 5 (4D 26)
NR8: Cost 3D 12
Rosebay Cl. NR6: Norw 2C 16
Rosebery Av. NR14: Por 4D 40
Rosebery Bus. Pk. NR14: Por 6C 40
Rosebery Ct. NR7: Thor And 3E 29
Rosebery Rd. NR3: Norw 6C 16
NR13: Gt P 1A 30
Rose Cotts. NR10: Hor F 2B 10
Rosedale Cres. NR1: Norw 4F 27
Rose Dr. NR4: Cring 2C 34
Rosefields NR13: B'all 3G 31
Rose La. NR1: Norw 5D 5 (4D 26)
Rosemary La. NR3: Norw 2B 4 (2C 26)
Rosemary Rd. NR7: Spro 3G 17
NR13: Blof 3F 21
Rosetta Rd. NR10: Spix 2H 11
Rose Valley NR2: Norw 4A 26
Roseville Cl. NR1: Norw 4G 27
Rose Wlk. NR13: B'all 4E 31
Rose Yd. NR3: Norw 1B 4 (2C 26)
Rosslare NR4: Norw 2H 35
Rossons Rd. NR8: Tav 4F 7
Rostwold Way NR3: Norw 5C 16
Rotary Ct. NR6: Lwr H 5F 15
Rotary Ho. NR1: Norw 8F 5
Rothbury Cl. NR18: Wym 4C 38
Rothbury Rd. NR18: Wym 4D 38
Rouen Rd. NR1: Norw 5D 5 (4D 26)
Roundhead Ct. NR7: Thor And 2E 29
Round Ho. Way NR4: Cring 2C 34
Roundtree Cl. NR7: Spro 5G 17
Roundtree Cl. Ind. Est. NR7: Spro 5G 17
Roundtree Trad. Est. NR7: Spro 5G 17
Roundtree Way NR7: Spro 5G 17
Roundway Down NR7: Thor And 1E 29
Round Well Rd. NR5: New C 6G 13
Rowan Cl. NR18: Wym 3F 39
Rowan Ct. NR5: New C 6A 14
NR7: Spro 4A 18
Rowan Gdns. NR9: Hether 5C 32
Rowan Way NR4: Cring 2C 34
Rowington Rd. NR1: Norw 8B 5 (5C 26)
Rowland Ct. NR1: Norw 8D 5 (5D 26)
Rowton Heath NR7: Thor And 1E 29
Roxley Cl. NR7: Thor And 4C 28
Royal Arc. NR2: Norw 5C 5
Royal Arch Ct. *NR2: Norw* *3B 26*
(off Earlham Rd.)
Royalist Dr. NR7: Thor And 2E 29
Royal Oak Ct. NR1: Norw 6D 5
Rufus St. NR8: Cost 2D 12
Rugge Dr. NR4: Norw 1F 35
Rumsey Wells Pl. NR2: Norw 4B 4
Runcton Cl. NR5: Norw 2C 24
The Runnel NR5: Bow 3A 24
Runnymede *NR3: Norw* *2C 4*
(off Golden Dog La.)
Rupert St. NR2: Norw 5B 26
(not continuous)
Rushmore Cl. NR7: Spro 2F 17
Rushmore Rd. NR7: Spro 2F 17
Ruskin Rd. NR4: Norw 5F 25
NR5: New C 6C 14
Russell Av. NR7: Spro 4F 17
NR10: Spix 2G 11
Russell St. NR2: Norw 2B 26
Russell Ter. NR14: Tro 1G 37
Russell Way NR18: Wym 5D 38
Russet Gro. NR4: Norw 4F 25
Rustens Mnr. Rd. NR18: Wym 3D 38
Rutland St. NR2: Norw 5B 26
Rydal Cl. NR5: Norw 3D 24
Rye Av. NR3: Norw 4A 16
Rye Cl. NR3: Norw 5A 16
Ryrie Ct. NR4: Norw 1G 35

S

Sadler Rd. NR6: Helle 6G 9
Saffron Sq. NR3: Norw 4B 16
Sainsbury Cen. for Visual Arts 6C 24
St Alban's Rd. NR1: Norw 6C 26
St Andrew's & Blackfriars' Halls 3C 4
St Andrews Av. NR7: Thor And 3D 28
St Andrews Bus. Pk. NR7: Thor And 3E 29
St Andrew's Cl. NR13: Blof 2G 31
St Andrews Cl. NR7: Thor And 3D 28
NR14: Fram E 3E 41
NR14: Por 4D 40
St Andrews Dr. NR4: Norw 3F 35
St Andrews Hall Plain NR3: Norw 3C 4 (3D 26)
St Andrews Hill NR2: Norw 4C 4 (3D 26)
St Andrews Pk. NR7: Thor And 3E 29
St Andrew's Rd. NR6: Helle 1E 15
St Andrews Sq. NR7: Thor And 3E 29
St Andrews St. NR2: Norw 4C 4 (3C 26)
St Andrew's Way NR13: Blof 2G 31
St Annes Cl. NR13: B'all 5H 31
St Annes Rd. NR14: Fram E 4D 40
St Ann La. NR1: Norw 6E 5 (4E 27)
St Augustines Ga. *NR3: Norw* *1C 26*
(off Waterloo Rd.)
St Augustines St. NR3: Norw 1B 4 (1C 26)
St Barnabas Ct. *NR2: Norw* *2B 26*
(off Orchard St.)
St Bartholomews Cl. NR2: Norw 1A 26
St Benedicts St. NR2: Norw 3A 4 (3B 26)
St Catherine's Rd. NR7: Thor And 1C 28
St Clements All. NR3: Norw 2C 4
St Clements Hill NR3: Norw 6D 16
St Clements Way NR13: B'all 3E 31
St Crispins Rd. NR3: Norw 1A 4 (2C 26)
St Davids Dr. NR13: Thor E 4E 19
St David's Rd. NR9: Hether 6C 32
St Edmund Cl. NR14: Caist E 2A 40
St Edmund's Cl. NR6: Lwr H 6F 15
NR8: Cost 2A 14
St Edmunds Ct. *NR18: Wym* *1G 39*
(off Poll Cl.)
St Edmund's Ri. NR8: Tav 5F 7
St Edmund's Rd. NR8: Tav 4F 7
St Edmunds Wharf NR3: Norw 2D 4
St Ethelberts Gate 3D 4
St Faiths Crematorium 1A 10
St Faiths La. NR1: Norw 4D 4 (3D 26)
St Faiths Rd. NR6: Old C 2C 16
St George Loke *NR7: Spro* *3E 17*
(off School La.)
St Georges All. NR3: Norw 2B 4
St Georges St. NR3: Norw 2B 4 (2C 26)
St Giles St. NR2: Norw 4A 4 (3C 26)
St Giles Ter. NR2: Norw 4A 4
St Gregory's All. NR2: Norw 4B 4
St Gregory's Bk. All. *NR2: Norw* *4B 4*
(off Charing Cross)
St Gregory's Cen. for the Arts 4B 4
St Helena Way NR10: H'ford 1F 9
St Helen's Sq. NR1: Norw 2E 4 (2E 27)
St James Cl. NR3: Norw 1F 4 (2E 27)
St James Ct. NR3: Norw 1D 4 (2D 26)
St James Ho. NR3: Norw 1F 4
St James Mdw. NR3: Norw 2F 4 (2E 27)
St James Mill NR3: Norw 1D 4 (2D 26)
St John Maddermarket NR2: Norw 4B 4 (3C 26)
St John's All. NR2: Norw 4B 4
St John's Cl. NR1: Norw 1D 36
NR9: Hether 6C 32
St John St. NR1: Norw 5D 5 (4E 27)
St Julians All. NR1: Norw 6D 5 (4D 26)
St Laurence Av. NR13: B'all 3D 30
St Lawrence Cl. NR2: Norw 4A 4

St Lawrence Dr. NR4: Cring 2D **34**
St Lawrence La. NR2: Norw 4B **4** (3C **26**)
St Lawrence Lit. Steps *NR2: Norw 3A 4*
(off Westwick St.)
St Lawrence Steps *NR2: Norw 3B 4*
(off Westwick St.)
St Leonards Cl. NR18: Wym 2D **38**
St Leonards Rd. NR1: Norw 3F **27**
St Leonard's Ter. NR1: Norw 3F **27**
St Margarets All. NR2: Norw 3A **4**
St Margarets Cl. NR8: Thor Mar 2A **8**
St Margarets Dr. NR7: Spro 2G **17**
St Margarets Gdns. NR12: Hov 2C **42**
St Margarets St. NR2: Norw 3A **4** (3C **26**)
St Martin at Bale Ct. NR1: Norw 5D **5**
St Martin at Palace Plain
NR3: Norw 2D **4** (2D **26**)
St Martins at Oak Wall La. NR3: Norw 1A **4**
St Martin's Cl. NR3: Norw 1A **4** (1C **26**)
St Martin's La. NR3: Norw 2A **4** (2C **26**)
St Martin's Rd. NR3: Norw 1A **4** (1C **26**)
St Marys All. NR3: Norw 2B **4**
St Mary's Cl. NR12: Wrox 3A **42**
NR13: Gt P 6A **20**
NR14: Alp 4H **41**
St Marys Cl. NR10: Hor F 2B **10**
St Marys Gro. NR7: Spro 2H **17**
St Mary's Plain NR3: Norw 2B **4** (2C **26**)
St Mary's Priory
Norwich **6F 27**
St Marys Rd. NR3: Norw 1C **26**
NR14: Por 4D **40**
St Matthews Rd. NR1: Norw 4F **4** (3E **27**)
St Michael at Pleas NR3: Norw 3D **4**
St Michaels Way NR13: B'all 5H **31**
St Michael Ter. *NR1: Norw 3F 27*
(off St Leonards Rd.)
St Mildreds Rd. NR5: Norw 3C **24**
St Miles All. NR3: Norw 2B **4**
St Olaves Rd. NR3: Norw 1D **26**
St Paul's Cl. NR6: Helle 2H **15**
NR10: H'ford 1G **9**
St Paul's Sq. NR3: Norw 1D **4**
St Peter Hungate Church **3C 4**
St Peters Cl. NR4: Cring 3E **35**
St Peters Ct. NR1: Norw 5D **5** (4D **26**)
St Peters Dr. NR9: E'ton 5A **12**
St Peters St. NR2: Norw 4B **4** (3C **26**)
St Peter's Way NR10: Spix 2G **11**
St Philips Rd. NR2: Norw 3A **26**
St Saviours All. NR3: Norw 1C **4**
St Saviours La. NR3: Norw 2C **4** (2D **26**)
Saints Ct. NR1: Norw 6C **5**
St Simon Cl. NR8: Cost 2D **12**
St Simon Ct. NR3: Norw 3D **4**
St Stephens Arc. NR2: Norw 6B **5**
St Stephens Plain *NR1: Norw 6C 5*
(off St Stephens St.)
St Stephens Rd. NR1: Norw 8A **5** (5C **26**)
St Stephens Sq. NR1: Norw 7A **5** (5C **26**)
St Stephens St. NR1: Norw 6B **5** (4C **26**)
St Swithins All. NR2: Norw 3A **4**
St Swithins Rd. NR2: Norw 3A **4** (3C **26**)
St Swithins Ter. *NR2: Norw 3A 4*
(off St Benedicts St.)
St Thomas Dr. NR18: Wym 6D **38**
St Thomas Rd. NR2: Norw 3H **25**
St Vedast St. NR1: Norw 4E **4** (3E **27**)
St Walstan's Cl. NR8: Tav 5G **7**
St Walstans Cl. NR5: New C 6G **13**
St Walstan's Rd. NR8: Tav 4G **7**
St Williams Way NR7: Thor And 1H **27**
Saker Cl. NR7: Thor And 1E **29**
Sale Rd. NR7: Norw 5A **18**
Salhouse Rd. NR7: Norw, Rack, Spro 5H **17**
NR12: Hov 1D **42**
NR12: Wrox 5A **42**
NR13: Lit P 1C **20**
NR13: Rack 1G **19**
Salhouse Rd. Ind. Est. NR7: Spro 5H **17**
Salisbury Rd. NR1: Norw 4G **27**
Salter Av. NR4: Norw 4F **25**
Salvia Cl. NR18: Wym 2G **39**
Salvin Ct. NR5: Norw 2C **24**
Sam Smith Way NR13: Rack 1G **19**
Samson & Hercules Ho. NR3: Norw 3D **4**
Samson Rd. NR6: Helle 3G **15**
Samuel Rd. NR1: Norw 1G **27**
Sandhole La. NR13: Lit P 2B **20**
Sandholme Cl. NR1: Norw 1G **27**
Sandringham Ct. NR2: Norw 8A **5**
Sandringham Rd. NR2: Norw 3A **26**
Sandy La. NR1: Norw 3D **36**
NR4: Norw 2C **36**
NR8: Tav 5F **7**
NR9: E'ton 2A **12**
NR10: H'ford 1F **9**
Santolina Cl. NR5: New C 6C **14**
Sapphire Way NR6: Norw 2A **16**
Saracen Rd. NR6: Helle 1G **15**
Sarah W. Cl. NR2: Norw 7A **5** (5B **26**)
Sarah Williman Cl. NR5: Norw 4D **24**
Saunders Ct. NR1: Norw 3F **27**
Savery Cl. NR5: Norw 3C **24**
Sawmill Cl. NR18: Wym 3C **38**
Sawyer Cres. NR9: Hether 3F **33**
Sawyers Cl. NR5: New C 6H **13**
Saxoncote Av. NR5: Bow 3B **24**
Saxonfields NR14: Por 5C **40**
Sayers St. NR2: Norw 2B **26**
(not continuous)
Scarlet Rd. NR4: Norw 2C **36**
Scarnell Rd. NR5: Norw 3E **25**
Sceptre Cl. NR6: Helle 4H **15**
Scholars Ct. NR3: Norw 2B **4**
School Av. NR7: Thor And 3C **28**
School Cl. NR13: Blof 1G **31**
School La. NR2: Norw 4C **4**
NR7: Spro 3E **17**
NR7: Thor And 3A **28**
NR9: Lit Mel 1F **33**
NR10: H'ford 2G **9**
School Rd. NR8: Dray 4A **8**
NR13: Blof, Lit P 4C **20**
School Ter. NR14: Tro 1G **37**
Scoles Grn. NR1: Norw 5D **5**
Scotch Hill Rd. NR8: Tav 4E **7**
Scott Cl. NR7: Spro 3B **18**
Scott Rd. NR1: Norw 4G **27**
Scott's Ct. NR1: Norw 6C **5**
Scott's Yd. NR1: Norw 7D **5**
Seabrook Ct. NR5: Bow 2B **24**
Seaforth Dr. NR8: Tav 5H **7**
Seaman Twr. NR3: Norw 5H **15**
The Seates NR8: Thor Mar 3G **7**
Sebald Cres. NR14: Por 4B **40**
Sebald Ho. *NR2: Norw 5G 25*
(off Kinghorn Rd.)
Sedman Wlk. *NR5: Bow 1B 24*
(off Rawley Rd.)
Sego Va. NR8: Tav 5H **7**
Seppings Way NR13: Thor E 4E **19**
Serotine Av. NR9: Hether 4C **32**
Seton Rd. NR8: Tav 4H **7**
Sewell Barn Theatre **5D 16**
Sewell Ct. NR6: Old C 6E **11**
Sewell Pk. Sports Cen. **5D 16**
Sewell Rd. NR3: Norw 5D **16**
Shack La. NR13: Blof 1E **31**
Shakespeare Way NR8: Tav 5G **7**
Sheep Mdw. Cl. NR5: New C 6A **14**
Sheffield Rd. NR18: Wym 2D **38**
Shelduck Way NR7: Spro 3A **18**
Shelley Dr. NR8: Tav 5G **7**
Shepherd Cl. NR5: Norw 4E **25**
Shepherd Purse Way NR5: Bow 2C **24**
Shepherds Cl. NR10: H'ford 2F **9**
Shepherd Way NR8: Thor Mar 3H **7**
Sherbourne Pl. NR1: Norw 7E **5** (4E **27**)
Sheridan Cl. NR8: Dray 5A **8**
Sherwell Rd. NR6: Helle 1F **15**
Sherwood Rd. NR4: Norw 2B **36**
Sherwyn Ho. *NR3: Norw 2B 4*
(off Winterton La.)
Shetland Pl. NR2: Norw 2B **26**
Shibleys Ct. NR2: Norw 4A **4**
Shillgate Way NR8: Thor Mar 3E **7**
Shillito Rd. NR13: Blof 1H **31**
Shipfield NR3: Norw 5E **17**
Shipstone Rd. NR3: Norw 1C **26**
Shire Hall, Royal Norfolk Regimental Mus.
4D 4 (3D 26)
The Shires NR8: Thor Mar 3A **8**
Shoemaker Ct. NR9: Hether 3F **33**
Shooters Cl. NR8: Tav 4G **7**
Shop La. NR9: Hether 4F **33**
Shorncliffe Av. NR3: Norw 6A **16**
Shorncliffe Cl. NR3: Norw 6B **16**
Shotesham Rd. NR14: Por 6B **40**
Showmens Guild Cvn. Site 5E **17**
Shreeve Rd. NR13: Blof 1H **31**
The Shrublands *NR2: Norw 3A 26*
(off W. Pottergate)
NR10: H'ford 1F **9**
Sidell Cl. NR4: Cring 4D **34**
Sidestrand NR1: Norw 7F **5**
The Sidings NR1: Norw 4H **27**
Sidney Rd. NR8: Cost 3A **14**
Sienna M. NR1: Norw 2G **27**
Sigismund Rd. NR1: Norw 8B **5** (6C **26**)
Silfield Av. NR18: Wym 6E **39**
Silfield Cres. NR18: Wym 6E **39**
Silfield Rd. NR18: Silf, Wym 6D **38**
Silkfields NR3: Norw 2A **4** (2C **26**)
Silk Mill Rd. NR6: Helle 3A **16**
Silver Birch Ct. NR3: Norw 5H **15**
Silver Haven *NR3: Norw 1E 27*
(off Mousehold Av.)
Silver Rd. NR3: Norw 1E **4** (6E **17**)
Silver St. NR3: Norw 1D **4** (1D **26**)
SILVER TRIANGLE 1E **27**
Silvo Rd. NR8: Cost 1D **12**
Simpson Way NR18: Wym 1G **39**
Singer Ct. *NR3: Norw 2C 4*
(off Calvert St.)
Sir Alfred Munning's Rd.
NR5: New C 4D **12**
NR8: Cost 4D **12**
Sir Thomas Beevor Cl. NR18: Wym 3D **38**
Siskin Cl. NR8: Cost 2D **12**
Sixteen Acre Rd. NR2: Norw 4G **25**
Skedge Way NR13: Blof 4E **21**
Skelton Rd. NR7: Norw 1H **27**
Skinners La. NR12: Wrox 5A **42**
Skipping Block Row NR18: Wym 1H **39**
Skippon Way NR7: Thor And 6E **19**
Skoner Rd. NR5: Bow 1C **24**
Skye Cl. NR5: Bow 1B **24**
Slade La. NR14: Fram P, Yelv 1G **41**
Sleaford Grn. NR3: Norw 5B **16**
Smeat St. NR5: Bow 2C **24**
Smee La. NR13: Gt P 1G **29**, 1A **30**
(not continuous)
Smithdale Rd. NR5: New C 6C **14**
Smithfield Rd. NR1: Norw 6D **26**
Smithson Cl. NR18: Wym 3D **38**
Smock Mill Loke NR18: Wym 3C **38**
Snowberry Cl. NR8: Tav 3E **7**
Snowdrop St. NR18: Wym 2G **39**
Softley Dr. NR4: Cring 1D **34**
Solario Rd. NR8: Cost 2D **12**
Sole Cl. NR10: H'ford 2G **9**
Soleme Rd. NR3: Norw 5A **16**
Somerleyton Gdns. NR2: Norw 4B **26**
Somerleyton St. NR2: Norw 4B **26**
Somerset Way NR8: Tav 4D **6**
Somme Cl. NR18: Wym 2G **39**
Sonya Ter. NR1: Norw 2G **27**
Sorrel Ho. NR5: Bow 1B **24**
Sotherton Rd. NR4: Norw 6G **25**
Southalls Way NR3: Norw 6E **17**
Southall Way NR7: Spro 3C **18**
The South Asia Collection **4A 4 (3C 26)**
South Av. NR7: Thor And 4B **28**
South Cft. NR9: Hether 5C **32**
Southerwood NR6: Norw 2C **16**
Southfield La. NR13: W'wick 1E **21**
Sth. Gage Cl. NR7: Spro 3A **18**
Southgate La. NR1: Norw 8E **5** (5E **27**)
Sth. Hill Cl. NR7: Thor And 1C **28**
Sth. Hill Rd. NR7: Thor And 6C **18**
South Pk. Av. NR4: Norw 6F **25**
South Wlk. NR13: Thor E 5E **19**
Southwell Rd. NR1: Norw 8B **5** (5C **26**)
NR10: Hor F 2H **9**
Sth. Wood Dr. NR14: Caist E 2A **40**
Sovereign Ho. NR3: Norw 1C **4**
Sovereign Way NR3: Norw 1C **4**
Sparhawk Av. NR7: Spro 3H **17**
Sparhawk Cl. NR7: Spro 3H **17**
Spar Rd. NR6: Norw 2B **16**
Sparrows Hill NR9: Baw 4C **22**
Speedwell Rd. NR18: Wym 4E **39**
Speedwell Way NR5: Bow 4A **24**
Speke St. NR2: Norw 2H **25**
Spelman Rd. NR2: Norw 5H **25**
Spencer Cl. NR13: Lit P 2C **20**
Spencer Rd. NR6: Norw 2B **16**
Spencer St. NR3: Norw 1D **26**
Spindle Cl. NR18: Wym 4E **39**
Spindle Rd. NR6: Norw 3C **16**
Spink's La. NR18: Wym 2G **39**
Spinney Cl. NR7: Thor And 1C **28**
Spinney Rd. NR7: Thor And 1B **28**
SPIRE NORWICH HOSPITAL **4B 24**
Spitalfields NR1: Norw 2F **27**
Spitfire Rd. NR6: Norw 1B **16**
SPIXWORTH 2H **11**
Spixworth Rd. NR6: Old C 4D **16**
NR10: Hor F 2A **10**
Sportspark
Sports Cen. & Swimming Pool **5E 25**
Springbank NR1: Norw 1D **36**
Springdale Cres. NR13: B'all 3D **30**
Springdale Rd. NR13: B'all 3D **30**
Springfield Rd. NR7: Norw 5A **18**
NR8: Tav 4F **7**
Springfields NR14: Por 4C **40**
Springwood NR8: Thor Mar 4H **7**
SPROWSTON 3G **17**
Sprowston Manor Golf Course **1B 18**

Sprowston Park & Ride 1A 18
Sprowston Retail Pk. 5H 17
Sprowston Rd. NR3: Norw 6D 16
Spruce Cres. NR14: Por 4C 40
Spur Ind. Est. NR18: Wym 4D 38
Spur La. NR14: Fram E 2C 40
Spynke Rd. NR3: Norw 4A 16
The Square NR4: Norw 5D 24
NR8: Thor Mar 3H 7
Squire's Haven NR1: Norw 4F 27
Stacy Rd. NR3: Norw 1D 26
Stafford Av. NR5: New C 6A 14
Stafford St. NR2: Norw 3H 25
Staithe La. NR13: B'all 4F 31
Staitheway Rd. NR12: Wrox 3B 42
Stalham Rd. NR12: Hov 2C 42
Stalham Rd. Ind. Est. NR12: Hov 1D 42
Stamp Office Yd. NR3: Norw 3C 4
Standley Ct. NR18: Wym 4C 38
Stanfield Rd. NR18: Wym 5G 39
Stanford Ct. NR5: Norw 3F 25
Stanford Cres. NR13: Lit P 2C 20
Stanley Av. NR7: Norw 4H 27
Stanley Rd. NR13: B'all 5G 31
Stanleys La. NR18: Wym 6D 38
Stanmore Cl. NR7: Thor And 3B 28
Stanmore Rd. NR7: Thor And 3B 28
Stannard Ct. NR7: Thor And 4A 28
Stannard Pl. NR3: Norw 2C 4
Stannard Rd. NR4: Norw 4G 25
Stan Petersen Cl. NR1: Norw 3F 27
Starling Ct. NR8: Cost 2D 12
Starling Rd. NR3: Norw 1C 26
Starling St. NR8: Cost 2E 13
Statham Cl. NR4: Norw 1A 36
Station App. NR1: Norw 5F 5 (4E 27)
NR18: Wym 6D 38
Station Cotts. NR9: Hether 6H 33
Station Halt NR13: B'all 4C 30
Station La. NR9: Hether 4G 33
(not continuous)
Station New Rd. NR13: B'all 4G 31
Station Rd. NR8: Dray 6A 8
NR12: Hov 2B 42
NR13: B'all 4F 31
NR18: Wym 5D 38
Staunford Ct. NR2: Norw 1A 26
Stearn Cl. NR9: E'ton 5A 12
Steepgreen Cl. NR1: Norw 1H 27
Steeple Chase NR8: Thor Mar 3A 8
Stepping La. NR1: Norw 5D 5 (4D 26)
The Steps NR2: Norw 3A 26
Stevenson Rd. NR5: Norw 2C 24
NR12: Wrox 5A 42
Steward Cl. NR18: Wym 3E 39
Steward St. NR3: Norw 1D 4 (1D 26)
Stile La. NR18: Wym 3C 38
Stillington Cl. NR7: Spro 4G 17
Stimpson Loke NR8: Cost 4B 14
Stirling Cl. NR8: Thor Mar 2A 8
Stirling Rd. NR6: Norw 1B 16
Stocks Hill NR9: Baw 3E 23
Stocks La. NR13: Blof 2G 31
Stockwell Rd. NR8: Cost 2D 12
Stoke Rd. NR1: Arm 2E 37
NR14: Arm 2E 37
NR14: Por 3B 40
Stone Breck NR5: New C 5H 13
Stone Ho. Cl. NR3: Norw 5C 16
Stonehouse Rd. NR7: Spro 3G 17
Stonemasons Ct. NR3: Norw 1B 4
Stone Rd. NR3: Norw 6B 16
NR13: Stru 6H 31
Stony Gro. NR8: Cost 2C 12
Stracey Rd. NR1: Norw 4F 27
Strangers Ct. NR2: Norw 4B 4 (3C 26)
Strangers' Hall 4B 4
Stratford Cl. NR1: Norw 1E 37
Stratford Cres. NR4: Cring 2D 34
Stratford Dr. NR1: Norw 1D 36
Strayground La. NR18: Wym 6C 38
The Street NR8: Cost 3H 13
NR8: R'land 4A 6
NR8: Tav 4E 7
NR13: B'all 3E 31
NR13: Blof 1G 31
NR14: Fram E, Por 3C 40
NR14: Fram P 1D 40
NR14: Surl 6D 30
NR14: Tro 1G 37
Strumpshaw Rd. NR13: B'all 4G 31
Stuart Cl. NR9: Hether 4D 32
Stuart Ct. NR1: Norw 4F 4
Stuart Gdns. NR1: Norw 4E 4 (3E 27)
Stuart Rd. NR1: Norw 8F 5 (5E 27)
Stylman Rd. NR5: Bow 2B 24
Suckling Av. NR3: Norw 4A 16
Suckling La. NR9: Hether 6E 33
NR14: Fram P 1E 41
Suffield Cl. NR4: Cring 4E 35
Suffield Ct. NR1: Norw 2E 4 (2E 27)
NR3: Norw 5C 16
Suffolk Rd. NR4: Norw 5D 24
Suffolk Sq. NR2: Norw 4B 26
Suffolk Ter. NR4: Norw 6D 24
Suffolk Wlk. NR4: Norw 6E 25
Sukey Way NR5: Bow 3A 24
Summer Cl. NR14: Fram E 3D 40
Summer Dr. NR12: Hov 1C 42
Sumpter Rd. NR4: Norw 6F 25
Suncroft NR1: Norw 1E 37
Sunderland Cl. NR6: Norw 1B 16
Sun La. NR3: Norw 6C 16
Sunningdale NR4: Norw 1H 35
Sunny Cl. NR5: New C 6C 14
Sunny Ct. NR5: New C 6C 14
Sunny Gro. NR5: New C 6C 14
Sunny Hill NR1: Norw 1D 36
Sunnyside Av. NR14: Por 4C 40
Supple Cl. NR1: Norw 2H 27
Surlingham Church Marsh Nature Reserve 6B 30
Surrey Cl. NR7: Spro 2H 17
Surrey Gro. NR1: Norw 7C 5 (4D 26)
Surrey St. NR1: Norw 6C 5 (4D 26)
Sursham Av. NR6: Spro 3E 17
Sussex St. NR3: Norw 1A 4 (2C 26)
Suters Dr. NR8: Thor Mar 3H 7
Sutherland Av. NR6: Helle 3H 15
Suton La. NR18: Suton 6B 38
Sutton Ct. NR6: Helle 2E 15
Sutton Dr. NR18: Wym 2F 39
Sutton Gdns. NR18: Wym 2F 39
Swafield St. NR5: Bow 2A 24
The Swale NR5: Bow 3A 24
Swallow Dr. NR18: Wym 6F 39
Swallow Tail Cl. NR5: Bow 4A 24
Swan La. NR2: Norw 4C 4
NR7: Spro 2A 18
Swan Plain NR10: Hor F 2A 10
Swansea Rd. NR2: Norw 4A 26
Swansgate NR6: Old C 1D 16
Swan St. NR10: Hor F 2A 10
Swanton Rd. NR2: Norw 1H 25
Swatman Gro. NR18: Wym 1G 39
Sweet Briar Ind. Est. NR3: Norw 6G 15
Sweetbriar La. NR6: Spro 6G 11
Sweet Briar Retail Pk. 5G 15
Sweet Briar Rd. NR6: Norw 6G 15
Swift Ct. NR3: Norw 2A 4
Swinbourne Cl. NR6: Norw 4C 16
Swindells Cl. NR5: New C 5B 14
Sycamore Av. NR18: Wym 3E 39
Sycamore Ct. NR4: Cring 2D 34
Sycamore Cres. NR2: Norw 2G 25
Sydney Cl. NR10: Spix 2G 11
Sydney Rd. NR10: Spix 2F 11
Sylvan Cl. NR6: Helle 1F 15
Sylvan Way NR8: Tav 5H 7
NR13: Blof 3F 21
Symonds Cl. NR13: Blof 1H 31
Sywell Cl. NR6: Old C 1E 17

T

Tagg Way NR13: Rack 1F 19
Tailor Pl. NR9: Hether 3E 33
Tailors Row NR3: Norw 6A 16
Talbot Cl. NR18: Wym 3D 38
Talbot Sq. NR3: Norw 1A 4 (2C 26)
Taleworth Cl. NR5: Bow 2B 24
Tamarind M. NR4: Norw 2F 35
Tanager Cl. NR3: Norw 4C 16
Tanners Ct. NR3: Norw 1B 26
Tansy Cl. NR6: Norw 3C 16
TAVERHAM 4G 7
Taverham Chase NR8: Tav 5G 7
Taverham La. NR8: Cost 5E 7
TAVERHAM PARK 4E 7
Taverham Pk. Av. NR8: Tav 5D 6
Taverham Rd. NR8: Dray, Tav 5F 7
Taverners Sq. NR3: Norw 1E 4
Taylor Av. NR4: Cring 4D 34
Taylor Rd. NR5: Norw 3D 24
Taylor's Ct. *NR3: Norw* 6D 16
(off Magdalen Rd.)
Taylor's La. NR6: Norw, Old C 1C 16
Taylors Sq. NR14: Por 4B 40
Taylor Way NR13: Lit P 5C 20
Teal Dr. NR8: Cost 2E 13
Telegraph La. E. NR1: Norw 3F 27
Telegraph La. W. NR1: Norw 3F 27
Telford Cl. NR3: Norw 6G 15
Templemere NR3: Norw 5F 17
Temple Rd. NR3: Norw 6D 16
Ten Bell Ct. NR2: Norw 3A 4 (3B 26)
Ten Bell La. NR2: Norw 4A 4 (3C 26)
Tenison Ct. *NR4: Norw* 2F 35
(off Eaton St.)
Terence Av. NR7: Spro 3F 17
The Terrace NR1: Norw 3F 27
Terrace Wlk. NR1: Norw 8D 5
Tesmonde Cl. NR5: Bow 2H 23
Thacker Way NR5: Bow 3A 24
Thatched Pavilion Ct. NR1: Norw 6E 27
Theatre Royal 5B 5 (4C 26)
Theatre St. NR2: Norw 5A 5 (4C 26)
Theobald Rd. NR1: Norw 4C 36
The Thicket NR8: Thor Mar 3H 7
Thickthorn Park & Ride 4B 34
Thirlmere NR9: Hether 4E 33
Thistle Cl. NR5: Bow 4A 24
Thistledown Rd. NR10: H'ford 2F 9
Thomas Glover Ct. NR3: Norw 5B 16
Thomas Tawell Ho. NR3: Norw 1C 4
Thomas Vere Rd. NR7: Thor And 2C 28
Thomas Way NR10: H'ford 1G 9
Thomas Wyatt Cl. NR2: Norw 8A 5 (5C 26)
Thompson Rd. NR7: Thor And 1C 28
Thompsons Yd. NR3: Norw 2D 4 (2D 26)
Thor Cl. NR7: Thor And 2B 28
Thor Loke NR7: Thor And 2B 28
Thornfield Way NR7: Norw 1A 28
Thornham Cl. NR7: Spro 5G 17
Thornham Dr. NR7: Spro 5G 17
Thornham Rd. NR7: Spro 5G 17
Thorn La. NR1: Norw 6D 5 (4D 26)
Thoroughfare Yd. NR3: Norw 2C 4
Thorpe Av. NR7: Thor And 1B 28
Thorpe Cl. NR7: Thor And 2C 28
THORPE END 4F 19
Thorpe Hall Cl. NR7: Thor And 4H 27
THORPE HAMLET 3F 27
Thorpe Hgts. NR1: Norw 4F 4
THORPE MARRIOTT 3H 7
Thorpe M. NR7: Thor And 4C 28
Thorpe Rd. NR1: Norw 5F 5 (4E 27)
THORPE ST ANDREW 1B 28
Thor Rd. NR7: Thor And 2B 28
Three Acre Cl. NR12: Hov 1B 42
Three Cnr. Dr. NR6: Old C 1E 17
Three King La. NR2: Norw 4A 4 (3C 26)
Three Mile La. NR5: New C 6A 14
Three Score Rd. NR5: Bow 3A 24
Three Tuns Ct. NR1: Norw 5D 5
Throckmorton Yd. NR3: Norw 1C 4 (1D 26)
Thunder La. NR7: Thor And 6B 18
Thurlby Rd. NR5: Bow 1H 23
Thurling Loke NR7: Norw 6B 18
Thurling Plain NR7: Norw 6B 18
Thurlow Cl. NR5: Bow 1H 23
Thurston Cl. NR5: Bow 1A 24
Tiercel Av. NR7: Spro 3H 17
Tillett Cl. NR3: Norw 5D 16
Tillett Rd. NR3: Norw 5D 16
Tillett Rd. E. NR3: Norw 5D 16
Tills Cl. NR6: Spro 3E 17
Tills Rd. NR6: Spro 2E 17
Timberhill NR1: Norw 5C 5 (4D 26)
Timothy Cl. NR1: Norw 1G 27
Tinker's La. NR13: Stru 6H 31
Tipperary Av. NR18: Wym 2G 39
Tippett Cl. NR5: Bow 3A 24
Tizzick Cl. NR5: Bow 4A 24
Toad La. NR13: Gt P 5H 19
Todd La. NR2: Norw 6B 26
Toftes Pl. NR5: Bow 1C 24
Tollgate Way NR5: Bow 4B 24
Tollhouse Rd. NR5: Norw 2F 25
Tolwin Wlk. NR3: Norw 6E 17
Tolye Rd. NR5: Bow 2A 24
Tombland NR3: Norw 3D 4 (3D 26)
Tombland All. NR3: Norw 3D 4
Tortoiseshell Way NR18: Wym 4F 39
Tottington Cl. NR5: Bow 1A 24
Tower Cl. NR8: Cost 3F 13
Tower Hill NR7: Thor And 3A 28
NR8: Cost 3F 13
Tower Hill Pk. NR8: Cost 3F 13
The Towers NR1: Norw 8F 5
Town Cl. Rd. NR2: Norw 6B 26
Town Grn. NR18: Wym 4C 38
Townhouse Rd. NR8: Cost 3H 13
Townsend Rd. NR4: Norw 2B 36
Townshend Ct. NR1: Norw 8B 5 (6D 26)
Tracey Rd. NR7: Thor And 6B 18
Trafalgar Sq. NR14: Por 5C 40
Trafalgar St. NR1: Norw 8C 5 (5D 26)
Trafford Rd. NR1: Norw 8B 5 (5C 26)
Trafford Wlk. NR12: Wrox 5A 42
Trafford Way NR10: Spix 2H 11

Traverse St. NR3: Norw .6C **16**
Treeview Ct. NR3: Norw .1E **27**
Tremaine Cl. NR6: Lwr H .6E **15**
Trendall Rd. NR7: Spro .3H **17**
Trident Dr. NR1: Norw .2F **27**
Trilithon Cl. NR6: Lwr H .5E **15**
Trimming Wlk. NR8: Tav .5H **7**
Trinity St. NR2: Norw .4B **26**
Triumph Ct. NR5: New C .6G **13**
Trix Rd. NR2: Norw .5B **26**
Trory St. NR2: Norw .4B **26**
Troutbeck NR9: Hether .4E **33**
Trowse By-Pass NR14: Tro .2F **37**
TROWSE MILLGATE .1F 37
TROWSE NEWTON .1G 37
Trowse Sports Hall .1G 37
Truman Cl. NR5: Norw .4D **24**
Tubby Dr. NR14: Por .4B **40**
TUCKSWOOD .2B 36
Tuckswood Cen. NR4: Norw .2B **36**
Tuckswood La. NR4: Norw .1B **36**
Tudor Ct. NR1: Norw .8D **5** (5D **26**)
Tulip Gdns. NR4: Cring .3D **34**
Tulip Tree Dr. NR14: Fram E .3C **40**
Tungate Cres. NR4: Cring .4E **35**
Tunstall Cl. NR5: Bow .2B **24**
Tunstead La. NR12: Hov .1C **42**
Tunstead Rd. NR12: Hov .2B **42**
Turnberry NR4: Norw .2H **35**
Turner Cl. NR18: Wym .3F **39**
Turner Rd. NR2: Norw .2H **25**
Turners Sq. NR1: Norw .5D **5**
Turnham Grn. NR7: Thor And .1E **29**
Turnpike Cl. NR6: Lwr H .5G **15**
Tusser Rd. NR8: Tav .5H **7**
Tusting Cl. NR7: Spro .3E **17**
Tuttles La. E. NR18: Wym .2D **38**
Tuttles La. W. NR18: Wym .2A **38**
Twelve Acre Rd. NR2: Norw .5G **25**
Twickenham Rd. NR6: Norw .2A **16**
Two Brewers Yd. NR3: Norw .1C **4**
Two Saints Cl. NR12: Hov .1C **42**

U

Ullswater Dr. NR9: Hether .4E **33**
Unicorn Yd. NR3: Norw .2A **4** (2C **26**)
Union Pl. NR4: Norw .5E **25**
Union St. NR2: Norw .6A **5** (5B **26**)
University Dr. NR4: Norw .4D **24**
University of East Anglia
Bob Champion Research & Education Building .6A **24**
Main Campus .6D **24**
Quadram Institute .6A **24**
University Plain NR4: Norw .5E **25**
University Technical College Norfolk .4B **36**
UNIVERSITY VILLAGE .4D 24
Unthank Rd. NR2: Norw .6H **25**
NR4: Norw .1F **35**
Upgate NR14: Por .4E **41**
Uphalle NR8: Thor Mar .4G **7**
Uplands Ct. NR4: Norw .6H **25**
Up. Breckland Rd. NR5: New C .6A **14**
Upper Cl. NR1: Norw .3D **4** (3D **26**)
Up. Goat La. NR2: Norw .4B **4** (3C **26**)
Up. Green La. NR3: Norw .1C **4** (2D **26**)
UPPER HELLESDON .4A 16
Up. King St. NR3: Norw .4D **4** (3D **26**)
Up. St Giles St. NR2: Norw .4A **4** (3B **26**)
Up. Stafford Av. NR5: New C .6A **14**
UPPER STOKE .4A 40
Upton Cl. NR4: Norw .1H **35**
Upton Rd. NR4: Norw .6H **25**
Utting Cl. NR14: Por .4B **40**

V

Vale Cl. NR10: H'ford .2G **9**
Vale Grn. NR3: Norw .6H **15**
Valentine St. NR2: Norw .3B **26**
The Valley Dr. NR1: Norw .6G **17**
Valley Rd. NR5: New C .6C **14**
Valleyside NR18: Wym .5D **38**
Valley Side Rd. NR1: Norw .1H **27**
Valley Vw. Cres. NR5: New C .6A **14**
Valpy Av. NR3: Norw .6H **15**
Vancouver Rd. NR7: Norw .1H **27**
Vane Cl. NR7: Thor And .2E **29**
Vanguard Chase NR5: New C .6G **13**
Vanguard Ct. NR2: Norw .1A **26**
Varvel Av. NR7: Spro .3H **17**
Varvel Cl. NR7: Spro .4H **17**
NR13: B'all .2D **30**
Vauxhall St. NR2: Norw .5A **5** (4B **26**)
Vawdrey Rd. NR8: Dray .4A **8**
Venables Cl. NR1: Norw .2G **27**
Vera Cl. NR13: Rack .2G **19**
Vera Rd. NR6: Helle .3A **16**
NR13: Rack .1G **19**
Verbena Dr. NR18: Wym .2F **39**
Verbena Rd. NR4: Cring .2C **34**
Vetch Cl. NR18: Wym .4E **39**
Vicarage Cl. NR8: Cost .2A **14**
Vicarage Ct. NR7: Spro .4F **17**
Vicarage Rd. NR3: Norw .6B **16**
Vicar St. NR18: Wym .4C **38**
Victoria Cl. NR8: Tav .5F **7**
Victoria Rd. NR8: Tav .5F **7**
Victoria St. NR1: Norw .7B **5** (5C **26**)
Victoria Way NR5: New C .5C **14**
Victory Av. NR14: Por .5B **40**
Victory Gro. NR5: New C .6F **13**
Victory Ho. NR4: Norw .5E **25**
Vienna Apts. NR7: Thor And .4H **27**
Village Cl. NR5: Norw .4D **24**
Villavon Way NR13: Blof .3G **21**
Vimy Dr. NR18: Wym .4E **39**
Vimy Ridge NR18: Wym .4E **39**
Vincent Rd. NR1: Norw .2F **27**
Viola Cl. NR4: Cring .3D **34**
Violet Elvin Ct. NR4: Norw .4G **25**
Violet Rd. NR3: Norw .6E **17**
Virginia Cl. NR7: Spro .3H **17**
Vue Cinema .5C 5 (4D 26)
Vulcan Cl. NR9: Hether .4D **32**
Vulcan Rd. Ind. Est. NR6: Norw .2B **16**
Vulcan Rd. Nth. NR6: Norw .2B **16**
Vulcan Rd. Sth. NR6: Helle .3B **16**

W

Waddington Ct. NR2: Norw .2A **26**
Waddington St. NR2: Norw .2A **26**
Wades Yd. NR2: Norw .4D **4**
Waggon & Horses La. NR3: Norw .3C **4** (3D **26**)
Wakefield Rd. NR5: Norw .3D **24**
Wakehurst Cl. NR4: Norw .2G **35**
Walcot Cl. NR5: Bow .2C **24**
Waldeck Rd. NR4: Norw .6H **25**
Waldegrave NR5: Bow .1B **24**
Waldemar Av. NR6: Helle .2A **16**
Waldemar Pk. NR6: Helle .2A **16**
Wales Sq. NR1: Norw .4E **4** (3E **27**)
Waller Cl. NR7: Thor And .6E **19**
Wall La. NR3: Norw .1D **26**
Wall Rd. NR3: Norw .5D **16**
Walnut Cl. NR8: Thor Mar .3G **7**
The Walnuts NR4: Norw .1A **36**
Walnut Tree Dr. NR14: Fram E .2C **40**
Walpole Gdns. NR2: Norw .5A **5**
Walpole St. NR2: Norw .5A **5** (4B **26**)
Walsingham Dr. NR8: Thor Mar .2H **7**
Walters Rd. NR8: Tav .5G **7**
Walton Rd. NR1: Norw .6D **26**
Waring Rd. NR5: Norw .3C **24**
Warman's Cl. NR9: Baw .3E **23**
War Memorial Cotts. NR7: Spro .5G **17**
Warminger Ct. NR1: Norw .6D **5** (4D **26**)
Warnett Rd. NR7: Norw .6A **18**
The Warren NR6: Old C .3D **16**
NR9: Baw .3E **23**
NR10: Hor F .1A **10**
Warren Av. NR6: Helle .2H **15**
Warren Cl. NR6: Old C .3D **16**
NR10: H'ford .2F **9**
Warrenwood Ct. NR3: Norw .4H **15**
Warwick Dr. NR18: Wym .2D **38**
Warwick St. NR2: Norw .4A **26**
Wash La. NR14: Por .5D **40**
The Waterfront .6E 5
Watergate .4F 4 (3E 27)
The Watering NR3: Norw .1B **26**
Water La. NR3: Norw .3B **4** (3D **26**)
NR4: Cring .2D **34**
NR7: Thor And .4A **28**
NR13: Gt P, Lit P .6A **20**
WATERLOO .2B 10
Waterloo Cl. NR10: Hor F .2A **10**
Waterloo Pk. Av. NR3: Norw .6B **16**
Waterloo Pk. Cl. NR3: Norw .6B **16**
Waterloo Rd. NR3: Norw .1C **26**
NR10: Hor F .2B **10**
Waterman Rd. NR2: Norw .2G **25**
Watermans Yd. NR2: Norw .3A **4**
The Watermill NR14: Tro .1F **37**
The Waterside NR6: Helle .4E **15**
Waterside NR1: Norw .2F **4** (2E **27**)
Waterworks Rd. NR2: Norw .2H **25**
Watkin Rd. NR4: Norw .3B **36**
Watling Rd. NR7: Norw .5A **18**
Watlings Ct. NR2: Norw .4A **4**
Watson Gro. NR2: Norw .1A **26**
Watton Rd. NR4: Coln .5E **23**
NR9: Baw, Gt Mel, Lit Mel .5A **22**
Watts Ct. NR2: Norw .5A **5**
Waveney Cl. NR12: Hov .1D **42**
Waveney Dr. NR2: Norw .6C **26**
NR12: Hov .2C **42**
Waveney Rd. NR4: Norw .5E **25**
Waverley Rd. NR4: Norw .1H **35**
Waxwing Way NR8: Cost .2E **13**
Weatherby Rd. NR5: Bow .1G **23**
Weaver Cres. NR9: Hether .3F **33**
Weavers Cl. NR10: Hor F .2A **10**
Weavers La. NR2: Norw .5B **5**
Webb Dr. NR13: Rack .1G **19**
Webdell Ct. NR1: Norw .2E **37**
Webster Cl. NR5: Bow .1C **24**
Wellesley Av. Nth. NR1: Norw .2G **27**
Wellesley Av. Sth. NR1: Norw .3G **27**
Wellesley Cl. NR14: Por .5C **40**
Wellington Grn. NR2: Norw .3A **4**
Wellington La. NR2: Norw .3A **4** (3B **26**)
Wellington Rd. NR2: Norw .3A **26**
Well Loke NR3: Norw .4A **16**
Welsford Rd. NR4: Norw .2A **36**
Wendene NR5: Bow .2A **24**
Wenman Ct. NR5: Bow .1A **24**
Wensum Cres. NR6: Helle .4E **15**
Wensum Dr. NR2: Norw .6C **26**
Wensum Mdws. Rd. NR6: Helle .3E **15**
Wensum St. NR3: Norw .3D **4** (3D **26**)
Wensum Valley Cl. NR6: Helle .3E **15**
Wensum Valley Golf Course .3D 6
Wensum Wlk. NR8: Thor Mar .2A **8**
Wentworth Grn. NR4: Norw .1G **35**
Wessex St. NR2: Norw .7A **5** (4B **26**) (not continuous)
Westacre Dr. NR6: Old C .6D **10**
West Cl. NR5: New C .5B **14**
West Cft. NR9: Hether .5C **32**
WEST EARLHAM .3D 24
West End NR8: Cost .2F **13**
W. End Av. NR8: Cost .2F **13**
NR13: B'all .3C **30**
W. End St. NR2: Norw .2A **26**
Western Av. NR7: Thor And .3B **28**
Westfield Rd. NR13: B'all .3F **31**
Westfield Vw. NR4: Norw .2F **35**
West Ga. NR18: Wym .4C **38**
Westgate NR6: Helle .2G **15**
Westgate Cl. NR2: Norw .5H **25**
Westgate Ct. NR18: Wym .4C **38**
Westgate Gdns. NR18: Suton .6B **38**
WEST GREEN .6B 40
West La. NR10: Hor F .3H **9**
NR13: B'all .4B **30**
Westlegate NR1: Norw .6C **5** (4D **26**)
Weston Cl. NR13: Blof .3F **21**
Weston Ct. NR6: Spro .1E **17**
Weston Rd. NR3: Norw .4B **16**
NR6: Norw .4B **16**
NR8: R'land .4A **6**
NR9: E'ton .2A **12**
Weston Wood Cl. NR7: Thor And .3B **28**
Weston Wood Rd. NR7: Thor And .3A **28**
West Pde. NR2: Norw .3A **26**
WEST PORINGLAND .6B 40
West Pottergate NR2: Norw .3B **26**
West Rd. NR5: New C .5B **14**
West Vw. NR14: Por .6C **40**
West Vw. Rd. NR13: Blof .1G **31**
Westwick St. NR2: Norw .2A **4** (3C **26**)
West Wing NR7: Thor And .3E **29**
Westwood Dr. NR6: Helle .1E **15**
Westwood Gdns. NR18: Wym .2B **38**
Westwood Ho. NR2: Norw .3H **25**
Whartons Ct. NR18: Wym .5C **38**
Wharton's La. NR18: Wym .6C **38**
Wheatacre Cl. NR10: H'ford .2F **9**
Wheat Flds. NR8: Thor Mar .3A **8**
Wheatley Rd. NR2: Norw .2G **25**
Wheeler Cres. NR9: E'ton .5A **12**
Wheeler Rd. NR3: Norw .6H **15**
Wheel Rd. NR14: Alp .5G **41**
Wherry Rd. NR1: Norw .6E **5** (4E **27**)
Whiffler Rd. NR3: Norw .4H **15**
Whiskerd Way NR8: Cost .2E **13**
Whistlefish Ct. NR5: Norw .2F **25**
Whitebeam Ct. NR5: Norw .2E **25**
White Farm La. NR7: Thor And .3H **27**
Whitefriars NR3: Norw .1D **4** (2D **26**)
White Gates NR5: New C .6H **13**
Whitegates Cl. NR9: Hether .5D **32**
Whitehall Rd. NR2: Norw .4A **26**
White Horse La. NR14: Arm, Tro .3E **37**
White Horse M. NR14: Tro .1G **37**

Whitehorse St. NR18: Wym 5C **38**
White Ho. Ct. NR3: Norw 4B **16**
White Ho. Gdns. NR14: Por 4E **41**
White Lion St. NR2: Norw 5C **5** (4D **26**)
White Lodge Bus. Est. NR4: Norw 3C **36**
White Rose Cl. NR5: Norw 1E **25**
White Swan Wlk. NR2: Norw 1A **26**
Whitethorn Cl. NR6: Norw 2C **16**
White Woman La. NR6: Old C, Spro 1E **17**
Whiting Rd. NR4: Norw 2C **36**
Whitley Cl. NR6: Norw 1B **16**
WHITLINGHAM 5D 28
Whitlingham Adventure **5H 27**
Whitlingham Country Pk. **5H 27**
Whitlingham Country Pk. Vis. Cen. **5H 27**
Whitlingham Hall NR14: Tro 1H **37**
Whitlingham La. NR7: Thor And 4C **28**
NR14: Tro 1G **37**
Whitwell Rd. NR1: Norw 2F **27**
Whitworth Ct. NR6: Norw 1B **16**
Wiffens Loke NR9: Hether 4D **32**
Wilberforce Rd. NR5: Norw 3C **24**
Wilby Rd. NR1: Norw 2D **36**
Wild Apple Cl. NR5: Bow 2B **24**
The Wilderness NR13: Post 5H **29**
Wilderness Rd. NR8: Cost 2D **12**
Wilde Rd. NR13: Rack 1F **19**
Wild Rd. NR3: Norw 6C **16**
Wilfred Owen M. NR18: Wym 2G **39**
Wilkins Ct. NR5: Norw 2D **24**
Wilkinson Rd. NR13: Rack 1F **19**
Wilks Farm Dr. NR7: Spro 2F **17**
Willets Ct. NR2: Norw 4A **4**
William Booth St. NR2: Norw 5B **5** (4C **26**)
William Childerhouse Way NR5: Bow 2A **24**
William Cl. NR18: Wym 2D **38**
William Frost Way NR5: New C 4D **12**
William Kett Cl. NR1: Norw 3F **27**
William Mear Gdns. NR1: Norw 3G **27**
William Peck Cl. NR10: Spix 2F **11**
William Peck Rd. NR10: Spix 2F **11**
William's Loke NR7: Thor And 1A **28**
Williamson Cl. NR7: Norw 5H **17**
William White Pl. *NR1: Norw 2F **27***
(off Gas Hill)
Willis St. NR3: Norw 1D **4** (2D **26**)
Willoughby Way NR13: Rack 1F **19**
Willow Cl. NR13: B'all 5G **31**
NR18: Wym 3E **39**
Willowcroft Way NR4: Cring 3D **34**
Willow Herb Wlk. NR18: Wym 4F **39**
Willow La. NR2: Norw 4A **4** (3C **26**)
The Willows NR2: Norw 2G **25**
Wilson Rd. NR1: Norw 4G **27**
Winalls Yd. NR1: Norw 7C **5** (4D **26**)
Winceby Cl. NR7: Thor And 1E **29**
Winchcomb Rd. NR2: Norw 2G **25**
Winchester Twr. *NR2: Norw 4B **26***
(off Johnson Pl.)
Windmill Cl. NR14: Por 5C **40**
Windmill Ct. NR3: Norw 5F **17**
Windmill La. NR8: Cost 3B **14**
Windmill Rd. NR3: Norw 5E **17**
Windsor Chase NR8: Thor Mar 4G **7**
Windsor Pk. Gdns. NR6: Spro 1F **17**
Windsor Rd. NR6: Helle 1G **15**
Wingate Way NR2: Norw 2B **26**
Wingfield Rd. NR3: Norw 1C **26**
Winkles Row NR1: Norw 8F **5**
Winners Wlk. NR8: Thor Mar 2H **7**
Winsford Way NR5: Norw 6D **14**
Winstanley Rd. NR7: Thor And 1E **29**
Winter Rd. NR2: Norw 3H **25**
Winterton La. NR3: Norw 2B **4** (2C **26**)
Wisteria Dr. NR18: Wym 1G **39**
Witard Cl. NR7: Norw 6A **18**
Witard Rd. NR7: Norw 6A **18**
Withy Way NR8: Thor Mar 4H **7**
WITTON 1C 30
Witton La. NR13: Lit P, Witt 5C **20**
Woburn St. NR2: Norw 4B **26**
Wodehouse Cl. NR18: Wym 2A **38**
Wodehouse St. NR3: Norw 1D **26**
Wolfe Rd. NR1: Norw 2G **27**
Wolfson Cl. NR4: Norw 5E **25**
Womersley Cl. NR1: Norw 2G **27**
Womersley Rd. NR1: Norw 2G **27**
Wood Avens Way NR18: Wym 4F **39**
Woodbastwick Rd. NR13: Blof 1F **21**
Woodcock Cl. NR3: Norw 4C **16**
Woodcock Hill NR8: Cost 2C **12**
Woodcock Rd. NR3: Norw 4B **16**
Woodcote NR9: Hether 5D **32**
Woodcroft Cl. NR7: Spro 5B **18**
Woodforde Rd. NR7: Norw 5A **18**
Woodgate NR4: Cring 4D **34**
Woodgrove Pde. *NR3: Norw 4C **16***
(off Woodcock Rd.)
Woodham Leas NR6: Old C 1D **16**
Wood Hill NR8: Tav 5G **7**
Woodhill Ri. NR5: Norw 1D **24**
Woodland Cl. NR6: Helle 1E **15**
Woodland Ct. NR18: Wym 3F **39**
Woodland Dr. NR6: Old C 1D **16**
NR13: Thor E 5E **19**
Woodland Rd. NR6: Helle 1E **15**
Woodlands NR8: Tav 3E **7**
Woodlands Av. NR14: Fram E 2C **40**
Woodlands Cres. NR7: Thor And 6D **18**
Woodlands Rd. NR5: New C 5B **14**
Woodpecker Ct. *NR8: Cost 2D **12***
(off Woodpecker Way)
Woodpecker La. NR4: Cring 2C **34**
Woodpecker Way NR8: Cost 2E **13**
Woodrow Pl. NR1: Norw 3G **27**
Woodruff Cl. NR6: Norw 2C **16**
Woods Cl. NR6: Helle 4G **15**
NR9: Hether 5C **32**
Woodside Cl. NR8: Tav 4F **7**
Woodside Ct. NR1: Norw 8F **5** (6E **27**)
Woodside Rd. NR7: Norw 5B **18**
Wood St. NR1: Norw 8A **5** (5C **26**)
Wood Vw. Ct. NR5: New C 5B **14**
Woodview Rd. NR6: Helle 2F **15**
NR9: E'ton 5A **12**
Woodward Rd. NR3: Norw 5A **16**
Woolgate Ct. *NR2: Norw 3A **4***
(off St Swithins Rd.)
Woolner's La. NR14: Fram P 1F **41**
Worcester Rd. NR5: New C 6F **13**
Wordsworth Rd. NR5: Norw 3D **24**
Wortham Cl. NR5: Bow 1B **24**
Wramplingham Rd. NR18: Wym 1E **39**
Wrench Rd. NR5: Norw 3E **25**
Wren Cl. NR4: Norw 1F **35**
Wrenningham Rd. NR6: Old C 1D **16**
Wrights Ct. NR3: Norw 3C **4**
WROXHAM 2B 42
Wroxham Miniature Worlds **1B 42**
Wroxham Rd. NR7: Spro 4F **17**
Wroxham Station
Bure Valley Railway **1B 42**
Wycliffe Rd. NR4: Norw 6E **25**
Wylde Cft. NR8: Thor Mar 2G **7**
Wymer St. NR2: Norw 3B **26**
WYMONDHAM 4C 38
Wymondham Abbey Station
Mid Norfolk Railway **5B 38**
Wymondham Bus. Pk. NR18: Wym 3G **39**
Wymondham Dell Indoor Bowls Club **4E 39**
Wymondham Heritage Mus. **5D 38**
Wymondham Leisure Cen. **4D 38**
Wymondham Rd. NR18: Wickle, Wym 2A **38**
Wymondham Station (Rail) 6D 38
Wymondham Tourist Info. Cen. **5D 38**
Wyngates NR13: Blof 1H **31**

X

X Adventure Activities **1B 8**

Y

Yare Ct. NR7: Thor And 4A **28**
Yarefield Pk. NR4: Norw 4B **36**
Yare Valley Dr. NR4: Cring 1D **34**
Yare Valley Ri. NR13: B'all 4E **31**
Yarmouth Rd. NR7: Post, Thor And 4H **27**
NR13: Blof, Witt 2E **31**
NR13: Post 4H **29**
Yarn M. NR3: Norw 1D **4**
Yarrington Way NR5: Bow 1H **23**
Yaxley Way NR5: Bow 2B **24**
YELVERTON 4H 41
Yelverton Cl. NR6: Helle 2E **15**
Yelverton Rd. NR14: Fram E 3E **41**
Yew Ct. NR7: Spro 3A **18**
York All. NR1: Norw 5C **5**
York St. NR2: Norw 5A **26**
(not continuous)
Youngs Grn. NR1: Norw 2E **4** (2E **27**)

Z

Zipfel's Ct. NR3: Norw 1C **4**
Zobel Cl. NR3: Norw 5G **15**

Copyright of Geographers' A-Z Map Company Ltd.

No reproduction by any method whatsoever of any part of this publication is permitted without the prior consent of the copyright owners.

The representation on the maps of a road, track or footpath is no evidence of the existence of a right of way.

SAFETY CAMERA INFORMATION

PocketGPSWorld.com's CamerAlert is a self-contained speed and red light camera warning system for SatNavs and Android or Apple iOS smartphones/tablets. Visit www.cameralert.com to download.

Safety camera locations are publicised by the Safer Roads Partnership which operates them in order to encourage drivers to comply with speed limits at these sites. It is the driver's absolute responsibility to be aware of and to adhere to speed limits at all times.

By showing this safety camera information it is the intention of Geographers' A-Z Map Company Ltd. to encourage safe driving and greater awareness of speed limits and vehicle speed. Data accurate at time of printing.

Printed in China by RR Donnelley APS Co Ltd.